WHAT OTHERS SAY...

Pamela Christian has written an account of a dynamic Christian life that is instructive and illustrative of how a Christian should deal with Christian doctrine. Though the author leads us into many heavy subjects, *Renew Your Hope! Remedy for Personal Breakthroughs* avoids the deadening intellectualism that characterizes so much written on these subjects. It is, however, strong on personal experience and the application of Biblical truth to everyday life, I call Pamela Christian's perspective balanced and compliment her on how well she has integrated a Biblically balanced approach to life.
CHARLES H. KRAFT, Ph.D., Professor Emeritus of Anthropology and Intercultural Communication at Fuller School of Intercultural Studies, Author and International Speaker

Pamela Christian's first book in her trilogy is *Examine Your Faith! Finding Truth in a World of Lies*. This second volume is a perfect and necessary follow-up: *Renew Your Hope! Remedy for Personal Breakthroughs*. Having established the uniqueness and truthfulness of Christianity in her first book, she now digs deeply into the potential rewards available for anyone who appropriates and applies the promises inherent in biblical Christianity Because of her own experiences of suffering and adversity, she is able to skillfully explain the ingredients of a spirit-filled life of victory with the compassion and insight only someone who has struggled through great obstacles can adequately put into plain words. Pamela's passion for helping Christians grow in faith, and for unbelievers to experience the life-changing power of Jesus Christ, shines through on practically every page. Her many testimonies of struggles and victories through faith in God—both her own and others—adds subjective confirmation to the objective biblical evidences she presents, which together confirm the power of God for those who put their trust in Jesus. This book is a must read for anyone who desires to grow in faith and maturity as a follower of Jesus Christ.
DAN STORY, M.A. Christian Apologetics, Author and Speaker

So often, Christians find themselves embracing either the power and presence of the Holy Spirit to the exclusion of apologetics or immersed in strictly left brain, factual defenses for the faith, while lacking an understanding of the role of the Holy Spirit in our lives today. Pamela Christian provides the perfect balance—showing Christians how to experience the clarity, hope, and victory that is ours by the power and promises of God with the manifestation of the Gifts today through the lens of rational thought, logic, factual evidence, and a persuasive argument for the truth of God's Word. This book is a much needed resource for Christians to grow in all areas of their faith.

BOB DUTKO, Christian Apologist and Nationally Syndicated Radio Talk-show Host

Pamela Christian is a friend of mine and someone I see living and walking in faith. She has had many life challenges like so many of us. I have seen her stand firm on God's promises and refuse to give in and quit. I so love how Pamela takes you step by step to help you understand *faith*, how it works and how you can use your faith in God to enjoy His will in your life. *Renew Your Hope! Remedy for Personal Breakthroughs* is full of great real-life stories that bring home the message loud and clear. You will learn about the love of God and His promises that will help every Believer succeed when life throws a curve ball.

TOM BARKEY, Ph.D., Church of Grace Lead Pastor, and Author

Pamela Christian's *Renew Your Hope!* is "best-in-class" reading for anyone who wants their connection to God to move from a frustrated quest for personal happiness to realized victorious "hope-FULL-ness". But watch out, your faith just might become confident, vibrant, and expectant of God's presence, power, and purposes, superseding anything that resembles cautious, dutiful, try-hard, self-preserving Christianity.

REV. DAVID MILLER, Chief Encouragement Officer, LifeLetter Ministries

I love this book, and I love Pamela Christian! I have personally known her for many years, and she is the *real deal*—a committed, passionate Christian with a heart to help others experience all that is available to them through Christ. As with her first book, her loving heart is evident, but even more with *Renew Your Hope!* Pamela shares many personal experiences—her failures and successes—wanting you to find the confident hope and personal breakthroughs you need. There are many competing voices making it difficult to discover and live in life-giving truth and hope. But Pamela and *Renew Your Hope!* provide a compassionate and reliable guide.

NANCY STAFFORD Actress, Speaker, and Author of *The Wonder of His Love: A Journey into the Heart of God*

Hope and faith are bound together in love. Pamela Christian explains the reasons for our faith, our hope, and God's love in this beautifully-written book. You will learn so much about yourself and your faith journey as you pour through the pages.

Pam is a sincere Christian who can make the complex easy to understand—she walks the talk and knows the material about which she writes from personal experience. In today's confusing, and often immoral, society, *Renew Your Hope!* is a tool you will be able to use to navigate your way to a better faith life.
DEB HAGGERTY, Consultant, Editor, Speaker, and Christ-follower

As Pamela Christian clearly explains, belief is a necessary condition to see "mountain-moving faith" at work. If your faith is not as dynamic and transformational as you read about on the pages of Scripture, *Renew Your Hope! Remedy for Personal Breakthroughs* can help you unlock your mind and open up the paths for the victorious life Christ offers Believers.
ROBIN M BERTRAM, Executive Produce Freedom Today TV, Christian Women in Media National Regions Director

In the first book in her *Faith to Live By* series, Pamela Christian teaches the importance of having an 'examined faith', something that I advocate on a daily basis. In book two of the series, *Renew Your Hope!* Pamela builds upon that foundation and demonstrates how we can have an *effective faith*—a faith that gives us hope in the One in whom that faith is deservedly placed. With a correct understanding of biblical faith sadly lacking, not only in today's secular culture but also within Christianity itself, *Renew Your Hope!* is a much needed refresher course in not just what it means to have faith, but in putting that faith into practice as well.
GREG WEST, Founder and editor of The Poached Egg Christian Worldview and Apologetics Network National Staff Member at Ratio Christ Student Apologetics Alliance

After reading Pamela Christian's first book *Examine Your Faith, Finding Truth in a World of Lies*, I was really impressed with how gifted she is in communicating somewhat scholarly information so the average person can understand and personally relate. She has carried forward this same gift in her new book, *Renew Your Hope, Remedy for Personal Breakthroughs*. The book is educational, but also compellingly transformational. As she shares her story about her faith-walk, we get the opportunity to absorb her experiences for our own personal application and benefit to our lives. All points are grounded in God's Word. I thank Pam for taking the time to research and write this book. My faith is strengthened along with my appreciation for our Sovereign God.
RON HENRY, President, The Sterling Group, and Area Director for Fellowship of Companies for Christ International

"The secret to receiving answers to prayer is satisfying the conditions, which is not difficult. We are simply required to become disciples of Jesus and learn His ways. We can do nothing. What's important is that we *become*." I love this quote from Pamela's book. We think so often that we have to find the right formula, scour the Scriptures to see what we're missing and when we do everything just right God will answer our prayers. We should be searching Scripture all the time because there is a never ending living message to us but the purpose isn't to see a hidden formula. The purpose is to become more like Jesus. As we get more and more familiar with how He lived and reacted to the challenges of life, we are able to react to our great challenges with our new natures, becoming more and more like Him. This is our hope in Christ.

LINDY BOONE MICHAELIS, Author of *Heaven Hears*

Pamela Christian connected with me from the very beginning. I really like the fact that she is empathetic. Her personal stories and those from others are not the confessions of glass-bubble saints who know nothing of tragedy or pain. The stories are real and they simply move the heart to a higher plane. Whatever you've experienced personally, there is a story in *Renew Your Hope* that will usher in the healing. This alone would make the book worthy of your attention; however, Pamela has a wonderful ability to encourage her reader. I kept waiting for the hammer to drop where I felt unworthy or guilty or just not good enough. That didn't happen. Not only does she believe that you can do all things through Christ, she will show you how. So if you're not already sold, let me add one more incentive. Pamela understands why most Christians struggle in their faith, and it's not for all the reasons that one might assume. Most people haven't begun to understand who they are in Christ Jesus: Saints who have been washed clean, children of the most high God, over-comers by the power of the resurrection, faith warriors who are more than conquerors. Pamela understands the identity crisis handicapping many believers today. The gift she brings to this discussion is her ability to help you really live as Christ has already promised you can—yoke-free and victorious.

R. JAMES SHUPP, Th.M., M.Div., Lead Pastor, Movement Church, San Antonio, Texas and Author of *Who Killed My Church?*

Renew Your Hope!

Remedy for Personal Breakthroughs

Pamela Christian

Renew Your Hope!
Remedy for Personal Breakthroughs

Book Two in the *Faith to Live By* book series.

Copyright © 2014 Pamela Christian

All rights reserved. No part of this book may be used or reproduced by any means, graphic, electronic, or mechanical, including photocopying, recording, taping, or by any information storage retrieval system without the written permission of the publisher except in the case of brief quotations embodied in critical articles and reviews.

Pamela Christian's books may be ordered through booksellers or by contacting:
Pamela Christian Ministries
18032 Lemon Drive #C206
Yorba Linda, CA 92886
www.pamelachristianministries.com

Published by:
Protocol Ltd.
A Division of Christian Development Company, LLC
info@protocolpublishing.com

Unless otherwise indicated, Scripture quotations are from the ESV® Bible (The Holy Bible, English Standard Version®), copyright © 2001 by Crossway, a publishing ministry of Good News Publishers. Used by permission. All rights reserved.

Scripture quotations marked (NLT) are taken from the Holy Bible, New Living Translation, copyright 1996, 2005, 2007, by Tyndale House Foundation. Used according to permission of Tyndale House Publishers, Inc., Carol Stream, Illinois 60188. All rights reserved.

Because of the dynamic source of the Internet, any web addresses or links contained in this guide or the companion book may have changed since publication and may no longer be valid. The views expressed in this work are solely the views of the author.

ISBN-13: 978-0-9909421-4-6 (sc)
ISBN-10: 0990942147 (sc)
ISBN-13: 978-0-9909421-6-0 (e)
Library of Congress Control Number: 2014954089

Printed in the United States of America.
Pamela Christian Ministries date: 12/01/2014

"For we are his workmanship, created in Christ Jesus for good works, which God prepared beforehand, that we should walk in them."
Ephesians 2:10

There is no one other than our Savior and Lord, Jesus Christ, to whom this book, entire book series, and ministry work I am able to do, should be dedicated. May my words bring glory and honor to Him, and a great blessing and benefit to each one who benefits from these ministries. Amen.

CONTENTS

	Acknowledgments	xi
	Introduction	xiii

PART ONE—Conditions of Faith

1	Faith Personified—Christ is Our Hope	3
2	Faith Realized—Apprehend God's Promises	33
3	Faith Personalized—Identify with Christ	57
4	Faith Materialized—Operate in Your Authority	83

PART TWO—Developing Faith

5	Faith Exercised—Growing through Opposition	107
6	Faith Exemplified— Encouraging Examples of Faith	131
7	Faith Jeopardized—Claim Your Authority	157
8	Faith Amplified—Overcome with Knowledge	183

PART THREE—The Fruit of Faith

9	Faith Fortified—Celebrate Your Abundance	211
10	Faith Magnified—Hope Revitalized	239
	Chapter End Notes	249
	About the Author	259

ACKNOWLEDGEMENTS

No man is an Island. One person's work is a compilation of efforts from those who've gone before from the beginning of all time and Creation. We collectively glean what is necessary for us from that compilation. Because of this history, I find impossible the task of properly acknowledging everyone who has had a part in this or other ministry projects of mine. The best way I know how is to thank God openly with my words and my life—to become as the Apostle Paul encourages, a living sacrifice for Christ. May I do this more and more each day of my life on earth, for the glory of God, and the benefit of others.

This, the second book in my *Faith to Live By* series, has been as enjoyable to research and write as the first. I fully expect the entire project to be a work of joy for all of us. *Us* refers to several individuals to whom I am indebted and have come to love and highly esteem.

Dan Story is a mentor and encourager who has seen my unedited manuscripts in the most woeful condition, yet he believed in me. His ability to see a *diamond in the rough* is something for which I am eternally grateful.

I greatly appreciate Nikki Linen for her immediate embrace of my calling, and her personal and professional guidance as we seek to grow the ministry work God has assigned me.

Lorna Juarez is invaluable for her precious and faithful intercession in seeking the Lord's wisdom, guidance, and protection, and for her delight with the prospect of our collectively bringing glory to God.

My editor, Deb Haggerty, an outstanding professional in the publishing industry, is one whose expertise and support I don't ever want to be without.

Don Otis, publicist, imparts encouragement, direction, and *above and beyond* dedication that helps me to keep focused forward.

My husband, David, has consistently paved a way for me to have the freedom and flexibility to do the work God has called me to do.

I also wish to acknowledge the many men and women whose work preceded me. Their efforts have allowed me to study and grow with the goal of sharing the life-giving truths I've been blessed to find thus far, and expect to continue to discover.

INTRODUCTION

Life has a way of beating us down and eroding our optimism. None of us escape hardships in life. Whether we experience intermittent seasons of adversity and recovery or a long haul of difficulties with little to no reprieve, each of us fights the battle of holding out for hope at one point or another. For most of us, finding hope is especially difficult when we endure troubles that come to us through no fault of our own. The tragic death of a loved one, the destruction of a marriage, the unexpected loss of income, and serious health issues—these are some adversities that I have personally suffered. And if you experience a long term of adversity like I have, much more than your hope suffers—so does your faith.

I've written *Renew Your Hope! Remedy for Personal Breakthroughs* with profound compassion and understanding from personal experiences—mine along with those of others who have allowed me to tell their stories. We try to share our real and raw responses experienced during our times of suffering to encourage you. We know the kinds of worries, fears, and doubts that can erode our faith and extinguish our hope. But we've learned what is required to combat the negative thoughts and feelings, to breakthrough our circumstances into victory. We share the intentional, deliberate effort that we can and *must* take if we want to experience the hope and personal breakthroughs that God wants us to have.

Hebrews 11:6 is the focus verse for this *Faith to Live By* book series. The verse reveals a promise of God that we can expect to enjoy in this life if we meet the condition of the promise. "And without faith it is impossible to please him, for whoever would draw near to God must believe that he exists, and that he rewards those who diligently seek Him."[1] What we believe directly influences our hope. Faith is the fundamental element of hope. Because of the faith/hope relationship, the first book in the series is *Examine Your Faith! Finding Truth in a World of Lies*. That book provides what you need to have *essential faith*—that is, faith that allows you to be rightly related with the One True God—the same faith that satisfies the condition of the promise of Hebrews 11:6. If you have not confidently concluded that Christianity is the only faith that leads to the One True God, I respectfully ask you to read the first book in this series. If you are not a Believer, you will gain little from what you read here.

The message in this second book is how to have *effective faith*—faith that allows us to overcome our circumstances and experience personal breakthroughs—the victory Christ offers. Effective faith is a matter of deeply comprehending God's truth, then practicing what we have learned. However, and very sadly, the majority of people who profess the Christian faith aren't doing this—they don't know how to embrace such faith and, as a result, they struggle with hopelessness.

God does not want us to live hopeless, defeated lives. That's the very reason He personally, and at great cost, provided a way of escape. You not only have God's promises for a hope-filled life, you have His assurance—His guarantee. But unless you believe in God *and* know how to appropriate His promises, you can be unnecessarily subjected to defeat.

Of the estimated seventy-five percent of Americans who profess to be Christian, one-third are referred to as *Cultural Christians*—they are Christians in name sake only, without a vibrant faith. Another one-third are categorized as *Congregational Christians* who have some ties to a home church, but who do not practice the Christian faith in their daily lives. These statistics mean that roughly *sixty-six percent* of all who profess the Christian faith don't fully operate in the victory and joy Jesus died to provide *Christian Believers* in this earthly life![2] These statistics show there are a lot of people who need to have their hope renewed!

I've known rejection and despair. I've seen the ravages that alcoholism and addictions have on individuals and families. I've suffered serious financial trials and major life and death health issues. I've fought depression daily as the adversities of life all but consumed me. But I have found what you and many others are seeking. Hope! Personal breakthroughs are available *if* we truly want them. *If we want them* may seem like a strange condition. You may wonder, *why wouldn't a person want breakthroughs?* Let me explain.

I've known many people who, on a subconscious level, have become so familiar with their burdens, so identified with the life they've always known, that the prospect of a breakthrough is not on their radar. They have become so resigned to their personal situation that they have no hope for anything different. Many people remain in a perpetual state of hopelessness simply because living without hope is familiar to them. For these people, the effort required to make any change is not something they are willing to do.

Finding hope and overcoming tragedies begins with an act of one's will. No doubt this is why Jesus asked the man at the pool of Bethesda, who had been an invalid for thirty-eight years, "Do you want to be healed?"[3]

The man's response reveals he'd wanted to be healed for a long time, but felt no hope that he could be made whole. He explained that he had no one to help him, that by the time he could reach the healing waters, another person stepped in before him. Can you relate? Have you been trying to find the answers you need, but always come up short? Have you been dealing with a matter for so very long that you are nearly without hope?

The man at the pool of Bethesda believed he could only be healed if he were the first person to enter the healing waters. Imagine how unbelievable the situation must have seemed to him when Jesus, a stranger to him, simply stated, "Get up, take up your bed and walk."[4] He probably had thoughts run through his mind along the lines of, *are you nuts? Can't you see my condition? How do you expect me to get up, let alone walk?*

If Jesus were to ask you something totally unexpected with the promise that your hope would be fulfilled and your breakthrough finally realized, would you be willing to take a step of faith? Are you willing to reconsider the paths or lessons or methods you've been taught to follow, with the prospect of finding new direction and new hope that leads to your needed breakthroughs?

I am a fellow struggler with a heart of compassion, and I want to share what I have learned to help you discover the victorious life available through faith in Jesus. You can gain new hope. You can have personal breakthroughs. I am not saying that there is a formula or a specific recipe or a particular program to follow that will produce the results you want. But there are principles and conditions that you can learn, and actions you can take, to help you experience all God's promised benefits.

Renewing your hope and embracing the remedy for personal breakthroughs begins and ends with faith. Not the so-called popularized faith that claims we can have whatever we want if we have enough faith. That teaching, sadly, is unbiblical and has prevented many people from discovering the true and genuine hope that is available, in abundance, through faith!

Recognizing that our hope is empowered by our conviction of faith, and that our faith is directly affected by what we believe to be truth, my work is devoted to helping you ascertain matters of truth. Hope and faith are interrelated and both can direct us to the prospect of experiencing a positive outcome. However, only when we are utterly convinced of the truth can we persevere unto breakthroughs.

The Christian faith, when genuinely embraced, makes a person completely new—radically transformed from the inside out. Moreover, as

Christian Believers grow in their faith, they have access to the supernatural power of the Holy Spirit. The Spirit is given to guide and empower every Believer to transform their lives and even the world around them. *Renew Your Hope! Remedy for Personal Breakthroughs* is written to help you learn how to apply your Christian faith. To live that faith in such a way that you can experience every bit of the abundant life—the mountain-moving faith—of which Jesus spoke.

As difficult as experiencing a joy-filled victorious life in this fallen world may be, Christ said we can, so I don't want to settle for less. Neither should you.

What are you seeking God for in your life? What breakthroughs do you earnestly need? Have you been suffering for a long time under the same burdens so that you've become wearied, even in your faith? Jesus not only had much to say about faith, He demonstrated a faith that produced more miracles than the Bible could record. The Apostle John, who was among the first twelve of Jesus' followers wrote, "Now there are also many other things that Jesus did. Were every one of them to be written, I suppose that the world itself could not contain the books that would be written."[5]

Jesus' disciples performed many miracles once they learned how to apply faith as Jesus taught them. In John 14:12-14, Jesus says, "Truly, truly, I say to you, whoever believes in me will also do the works that I do; and greater works than these will he do, because I am going to the Father. Whatever you ask in my name, this I will do, that the Father may be glorified in the Son. If you ask me anything in my name, I will do it."[6]

Now can be your time to be restored to the fullness of God's promises of transformation and hope, which Christ suffered and died to provide you. You can truly renew your hope and discover the remedies for personal breakthroughs! If this sounds like something you're ready to explore, simply turn the page.

PART ONE

CONDITIONS OF FAITH

God's love is unconditional, but His promises aren't. There are conditions of faith that we must meet before we can lay any claim to God's promises. To prepare you to discover the hope you desire, and to experience the personal breakthroughs you need, take time to fully grasp the foundational concepts found in Part One of this book.

CHAPTER ONE

Faith Personified

Christ is Our Hope

What I've learned in my decades of life is that when we are up against hardships, we are in the perfect position for God to miraculously intervene in our lives. While God can and does work in our life when we are not suffering, we feel him doing so most intensely when we *are* suffering.

This book is written from the perspective that not only does God exist, He is a miracle-working God, actively involved in the real-world circumstances of people, especially those who invite Him to participate in their lives. I realize that not everyone believes this. Not everyone desires His involvement because they don't want to be subject to God—they want to be god or lord of their own lives. Additionally, many people, even some who believe in God, don't believe that the miraculous gifts described in the Christian Bible are available today. Still, I don't know of anyone who would refuse a miracle that made their life better. Do you?

Maybe you're one who struggles with the existence, nature, and involvement of God in the world today. When you come up against hardships that reveal the full extent of your human limitations, don't you secretly wish that some way, some how, you could get the help you need?

If so, I ask you to maintain an open mind as you read this book. You will learn important principles from the Bible and from real life testimonies—some from Scriptures, some my own, and some from people I know.

Hope's Prerequisite is Faith

Hope springs eternal is an oft-used phrase in poems, music, books, philosophical discussions, and more. But anyone who has lived much life on earth will admit, in honesty, that there are times we feel devoid of hope. These are the occasions when we can see absolutely no way our hope can be fulfilled. For hope to spring at all, let alone eternally, requires faith. Faith and hope are gifts from God. When we lack faith or hope, we have not properly *understood, acknowledged, believed, and received.* Consider the following word-picture.

> I have in my hand a very large and beautifully-wrapped gift that I am elated to give you. I think I'm even more excited about giving the gift to you than you will be to receive the present. Yet I know what is inside the package is something you want and need and will be ecstatic to have. I set the gift directly in front of you easily within your reach. And I'm so giddy that before you ever reach out to receive and open my present, I blurt out what's inside! But you don't respond. You don't even blink. My gift freely given to you from my heart is directly in front of you. The gift is completely yours for the taking, but you don't seem to realize that I and my gift even exist. Or if you know I exist, you don't know enough about me to accept what I'm offering. That's the problem.

Unless you believe that I exist, and that I have the ability to give you such a glorious gift, you will not even consider receiving the present. The gift is something you have greatly needed and for which you've longed. The only way you can reach out and embrace the gift I have for you is if you have faith in me—that I am real and am able to benefit you personally.

Hebrews 11:6 reads, "And without faith it is impossible to please him, for whoever would draw near to God must believe that he exists, and that he rewards those who diligently seek Him."[1]

Unless you believe, you will not receive—you will not receive faith or hope or anything else from God unless you believe and then, by faith, act on that belief to receive.

Assuming you are a skeptic, or a person whose hope and faith are dim, I offer you real and certain hope, provided you believe in God through faith in Jesus. If you have not settled this belief and faith in *Christ*, (the Greek title given Jesus that means Anointed One), the pages of this chapter may help you to do so. If you have settled your faith in Christ for salvation, but have difficulty believing Him for the breakthroughs you need, keep reading. The same process for acquiring *essential faith* (saving faith) applies for receiving *effective faith*, (demonstrated faith). Four simple steps in the following order comprise the process:

1. Understanding – to learn and gain knowledge/vision.
2. Accepting – to personally acknowledge as truth.
3. Believing – to stand, rely upon, trust, and expect.
4. Receiving – to personally obtain.

With such a simple process, why aren't more people embracing the many breakthroughs God wants for us? Because in our human reasoning, we often make what is simple amazingly difficult.

Understanding, Accepting, and Believing Christ

As God intended, within the Christian faith is power to overcome the evil of this world. Through faith in Jesus, also referred to as Christ, any human being can have hope. God wants you to be filled with hope and to see your hopes fulfilled—so much so that He made hope abundantly possible through faith in Christ.

I didn't know Christ until I was nearly thirty years old. Oh, I knew about Him, at least in part. My parents allowed me to attend church with our neighbors when I was young. I recall the Sunday school teacher telling me about Jesus and how He could be my forever friend. She explained that Jesus could save me from my sin and keep me from going to Hell, which she made clear was a very terrible place. At the tender young age of about five, I didn't exactly know what sin was, but I knew what a terrible place was. The violence, alcoholism, and abuse in my home had taught me that much. In response, I did what the Sunday school teacher suggested and prayed to ask Jesus to be my Forever Friend. I didn't fully understand what I was doing, and without any reinforcing instruction from my parents or other influencers in my life, I lived my life like many people today. I knew something about Jesus, but I didn't give Him or the Christian faith much consideration, though I believed I was a Christian and entitled to all the benefits of the faith.

Not until I was nearly thirty years old, when my entire life fell apart and everything I believed came crashing down, did I ever seriously considered Jesus again. The man I thought I would marry, and with whom I hoped I would spend the rest of my life, broke off our relationship, which literally broke me.

I recall the night, that dark painful night when I sat alone in my condominium. Hot tears streamed down my face uncontrollably while sobs from the depth of my being—a depth I'd never experienced before—consumed me. My thoughts drifted back to the Sunday school teacher's assurance that Jesus could help me. I found myself praying aloud, "Jesus, God, Heavenly Father," I really wasn't sure how to address Him. "If You are everything the Sunday school teacher said You are, if You are a loving and caring God who can help me with my life, then I need You now more than ever. I know I've lived my life on my own. I've lived as lord of my own life. But I'm willing for You to be Lord of my life if You can take my life and make something good of it. I now realize I need to be saved from much more than Hell. I need to be saved from the mess I've made of my life."

Although I had just a little understanding about Jesus and God, with uncertain hopefulness that God is as the Sunday school teacher explained, God responded to me immediately. Right there. Right then. In the midst of the greatest pain I'd ever known, I found real and certain Hope. God answered my prayer and I was instantly transformed. I didn't understand what had happened, but I knew the experience was real. God is real. Jesus is real. Hope is available, not only for me, but for you. In fact, hope is available for anyone who wants to embrace what is offered through faith in Christ.

Sadly, very few people know this or believe this. Many don't want the hope that Jesus offers because of wrong understanding—because they are deceived. Many people have a wholly incorrect understanding of God, Jesus, the Bible, and Christianity.

With these precious people in mind, perhaps including you, I devote my life to helping people discover and live in life-giving truth. Hope is available. Real and confident hope exists. Hope begins with personal *salvation*, which is to be restored into a right relationship with *God the Father*, through faith in *Jesus the Son*, by the power of the *Holy Spirit*. The Christian God is a *Triune God*—that is, He is one God who eternally exists as three persons. This God is the God and Creator of all that exists.

As the Creator of all that exists, God wants you to enjoy a victorious hope-filled life, able to overcome any adversities you encounter.

Biblical Understanding of a Victorious Life

God originally fashioned humanity in His image, fully-empowered to wield His imparted-authority over the earth and all that the earth contained. However, the first man and woman, deceived by the enemy of God, rejected God's authority. In so doing they rejected all that was good and *holy* and embraced all that is wicked and evil. Holy means to be dedicated or consecrated or set apart unto God.

But God's love for each individual descended from the first man and woman is so great that even though His authority had been rejected outright, He revealed a plan of redemption for all mankind. The moment the first man, Adam, and the first woman, Eve, admitted their *sin*—their rejection of God and all that was good—God cursed the enemy known as *Satan*. Then He explained the future difficulties Adam and Eve had brought into all Creation, and to all their descendents. Moved by His great love, God began to reveal His plan to redeem humanity from the ravages of sin, restoring to those who choose God, victory over evil—hope in place of despair.[2]

Evil entered into our world as a result of the first man and first woman's rejection of God's authority. However, *Believers*—those who place their faith in Jesus the Christ—can subdue evil and overcome many of the ravages and sufferings that exist on earth. Through Christ's imputed authority they have hope.

A victorious life on earth is not one that is devoid of all pain, sickness, disease, and suffering—that's life in heaven. A victorious life on earth is one that intentionally seeks God the Father's direction in order to do His will on earth. His will is revealed in His *Written Word*, the Bible, and in Jesus, referred to as God's *Living Word*. His will includes overcoming all sorts of evil, disease, pain, and suffering for the benefit of humanity while bringing glory to God. His will is entirely motivated by His character, which is love—supreme love from which all good originates according to 1 John 4:8. God revealed His love in the life, death, and resurrection of Jesus. Jesus is the One who proclaimed: "I have said these things to you, that in me you may have peace. *In the world you will have tribulation.* But take heart; I have overcome the world."[3] [Emphasis added] If there is any limitation in securing all that God offers—the abundant life that Christ died to provide—the cause is our limited thinking and understanding. Recall that *understanding* is the first step in the process of receiving.

God's View of Abundant Victorious Life

In John 10:10, Jesus is quoted: "I came that they may have life and have it abundantly."[4] The Greek word used for *abundantly* in that passage is *perisson*, which carries the additional meanings of special, unusual, superabundant … overflowing, over and above a certain quantity, a quantity so abundant as to be considerably more than what one would expect or anticipate.[5]

1 Corinthians 2:9 paraphrases the Old Testament passage from Isaiah 64:4. We read, "What no eye has seen, nor ear heard, nor the heart of man imagined, what God has prepared for those who love him."[6] The Apostle Paul informs us that God "…is able to do far more abundantly than all that we ask or think, according to the power at work within us."[7] (Ephesians 3:20) Clearly God desires us to have abundant life.

First, the life God offers is eternal *relationship* with Him. We read in John 17:3 Jesus' words, "And this is eternal life, that they know you the only true God, and Jesus Christ whom you have sent."[8] To personally know God is the greatest privilege we can have. While those who know God have authority and power in Jesus' name, which is wonderful, our greatest joy is to be that our "names are written in heaven." (Luke 10:19-20)[9]

Second, life is given to us by way of *regeneration* (explained more fully later in this chapter). In our natural-born physical condition we are enemies of God. Only when a person willfully chooses to believe in and receive Jesus as Savior and Lord is their spirit within them born-again—regenerated from death to life. Knowing God the Father through faith in Jesus Christ *is* life, and life abundant. While regeneration is most assuredly glorious enough, there is more!

Our eternal lives of faith in Christ begin the day we say *yes* to Jesus. From that moment on we are no longer our own as we've been bought with the very blood of Jesus.[10] Romans 8:32 reveals how God has demonstrated His love for us: "He [God] who did not spare his own Son but gave him up for us all, how will he [God] not also with him [Son] graciously give us all things?"[11] With faith in Christ we are adopted into the family of God and made joint heirs with Jesus, meaning that we share in all that belongs to Him.

By definition, a victorious life is one that overcomes opposition. If there is no opposition, there is nothing over which to have victory. With faith in Christ, and by partnering with God and His Holy Spirit who resides in Believers, we are transformed and we work with God in His plan. God's view of life abundant is not a life that never suffers. Abundant life is one that gains victory by going through the suffering of this world and being greatly improved by the process. In fact, *according to the degree that we partner with God*, we will realize victory, or not.

We were created by God with works of service in mind. We are each given spiritual gifts and natural talents in order to succeed in the unique purpose for our life. We can know God's perfect plan and purpose for ourselves, if we seek Him. God intends that we seek Him first, then all things will be added unto us, as promised in Matthew 6:25-34. When we submit to God and discover and live our God-intended purpose, even with opposition, we find true personal fulfillment. Nothing can operate optimally when used contrary to the created design. Therefore, we serve ourselves best to seek God and His planned purpose for our lives.

God knows our wants and desires—He knows our hearts. He knows the struggle suffered in lack and the relief enjoyed in plenty. What is considered abundant to one person, would not be abundant to another. God's love and interaction with each of us is distinct according to our uniquely individual situations and His plan for our lives.

The Abundance of the Heart Influences our Life

French Philosopher, Blaise Pascal, (1623-1662) is accredited the quote, "There is a God-shaped vacuum in the heart of every man which cannot be filled by any created thing, but only by God, the Creator, made known through Jesus.[12]

Humans are not only created with a heart-need to know God, but are made in God's image. Scriptures reveal that God is three Persons in One: Father, Son, and Holy Spirit. Being made in God's image, we are created in three-parts: body; soul, and spirit. The human soul and spirit are eternal, whereas the body is temporal. Specific to the heart of man, which refers to the soul and spirit, the Bible has much to say.

The word heart as used in the Old Testament is the Hebrew word *leb*, which means much more than the seat of human emotion or the physical heart organ. Heart means the unique essence of the individual soul (mind/intellect/will, heart/emotions, and distinct personality). When we place our faith in Christ, our eternal spirit is instantly made holy— transformed into an entirely new being that never before existed. Our body and soul however remain unchanged until we willingly cooperate with the Holy Spirit to transform us. We have an active and willful participation in the transforming of our *leb* and body. Based on Jeremiah 17:9-10, we should want to do the work: "The heart [*leb*] is deceitful above all things, and desperately sick; who can understand it? I the LORD search the heart [*leb*] and test the mind, to give every man according to his ways, according to the fruit of his deeds."[13]

As physical beings, we are naturally-oriented toward material things. But as Believers, our focus must first be on God. "Set your minds on things that are above, not on things that are on earth. For you have died, and your life is hidden with Christ in God.[14] (Colossians 3:2-3) In Matthew 6:19-20, we read the words of Jesus: "Do not lay up for yourselves treasures on earth, where moth and rust destroy and where thieves break in and steal, but lay up for yourselves treasures in heaven, where neither moth nor rust destroys and where thieves do not break in and steal."[15] Also in Matthew:

> Therefore I tell you, do not be anxious about your life, what you will eat or what you will drink, nor about your body, what you will put on. Is not life more than food, and the body more than clothing? ... Therefore do not be anxious, saying, 'What shall we eat?' or 'What shall we drink?' or 'What shall we wear?' For the Gentiles seek after all these things, and your heavenly Father knows that you need them all.[16]

Jeremiah 9:23-24 provides us with a bold and comforting statement from God:

> Thus says the LORD: Let not the wise man boast in his wisdom, let not the mighty man boast in his might, let not the rich man boast in his riches, but let him who boasts boast in this, that he understands and knows me, that I am the LORD who practices steadfast love, justice, and

righteousness in the earth. For in these things I delight, declares the LORD.[17]

When we learn to abide in Christ—when we live from our regenerated spirit instead of our natural inclinations—we experience the abundant life. Abundant life begins and ends with knowing God. J.I. Packer, author of the best-selling book *Knowing God*, wrote, "What makes life worthwhile is having a big enough objective, something which catches our imagination and lays hold of our allegiance, and this the Christian has in a way that no other person has. For what higher, more exalted, and more compelling goal can there be than to know God?"[18] Knowing God, in the sense of the Hebrew word, *yada*, is to have a personal, experiential knowledge of Him.[19] Having a personal relationship with God the Father through faith in Jesus Christ, by the power of the Holy Spirit, *this* is abundant life. And from this new platform, we can express God's love and power in ways that overcome natural circumstances and transform us more into the image of Christ.

The War of Good and Evil

Our world is at war and hungry for hope. You and I and every human being ever born are born into this war. The war is strategically-waged against humanity in an all out effort to prevent us from finding any measure of hope. And because of the numerous battles that have been won against humanity, many are on the verge of, or in, complete despair. What people don't realize is that Christ *is* our Hope. There is no other. The historical person named Jesus, known as Christ, is our only hope. However, through all time and history, people have sought to find other solutions out of hearts that reject God. Additionally, the war is so intense that even Christians—those who have discovered the hope of Christ—can unwittingly reject some of the promises of God and as a result feel hopeless or unfulfilled in their faith.

Many people reject God and His promises out of ignorance or deception. They don't know the realities concerning Jesus, and in turn they don't know the truth about God. From nearly the beginning of the human race, war has been declared against truth, in an effort by the enemy of God to prevent people from knowing God. And unless we properly know God—His nature and His character, will, and intentions for us—we cannot expect to find any hope.

Conditions for Effective Faith

There are several testimonies recorded herein to encourage you in your faith and to provide you with some very specific guidelines to follow when you are contending for God's intervention. Each situation is different, but there are some basic conditions that need to be satisfied in every instance in order for God to be willing to act. God will never act against the human will. He will not force Himself upon anyone. If you choose Him, you get Him, and all His promised benefits are available to you. If you don't, you don't. It's that simple.

If you have a need for something in your life that you cannot produce—if you need God to intervene in your life (and I assume you do or that that you will)—then you need to make certain you have satisfied the conditions that make His work on your behalf possible. Following is the first condition that must be satisfied.

Who Do You Say Jesus Is?

When deciding on religious faith, the one question that has resonated with humanity for over two thousand years was asked by Jesus. Addressing Peter, one of His first twelve disciples, Jesus asked, "But who do you say I am?"[20] By His very existence, Jesus poses the same question to every individual. Are you prepared to answer that question for yourself?

Throughout the centuries, few deny the historical reality of a significantly influential man named Jesus. Many, however, deny Who He claimed to be. Contemplating how much controversy there is over one Man Who, earthly speaking, came from very humble beginnings, had no educational degree, and a far from impressive occupation is interesting. Just His name alone causes some people to declare personal offense. The symbol for Jesus' life, the cross, is the subject of many lawsuits by those who don't want to allow *even a symbolic reference* to this man in public places. They attempt to deny, disregard, and wipe out over two thousands of years of *historical faith*, held by hundreds of millions of individuals: faith based on solid, objective, and verifiable evidence.

Those in the Old Testament era who believed in the coming of God's promised Redeemer/Deliverer and those in the New Testament era who look back and believe on the historical Redeemer/Deliverer named Jesus, share the same *faith conviction*. Anyone who places their faith in the promised Redeemer/Deliverer is spiritually transformed from being an enemy of God to being a member of God's family. This change is a super-natural spiritual transformation. Unless our faith is in Christ, we can have no hope. Let me explain.

Nicodemus was a Jewish religious leader who lived in the days of Jesus. In the Gospel according to John, we learn that Nicodemus sought Jesus *in the night* to inquire of Him. Jesus' response to Nicodemus was as follows,

"Truly, truly, I say to you, unless one is born again he cannot see the kingdom of God."

Understandably Nicodemus asked, "How can a man be born when he is old? Can he enter a second time into his mother's womb and be born?" Jesus answered,

> "Truly, truly, I say to you, unless one is born of water and the Spirit, he cannot enter the kingdom of God. That which is born of the flesh is flesh, and that which is born of the Spirit is spirit. Do not marvel that I said to you, 'You must be born again.' The wind blows where it wishes, and you hear its sound, but you do not know where it comes from or where it goes. So it is with everyone who is born of the Spirit.[21]

Having difficulty understanding what Jesus meant Nicodemus inquired further. Jesus replied:

> Are you the teacher of Israel and yet you do not understand these things? Truly, truly, I say to you, we speak of what we know, and bear witness to what we have seen, but you do not receive our testimony. If I have told you earthly things and you do not believe, how can you believe if I tell you heavenly things? No one has ascended into heaven except he who descended from heaven, the Son of Man. And as Moses lifted up the serpent in the wilderness, so must the Son of Man be lifted up, that whoever believes in him may have eternal life.
>
> For God so loved the world, that he gave his only Son, that whoever believes in him should not perish but have eternal life. For God did not send his Son into the world to

condemn the world, but in order that the world might be saved through him. Whoever believes in him is not condemned, but whoever does not believe is condemned already, because he has not believed in the name of the only Son of God. And this is the judgment: the light has come into the world, and people loved the darkness rather than the light because their works were evil. For everyone who does wicked things hates the light and does not come to the light, lest his works should be exposed. But whoever does what is true comes to the light, so that it may be clearly seen that his works have been carried out in God.[22]

Early in Jesus' ministry, He boldly claimed to be the promised Redeemer/Deliverer—far more than simply a good teacher as Nicodemus first thought.

Jesus' favorite reference to Himself was *Son of Man*, as you read in the above verse. This was His favorite reference because of His appointed mission as the promised Redeemer/Deliverer for humanity and because of his unique physical conception, explored later in this chapter.

Also in the above passage, Jesus' use of the pronouns, *We* and *Our*, reveals His claim to personhood with the *Triune God*. The study of the Triune God, or the *Trinity*, is fascinating. Beginning with the first book of the Old Testament, God reveals Himself—His nature—as three persons in One. Each is co-existent, co-eternal, and equal in power but with each emphasizing a different role. For now our focus is on God the Son, namely Jesus.

No other person in history has caused as much profound commotion as this man named Jesus. However, once you understand who He not only claimed, but proved Himself to be, you either love Him or hate Him. Those who are indifferent are those who don't properly understand the factual, historical life, death, and resurrection of Jesus. What about you? Do you love Him? Do you hate Him? Are you indifferent?

Consider that whether you love Him or hate Him, you believe in Him. After all, what logic is there in hating someone or something that you don't believe exists? What logic would there be to have *any emotion whatsoever* toward someone or something you don't believe exists?

Generally speaking, people don't deny the existence of a historical man Who was born as early as 4 BC and Who died as late as AD 36, named Jesus. What they seek to deny is Who He claimed to be. Clearly He claimed to be our Hope.

Understanding the History of the War

Before creating the universe, God created spiritual beings known as angels who operate under His authority.[23] God gave all His created beings *free-will*—decision-making capabilities. Free-will allows God's created beings to have complete control over the decision to worship God or not. God does not impose Himself or His ways on anyone.

Scriptures reveal the names of some of the angels. One angel is named Lucifer. We have limited knowledge of him. Scriptures reveal he was an archangel, perhaps one of the highest ranking. From the prophet Isaiah we know that this angel rebelled against God. "You said in your heart, *I will ascend to heaven; above the stars of God I will set my throne on high; I will sit on the mount of assembly in the far reaches of the north; I will ascend above the heights of the clouds; I will make myself like the Most High.*"[24]

We don't know why this angel, also known as Satan, sacrificed his high-ranking position to fight his Master. Charles H. Kraft, author of *I Give You Authority: Practicing the Authority Jesus Gave Us*, has a theory:

> Perhaps the thing that tipped him [Lucifer] in the direction [to rebel] was the rumor that God planned to create a new being, one that would carry God's own image, who would therefore displace Lucifer as second in authority over the universe. My theory is that this plan of God angered him beyond his ability to remain obedient to God, so he rebelled and set up his own kingdom.[25]

Through an act of his free-will, Lucifer became an enemy of God. We learn from Scriptures that he influenced a great number of heavenly hosts to join him. We don't know just how much authority and power as an archangel Lucifer was able to maintain in his rebellion. Regardless, he seems to have enough to disrupt the plans of God and His creatures. "This situation," as Kraft puts it, "has resulted in one of the great ironies of history—a being who uses the very power God allows him to oppose the God who gave it to him [in the first place]. But this irony is paralleled by another: the fact that God has done the same thing with humans. God has set certain limitations upon Himself by giving to humans and apparently angels, a certain amount of autonomy [through free-will] that we can use, if we choose, even to oppose the One who gives it to us."[26]

Scriptures reveal that Lucifer wasn't satisfied with seeking to establish his own kingdom. He is bent on destroying all that is important to God. This desire is rooted in pride—a penchant for self-importance and an unwillingness to submit to any authority except one's own.

Modern Day Rejection of God

Pride is the root-cause for humanity's continued rejection of God to this day. You may say, "But I believe in God. I am a Christian!" Perhaps you are among those who are identified as Cultural or Congregational Christians. You acknowledge that God exists, have perhaps even received Jesus as your Savior, but you do not submit your life to Him and His ways—you do not acknowledge Jesus as Lord. If you have remained lord of your life, then you merely know about Jesus—you have not placed your trust in Him. Scripture refers to such ideology as having a form of godliness but denying the power thereof.[27] And as I already shared, I attempted to live the first thirty years of my life in that manner.

For Adam and Eve, just as God had forewarned, rejection of His authority resulted in spiritual death, separating them from God and all that was good. Their choice led to sin, sickness, suffering, death, and evil entering into our world. Rejection of God is called sin. Sin never impacts just one person, but always impacts all the world.

Because Adam and Eve are the human father and mother of all humanity, every human born after them has *inherited* the same spiritually-dead condition. We are each born dead in sin—our spirit is dead. We are born enemies of God. We are born sinners capable of nothing good, in and of ourselves. Note that we are not considered sinners because we commit acts of sin. Rather we commit acts of sin because of our natural-born, inherited sin-nature. We cannot help ourselves, which is precisely why God promised, then fulfilled His promise to send us a Redeemer.

Jesus, the Promised Redeemer

God miraculously fulfilled His promise through the birth, life, death, and resurrection of Jesus. In God's wisdom, He chose the specific family line for Jesus—the lineage of King David. To a young virgin woman named Mary, God sent the angel Gabriel who proclaimed;

Do not be afraid, Mary, for you have found favor with

> God. And behold, you will conceive in your womb and bear a son, and you shall call his name Jesus. He will be great and will be called the Son of the Most High. And the Lord God will give to him the throne of his father David, and he will reign over the house of Jacob forever, and of his kingdom there will be no end.[28]

As she was a virgin, his words greatly perplexed Mary. She asked the angel Gabriel how this could be. The angel answered and said to her, "The Holy Spirit will come upon you, and the power of the Most High will overshadow you; therefore the child to be born will be called holy—the Son of God."[29]

To help our understanding, consider that the Holy Spirit of God miraculously caused Mary to become pregnant without sexual intercourse. In this way Jesus was conceived both fully human and fully God. In our quest to learn how to apply effective faith and to experience the hope Christ offers, we must understand that He operated primarily in His humanity while on earth. He intentionally subjected His human body and soul to the Father's will. "...who, though he [Jesus] was in the form of God, did not count equality with God a thing to be grasped, but emptied himself, by taking the form of a servant, being born in the likeness of men. And being found in human form, he humbled himself becoming obedient to the point of death, even death on a cross." (Philippians 2:6-8)

Jesus was fully human, and without relying on His divinity, He lived in His humanity, utterly reliant on His Spiritual relationship with God the Father, and lived a sinless life. He thereby became the One who could pay the debt of sin that we owe, but cannot pay because of our sin-nature. The Bible tells us that He was tempted in every way that sin is known to man, yet He did not sin. This unique purity of human existence, through willful reliance on God the Father, allowed Him to be the one suitable Sacrifice to redeem all of humanity.

We learn from reading 2 Corinthians 5:21, "For our sake he [God the Father] made him [Jesus] to be sin who knew no sin, so that in him [Jesus] we might become the righteousness of God." Jesus took on the sins of the world so that anyone who believes in Him will not perish but have everlasting life. His sinless life, lived out entirely in His humanity, was offered up as the supreme sacrifice. His tortured, body was put to death, death by crucifixion, then He was buried in a tomb. But three days later—as foretold by the Old Testament prophet Hosea, as referenced in the Old Testament by Jonah and as prophesied by Jesus Himself,[30]—by the power of the Holy Spirit, Jesus was bodily resurrected. Jesus' resurrection is the final act of His earthly mission and the fulfillment of God's promise to send a Redeemer. From this victory over sin, sickness, disease, and death all who believe and receive Jesus as Savior and Lord are given a new spirit, a new heart, and an opportunity for a new mind. In time we will also inherit our new bodies in Christ.[31] Jesus is the personification of God's promise. Through faith in Him, we are given the ability to overcome the sin of this world, and to enjoy the abundant, victorious life Christ offers.

Simply through faith in Jesus dying in our place, as the *Sacrificial Lamb of God* who fully paid the debt of sin for all who will believe and receive Him, we are restored to a full, pure relationship with God the Father, by the power of the Holy Spirit. Through faith in Jesus being Who He claimed to be, God offers a spiritually born-again new life—an utterly transformed spirit to anyone who chooses to believe in and receive Jesus as their personal Savior and Lord. Jesus was conveying these truths to Nicodemus. A spiritual birth is needed to restore us to God the Father, through faith in Jesus Christ, by the power of the Holy Spirit.

Not everyone will make this choice to be restored to God through faith in Christ. But understand, God never had the intention that man would be separated from Him and all that's good. God's preference for mankind was and is the perfect and holy world He created and the same eternal communion He intended for Adam and Eve. God still offers these things to anyone who will believe Him for His Word—His promises.

By Faith We Are New Creatures Capable of New Feats

Those who place their faith in Jesus Christ are made into utterly new creatures—spiritually-regenerated human beings that never existed before. We are fully made new creations in Christ! 2 Corinthians 5:17 reads, "Therefore, if anyone is in Christ, he is a new creation. The old has passed away; behold, the new has come." This should give you tremendously overwhelming joy! With faith in Christ, your old sinful nature, with all its shame, guilt, bondage, and enmity with God, has been destroyed and no longer exits. Moreover, your nature's been replaced with an utterly newly-born creation! This means that personal salvation provides us a new spirit allowing us to work with God to transform our mind, soul, and even our body in Christ!

As amazing as our new spirit being is, very sadly, personal salvation and confidence of eternal life in heaven is where the celebration stops for most Christians. Why? Because they have been deceived about God's motives—His plan, will, and intentions for them. They see God's "dos and don'ts" for living as restrictive and antiquated—no longer relevant. They prefer instead to live a life of their own choosing, within their own power and abilities. But when we understand the depths of God's love for us, and that all His "dos and don'ts" are for our own protection and good, the only rational response is to unabashedly embrace Him and all His ways. When we understand that He loves us, He created us, and He knows what is best for us, we'd be foolish not to embrace Him.

What Does Christ Mean to You?

If at this point you realize you have never fully understood the Christian faith and all that faith offers, is there any reason you can't embrace Him now? Jesus died to give you the opportunity to be rightly-related to God the Father through faith in Who Jesus claimed and demonstrated Himself to be. But more, He also died to give you the power to overcome the sin of this world—to live the abundant, victorious life He exemplified and taught His disciples to live.

Jesus' first twelve disciples were simple, ordinary men. They didn't have prominent positions in society. They weren't highly educated. Neither were they wealthy. But they found so much more than these earthly things through embracing Jesus as their Savior and Lord. They found hope in Christ that allowed them to enjoy peace and security in both times of plenty and in times of need. As a result of their faith in Christ, they lived and worked by the same power Christ prayerfully called upon through communion with God the Father. With hearts lined up with the Father and His plans and purposes, they fully embraced their new spiritual being. They learned how to cause the soul and body and the physical world to come under subjection to the power of Christ, through the Holy Spirit. They learned how and when to perform miracles, signs, and wonders for the benefit of people and the glory of God.

Christ still offers us the hope and the power to live victoriously in this life and into the life to come. If you want to be restored into a right relationship with God the Father, through faith in Christ, all you need to do is believe in Jesus for Who He is, and by believing, receive the Holy Spirit. Romans 10:8-13 reads:

> The word is near you, in your mouth and in your heart (that is, the word of faith that we proclaim); because, if you confess with your mouth that Jesus is Lord and believe in your heart that God raised him from the dead, you will be saved. For with the heart one believes and is justified, and with the mouth one confesses and is saved. For the Scripture says, "Everyone who believes in him will not be put to shame." For there is no distinction between Jew and Greek; for the same Lord is Lord of all, bestowing his riches on all who call on him. For "everyone who calls on the name of the Lord will be saved.[32]

A word of caution: many have sought to merely receive the power or gifts of God without desiring a personal relationship with Him. As stated earlier, I wanted Jesus to be my Savior to keep me from hell in my eternal life. But I wanted to remain lord of my temporal life. That is, until I made such a hopeless mess of my life that I needed someone greater than myself to save me. I share from experience: no one can have the power or enjoy the victory and promises of God without genuinely desiring a personal relationship with Him through faith in Christ.

Your first step in renewing your hope is to enter into a genuine personal relationship with God the Father, through faith in Jesus Christ, by the power of the Holy Spirit. If at this point you sense you earnestly desire this in a way you never have before, then simply proclaim your faith in Christ right where you are. You can pray this simple prayer, *Father God, I thank you for opening the eyes of understanding in my heart. Today, as never before, I believe in Jesus as the Son of God, whose personal sacrifice opened the way for me to be restored into a right relationship with You. I choose to receive Jesus as my personal Lord, so I can begin to walk in Your ways in this life. I thank You for this eternal Hope, and eagerly look forward to what You will do for me and through me, for Your glory and the benefit of many. Amen.*

If you prayed that prayer, take the time now to reflect on the meaning. Bask in God's pleasure with you. You have exchanged your naturally-born sinful condition for a supernaturally-born sinless condition. Your spirit has been made entirely new! I celebrate with all of heaven that your name is written in the *Lamb's Book of Life*. I pray you learn to effectively work out your new found faith into the abundant, victorious life Christ died to give you, and may this book be exceedingly helpful to that end.

Christ in Us is Our Hope and Glory

From the moment we say *yes* to Jesus as Savior and Lord, we are imbued with God's Holy Spirit. 2 Corinthians 1:22 and 2 Corinthians 5:5 clearly relate that we receive the Holy Spirit "who is the guarantee of our inheritance," according to Ephesians 1:14. As a Believer, your individual spirit has been made sinless and you have the indwelling of the Holy Spirit to guide and help you in all things. Considering how Jesus was conceived both fully human and fully God and that He relied on His Spiritual relationship—not the powers of deity—we have every reason to live according to Christ's example. As a Believer your new spirit has access to the full measure of the Holy Spirit who resides within you.

The Holy Spirit has many roles in God's scheme of things and therefore many descriptive names. A study about the Holy Spirit is recommended for all Believers to help us cement the reality and extent of the power and ability to which we have access. But for the sake of this introductory understanding, know that the Holy Spirit is the Third Person of the God-head. He is equal with God the Father and God the Son, yet is a distinct Person of the God-head. He has His own areas of ministry.

The Hebrew word uniformly used for the Holy Spirit is *rauch*, meaning "breath," "wind," or "breeze." The word spirit in the Greek is *pneuma*, also meaning "breath," or "blow." In Genesis, we read that God breathed on Adam to give him life. This gives us understanding that the Holy Spirit is the breath of life. He is also referred to as the power of God. Two major instances where we can learn of the ability of His power are found first in the development of all Creation, and also in the resurrection of Christ. He is referred to as the Spirit of the Lord, the fear (honor/reverence) of the Lord, the prophets/prophecy, wisdom, understanding, counsel, knowledge, might, life, unity, truth, conviction, adoption, sanctification, sound mind, supplication, union, communion, grace, judgment, and revelation. He is called our teacher, friend, and author of our faith. He is the source of God's power for us, ever available, and the fulfillment of our salvation in Christ. His gifts include spiritual baptism, indwelling accessibility, illumination, and internal guidance.

The same power that resurrected Jesus from the dead—the Holy Spirit—resides in Believers to empower us to *overcome*. The word overcome as used in the New Testament is the Greek word *nikao*, which means to subdue (literally or figuratively), to conquer, overcome, prevail, and get the victory. This word is used twenty-eight times in the New Testament and each time conveys that Believers have the power for total victory over all that comes against our faith.

The problem is that we haven't been sufficiently taught how to live as victorious Christians in this fallen world. Just as a child must be taught many things to successfully grow and mature and be an effective individual, so must we be trained-up as new supernaturally-born Believers to become successful, mature Christ-followers. We need to have a better understanding of the two worlds in which we live as born-again Believers. My prayer is that you find the teaching provided here helpful in guiding you to live out of your new spirit.

Living in Two Worlds

God has created the physical world within the spiritual world. Both co-exist. The physical world is subject to the spiritual world. In our natural physically-born state, we live according to the condition of the fallen physical world. However, those who become supernaturally born-again live in both the spiritual and the physical worlds. Furthermore, being spiritually renewed, Believers have the distinct ability to overcome the hostile physical world.

With the help of God's Holy Spirit, we can refuse to be influenced or controlled by this physical world. The Apostle Paul instructs Believers in Romans 12:1-2:

> I appeal to you therefore, brothers, by the mercies of God, to present your bodies as a living sacrifice, holy and acceptable to God, which is your spiritual worship. Do not be conformed to this world, but be transformed by the renewal of your mind, that by testing you may discern what is the will of God, what is good and acceptable and perfect.[33]

As mentioned, the moment a person is born-again, their spirit is completely regenerated and made holy, but their soul and body need to be subjected to their new spirit with the help of the Holy Spirit. Our soul and body are still targets of the enemy. In fact, the primary battleground of choice for the enemy of God is in our mind. This is why we're instructed to be diligent to take every thought captive, "For the weapons of our warfare are not of the flesh but have divine power to destroy strongholds. We destroy arguments and every lofty opinion raised *against the knowledge of God*, and take every thought captive to obey Christ."[34] [Emphasis added], (2 Corinthians 10:4-5)

Additionally, the Apostle John instructs Believers, "Do not love the world or the things in the world. If anyone loves the world, the love of the Father is not in him. For all that is in the world—the desires of the flesh and the desires of the eyes and pride of life—is not from the Father but is from the world. And the world is passing away along with its desires, but whoever does the will of God abides forever."[35] (1 John 2:15-17)

Born-again Believers are to be *in* this world but no longer *of* this world. This is true in terms of our new eternal spirit. But until our physical lives come to an end, we remain in this fallen world capable of being influenced by it, unless we are diligent about cooperating with the Holy Spirit's *sanctifying* [purifying] power.

Our free-will is not automated to *godly choices only* at the time we're born-again. Free-will would not be *free* if that were the case. God wants relationship with those who want relationship with Him, as demonstrated by all the choices we make, even in our daily lives. Obedience to God and His ways demonstrates our desire for Him.

Explaining more about the Christian's predicament of living in two worlds, Dr. Tom Barkey, Pastor of Church of Grace in Yorba Linda, California explains:

> The two worlds Believers live in are very different and yet quite similar. Just as the physical world has absolute laws such as the law of gravity, physics, mechanics, motion or thermodynamics, so are there absolute laws in the spiritual world. Physical beings remain in the physical world. Spiritual beings, on the other hand, can visit the physical world. Spiritual beings, both heavenly and demonic,

influence people as they are welcomed or entertained by individuals. The demonic spirits are enemies of God and all who belong to Him and they are consistently active seeking to ensnare Believers to destroy their testimony. Revelation 12:11 addressing the final defeat of Satan and his followers explains "And they [referring to Believers in Christ] have conquered him [the enemy] by the blood of the Lamb [Jesus] and by the word of their testimony, for they loved not their lives even unto death."[36] If Christians don't rely on the indwelling power and help of the Holy Spirit, they can become entangled with the sin of the world. Christians need to learn the laws of the spiritual world to overcome the hostility of physical world. Christians are uniquely capable of living in the physical world by the leading of their new spirit, guided by the Holy Spirit.

To be victorious Christians in this physical world, we need to learn the laws, instructions, and methods of the spiritual world. You'll find more about the laws of the spiritual world in Chapter Three. Once you understand the spiritual laws, in order to effectively operate within them and bring transformation to your physical world, you will need to follow these ten instructions. I call them the *Ten Commandments of Effective Faith:*

- Believe God
- Surrender Self to Jesus
- Rely on the Holy Spirit
- Study and apply the Word of God
- Maintain fellowship/accountability with other Believers
- Actively seek to mature your faith
- Obey God

- Resist the devil
- Operate in Christ's authority
- Expect God's best to occur

If you have faith in Christ, you have every reason to walk in hope. Not a hope that's akin to wishful thinking, but a confident hope—a certain hope that knows your victory is assured! You need to learn how to rightly apply sound faith. My goal for you is that you will be fully-equipped to experience all the breakthroughs you're entitled to according to God's will, by the time you finish reading this book.

In the next chapter, we'll learn the importance of a clear understanding about *faith in Christ* in order to have faith conviction that can move mountains.

CHAPTER TWO

Faith Realized

Apprehend God's Promises

Christ in us is our hope and glory.[1] This hope is available for anyone who desires to discover and live in life-giving truth. With the power of the Holy Spirit to overcome the obstacles in this life readily available, why don't we see more victorious Christians?

By reading the pages of the *Gospels*, (the books of Matthew, Mark, Luke, and John), we learn of the miracles that Jesus and His disciples performed. In verse after verse, Scriptures proclaim the power available to all who place their faith in Jesus. Based on Scriptures, we should find abounding hope in any circumstance! So why do hope and the supernatural breakthroughs people need seem elusive? As I wrote in the Introduction, hindering the miraculous has to do with unbelief.

Unbelief is a condition certain to prevent God from working in our lives. He will never work against the human will. Many who profess Christianity choose not to believe that miracles are available today. The two viewpoints are *Cessationists* (those who believe that the supernatural gifts revealed in Scripture died with the death of the last of the original Apostles) and *Continuationists* (those who believe that the supernatural gifts have never ceased to be available, but have merely not been properly accessed.) I explore this more in Chapters Five and Seven. For the purposes of this chapter, I'm assuming that you are one who would not reject the occurrence of a miracle if that miracle made your life better.

Accessing God's Promises

For the actualization of the miraculous, faith must be based in Christ—His power, will, and intentions for humanity in this earthly existence. Christ is referred to as the *Living Word* of God because He personified God's promise to send a Redeemer. In effect, He is the embodiment of all God's promises.

The Bible is referred to as the *Written Word* of God, because in Scripture we find all the recorded promises of God.

There are two primary Greek words that describe Scripture. Both are translated *word* in the New Testament.

Logos principally refers to the total inspired Word of God and to Jesus—the Living Word. *Logos* is found in John 1:1; Luke 8:11; Philippians 2:16; Hebrews 4:12; and other verses. Strictly defined, logos means logic.[2] However, in Greek philosophy, *logos* also referred to a universal, divine reason that acts according to the principle of the universe. Over time the word came to mean a mediating principle between God and the world and can be understood as God's Word or the Divine Wisdom, which is immanent in the world.[3]

The second Greek word translated *word* is *rhema*, which refers to the spoken word. *Rhema* literally means an *utterance* (individually, collectively, or specifically). Examples are found in Luke 1:38; 3:2; 5:5; and Acts 11:16.[4] As explained by Advanced Training Institute International, *rhema* is a verse or portion of Scripture that the Holy Spirit brings to our attention with application to a current situation or need for direction.[5]

Faith in God and His Word (all forms) is the kind of faith that pleases God and that brings Him to express His pleasure by blessing us in our spirit, soul, and physical existence. The very first miracle that comes through the four-step process of 1. Understanding; 2. Accepting; 3.

Believing; and 4. Receiving is that of redemption. Recreating our spirit-man is a miracle of spiritual redemption. The fact that God still redeems those who by faith in Jesus want to be reunited with Him is reason enough for me to believe that other miracles remain available today. Yet, the reality is we don't hear of, see, or experience many miraculous claims that are often dismissed as being natural world events.

Believe and You Shall Receive

Whether we realize the truth or not, we all receive according to what we believe. If you believe you are second-rate, you will never achieve first place. You will conduct your life, even your thought life, according to your beliefs. If on the other hand, you believe you are who God says you are through faith in Christ, you will experience life accordingly. We will receive according to what we believe, whether or not what we believe is true or good. This concept is entirely different from the so-called *Power of Positive Thinking*. We cannot *will* matters into existence. Only God can do that. We can, however, influence what reality we experience based on what we believe. We will receive according to what we believe, whether or not what we believe is true or good. When I travel and speak I ask my audiences, "Who in this room wants to live their life on the basis of a lie?" No one ever raises their hand to that question. How vitally important for us then, that we make certain we know and believe truth, which is found in God by faith in Jesus.

If we can learn to believe that God can do what He says He can do, which includes defying physical laws, then we position ourselves to experience the miraculous. God's intervention in your life for the good is available to you, if your faith is in Christ. Believe this!

Modern Day Miracle Battle of Life and Death

Natalie and Paul Valcarcel are two people I know who exemplify believing God for His Word. Natalie is an itty-bitty-sized person with a tremendous-sized faith. Her story of believing God against all odds and professional medical advice is one that is sure to inspire you to willfully demonstrate spiritual tenacity in your own trials.

When Natalie was twenty-nine years old, she began to experience such serious pain before her monthly periods that she writhed on the floor and thought that she would die from the pain alone. One day while at work, the pain became so severe that she was taken to the emergency room. The medical professionals performed an ultra-sound only to find a fibroid tumor.

The doctor assured Natalie that the tumor wasn't anything for her to worry about, that women have fibroids frequently. Noting the tumor was only six centimeters, the doctor concluded that nothing needed to be done. She was completely convinced that there was no reason for alarm.

This diagnosis came just two weeks before Natalie's wedding day. With her upcoming marriage to Paul in mind, naturally Natalie asked, "Is this going to affect my having children?" The doctor responded that many women with fibroids are able to conceive and that she considered Natalie's worry a non-issue.

Natalie and Paul were married, but within a few months she noticed that things just weren't the same as before. She felt the mass within growing, but was consistently told by her doctor not to worry.

About nine months after their wedding, Natalie decided to see the doctor again, especially since her level of discomfort was increasing. At this visit, the doctor reported that the mass was bigger than the original ultra-sound showed. She reported that the fibroid should probably be removed by a fairly simple surgery. In Natalie's words:

> I went in for surgery believing that Dr. Luna would simply remove the tumor and everything would be just fine. I believe that she had the same confidence as well. In the middle of my surgery while I was still under anesthesia, she came out to the waiting room where Paul and our families waited. She asked to speak to Paul and told him that the tumor was much bigger than she had thought and that they could not remove the tumor without taking the uterus. She came out to get permission from Paul to continue to proceed. She expressed that she felt I wasn't ready to wake up and find I'd undergone a hysterectomy. She told him with tears in her eyes *I hate when bad things happen to good people.* Paul told her not to perform the hysterectomy—that he wanted to talk to me first.
>
> When I came to, Dr. Luna told me she was unable to remove the tumor. She explained that I needed to recover and then they would attempt another surgery at a later date. Since she had vacation planned, we agreed that we'd use that time for my recovery and we'd plan the next procedure when she returned.

Several days later, the doctor called Natalie and explained that the tumor was enveloping the uterus. She told Natalie not to hold out any hope of conceiving at this stage due to the development and placement of the tumor. Based on all her medical experience and the threat of the tumor, the doctor recommended a hysterectomy. Natalie explains her phone conversation with the doctor:

> I trusted my doctor and listened to what she

> recommended. She wanted to start me on hormone therapy to get my body ready for surgery. She explained that hormones were the next immediate step. I felt a resistance within and I told her that I didn't feel like I wanted to do that right now. I needed to pray about it. I didn't want to make any decisions without prayer. I asked her to give me some time to pray and assured her that I was listening to her.
>
> After I hung up with Dr. Luna, I went to the Lord in prayer. I admit I was kind of mad and asked God, *What's happening?* I told Him as I sat on the couch still recovering, *I need to hear from you so I'm not leaving this spot until You show me what I need to do in this situation. I don't know what to do or how to handle this. But You do, so I'm going to sit here until you speak to me.*

Natalie then sat in utter silence and stillness. No television, no radio, no reading. She sat and listened, determined not to move until she heard from the Lord.

> I didn't hear anything from Him all day. When I went to bed that night I laid down and no sooner did my head reach the pillow than I heard Him say, *Be fruitful and multiply.* I thought, *Really? That's all You're going to tell me?* I naturally thought about the passage in Genesis where God instructs all of humanity to be fruitful and multiply and concluded that I already knew that instruction. A bit put off, I fell asleep.
>
> When I woke up the next morning, a bit perplexed that all I heard God say was *Be fruitful and multiply,* I decided to

look up every passage in Scripture where those words are used. I found five places in the Bible. In each instance, God was issuing a command, telling the person to do what He said, with the added admonition that what He said was going to happen. I remember thinking, *Okay, I understand now that you want me to be fruitful and multiply. You spoke to me with this command in such a way that it is going to happen. I believe You so I conclude that it is Your will for me to have children. But what do I do next? You're commanding my body to do this.* Then I heard God instruct me to read the story of Jacob. I thought, *What? The story of Jacob? What's that story got to do with my situation?* If God said read about Abraham and Sarah or Zacharias and Elizabeth that would make sense, but Jacob? Then I heard God tell me to read the whole story of Jacob.

After I read the story, and really pondered over the words, I realized that Jacob understood the power of blessing. He believed if he could just grab onto God's available blessing, that blessing would be his. He went to extremes to get blessings in his life. He lied, he deceived, and he wrestled. He did whatever he had to do to get a blessing spoken over him knowing that if the blessing was spoken, what was said would happen. So I asked God, *What blessings have been spoken over me that I may have discarded or not taken seriously or forgotten?* The Lord replied, *Your wedding blessing.*

With the fresh understanding from Jacob's story that what God commands is ours for the taking, I immediately called my mom to ask her about the blessing she insisted

Paul and I have spoken over us on our wedding day.

When Paul and Natalie were married, Natalie's mother insisted on having a blessing spoken over the two of them by both sets of parents. Her mother is a Believer, but not her father. Paul's parents are Believers. That her father agreed to participate was a miracle in itself. On the day of the wedding, their parents spoke Psalm 128 over Paul and Natalie. "Just before we ate our dinner following the wedding ceremony, we heard these words from our parents,"

> Blessed (happy, fortunate, to be envied) is everyone who fears, reveres, and worships the Lord, who walks in His ways and lives according to His commandments. For you shall eat [the fruit] of the labor of your hands; happy (blessed, fortunate, enviable) shall you be, and it shall be well with you. Your wife shall be like a fruitful vine in the innermost parts of your house; your children shall be like olive plants round about your table. Behold, thus shall the man be blessed who reverently and worshipfully fears the Lord. May the Lord bless you out of Zion [His sanctuary], and may you see the prosperity of Jerusalem all the days of your life; Yes, may you see your children's children. Peace be upon Israel! (Psalm 128, Amplified)

Natalie shares her response:
> At the time they spoke, I received their words as a nice general blessing from Scripture, and thought, *That was nice, Mom, thanks.* I dismissed the reading without paying much attention. But once I looked the psalm up and read the words, I realized that the blessing spoken over us was for

me personally as the wife and for Paul as the husband. I started thinking like Jacob and snatched this blessing.

Every day when I was in pain or not feeling well or the tumor seemed to have the upper hand, I would say, *Thank you, Lord, that I am a fruitful vine in the innermost parts of my home and that I will see my children around my table like olive plants. And I thank you that I will see my children's children.* I held on and prayed daily. I understood without a doubt the Lord's will was for me to have children.

The experience was very difficult for Natalie as the tumor continued to grow. The doctor would compassionately speak to Natalie stating that she didn't understand what Natalie was doing. Dr. Luna was convinced that Natalie couldn't have children based on the tumor she actually saw during the first attempt at surgery. She admonished Natalie stating, "You need to do something about this. I don't want so see you end up in the emergency room with your life on the line."

With respect for her doctor, Natalie replied, "I know. But I'm still praying." She didn't want to dismiss her doctor or come across that she was disrespecting her professional opinion. So she told the doctor, "I'm grateful for you, and I appreciate you being patient with me as I wait for a miracle." I was honest with her but not at all dismissive. She was respectful of me, too, but clearly quite frustrated with me at times."

Every six months Natalie was checked hoping that the doctor would say things were getting better. She also knew that she needed a witness to the miracle she was believing God for. What better person than the doctor who believed the prospect of conceiving a child was impossible?

Five years went by as the tumor grew. Natalie looked like she was six-months pregnant. People often asked her when she was due. She'd reply,

"No, I'm not pregnant. I have a fibroid tumor. But I'm believing God, and I know one day I will be pregnant."

The tumor growth demanded an incredible amount of blood. There were large arteries feeding the tumor. Her doctor sternly instructed Natalie to make the decision to have the hysterectomy, even threatening to make Natalie a ward of the state. In March, 2010, Dr. Luna told Natalie that she was putting her on a deadline—if Natalie didn't get the miracle she was waiting for within a couple of months, Dr. Luna would schedule the hysterectomy.

As the months went by, Natalie did her best to honor her doctor while still believing God for a miracle. The day before her scheduled doctor's visit, Natalie received a phone call from a friend. She asked if Natalie had ever heard of a procedure called fibroid embolization. Her friend had heard about the procedure on the radio, called the number given, and gave them Natalie's name and phone number. She told Natalie to expect a call from that doctor's office.

The same day the nurse consultant from the office running the radio advertisement called Natalie. Natalie told her of the seriousness of her condition. As Natalie now looked nearly full-term pregnant, clearly the fibroid was not a small tumor. The nurse explained the procedure to Natalie. Natalie took the information she'd learned with her to her appointment with Dr. Luna. She asked the doctor if she'd heard of the fibroid embolization procedure. Dr. Luna had, so Natalie then asked, "What do you think about the prospect for me, especially since a hysterectomy is so drastic?" Dr. Luna didn't think the procedure would work for me, but was willing to try because she'd seen me hold out so long for a miracle. Natalie recalls what this season was like for her:

> In my prayer time I clearly felt confirmation in my spirit that this was the direction to go. I wasn't daunted by my

doctor's claim that I'd be infertile. God was able to have Abraham and Sarah conceive even when they were way past their ability to do so. I thought, *If they had zero chances and God had them conceive, then if I have zero chances God can have me conceive.*

On the day of the embolization procedure, I felt the Spirit of God all over me comforting me that I was in His will. Just before I was prepped, one of the nurses asked me, *Do you want to have children?* I said *Yes*. She replied, *Then you shouldn't have this procedure, because there is no possibility you can get pregnant after this.* I assured her that I'd been apprised of the dangers but that I'd prayed about my situation, and I was confident that I was to do the embolization.

The nurse then went to the specialist who personally approached me with the same inquiry. They had a major concern about my decision. The doctor asked, *You do realize that this procedure causes infertility, don't you?* I replied, *I understand.*

They finally started the procedure. I was not put under any anesthesia and had been forewarned that the surgery would be extremely painful. I was told the doctor would be very generous with pain medication. Yet I felt no pain! I could have been given as much pain medication as I wanted, I simply needed to ask for it. But I didn't need medication. I felt nothing.

After the procedure, I still didn't need any pain medication. The nurses said I was really strong. And I told them that I really wasn't, that Christ was my strength, and He's all I needed. They tried to encourage me to take medication, believing I was in shock. So they gave me morphine which made me sick. I then insisted on taking none.

The specialist came in the next day to express that the operation was very successful. He explained, *We tell everyone if they want to get pregnant not to do this procedure. But in your case I think your chances of getting pregnant are better than before.* He said that the arteries to the fibroid were the largest he'd ever seen. He explained that the process is to sever the arteries and then to plug them by putting two or three pellets at the severed ends. But in my case, he had to use sixteen to eighteen pellets to accomplish the plugging. Clearly I'd been feeding a monster in my body.

We're now at the end of June, 2010. My husband was hired by Church of Grace to lead worship. Because of my need to recover from the embolism procedure, I didn't attend church with him until late July or early August. No one knew who I was. While sitting in the main sanctuary watching the worship team practice, a little lady named Mary, who had been praying over the people who would eventually sit in the then empty chairs, came up to me. *Hi, I don't think I've ever met you, my name is Mary.* I told her my name and who I was after which time she went back to praying over the chairs. About ten minutes later she came up to me again and asked, *Do you have children?* I replied, *No, not yet. We're believing for children.* Her face lit up, *You are? The reason I came over to you is because I was praying over on the other side and the Lord told me to tell you that you are going to have a child.* I explained a little of what I'd been through, and that

I was believing God for a miracle. She began jumping up and down, excited to have obeyed the Lord to speak His word and provide confirmation.

Based on Mary's prophetic word from the Lord, I expected the tumor would shrink as the blood flow ceased. Instead, the tumor developed more arteries and took on life again. The fibroid not only didn't shrink, but got bigger and lodged up into my ribs. I had a hard time sitting or breathing. My doctor was really frustrated with me and said, *I told you there was no guarantee the embolism procedure would work. Now things are getting worse and I have to put you on disability. Maybe pain in your ribs will be the thing that will push you to finally do the hysterectomy.* I replied, *Okay, just give me the weekend to pray, and I'll get back to you on Monday about the hysterectomy.*

I went home that Friday discouraged because I know what the Word says, and I believe God's promises, but everything seemed to negate them. I couldn't get physically comfortable. I was worried how we would pay our bills with me not working. So, I just prayed. I prayed until I got peace back again. I didn't physically feel better but I had the peace of God and that was all I needed. I prayed, *I know you have this, God, and I thank you for your promise.*

Sunday of that weekend, sitting in the parking lot of the church, while Paul was practicing with the band, I prayed and brought up all my concerns before the Lord. As I remained quiet, God spoke to me saying, *You will have a child. And you will have three. And this is how you will know—the Pastor will confirm it to you today.* I replied, *Lord, just as you say,*

I believe Your will will be done. I sat in the sanctuary where Pastor Tom Barkey was doing his rounds of shaking of hands and greetings before service. He shook my hand and went on his way. The service went on as usual, except at the end. That's when Pastor Tom said, *I'm going to do something a little different. The Lord just told me to do this now. This has happened to me three times before, and that is, the Lord has told me that someone here is going to have a baby. With two of the women that I have given this Word to before, they were pregnant within months. The other one it took a year before she got pregnant. This girl here today doesn't even know that I am talking about her, but when I shook her hand this morning, the Lord told me "pregnant". I asked the Lord, Do I tell her now? and the Lord said No. Tell her when I tell you to tell her. The Lord is telling me to tell her right now.* He then looked at me and said *Natalie, this is you. And this is what the Lord is saying to you right now 'Nothing is impossible with God!'* I said out loud, *The Lord told me that you would confirm this to me today.* He said to come up and tell them what the Lord told me. So I did, and then he prayed for me. That day I emailed my doctor and told her that I wasn't going to do the hysterectomy. This was November, 2010.

I still had no relief physically. Everything in the natural world went against everything the Lord was speaking to me. Everyday I had to make a conscious decision to believe what the Lord had spoken to me.

I went through the month of December with lots of pain and discomfort and prayed for the Lord to take the fibroid away. I managed to attend a New Year's Eve party with my husband where we praised the Lord for the New Year. When I woke up that New Year's Day morning, I was surprised that I slept the whole night. When I got up I realized I had no pain or discomfort at all! This grace was given to me for the next 4 months.

At the beginning of March, I had a very painful period. I closed the door to my bedroom to pray regarding the pain. I heard the Lord say, *This will be your last period.* I thanked the Lord and went out the door to the living room and told my husband, *This will be my last period!* My husband, not really paying attention to my statement, said, *Okay*, and continued watching T.V. And sure enough it was my last period! On April 11th, my birthday, I learned I was pregnant!

I emailed my doctor immediately and told her that my miracle came through! She emailed back the next day asking me to come in to have some blood work done to be certain the pregnancy was not tubal. I did, and my hormone levels were very good. Next she ordered an ultrasound. Finding the uterus took a long time because of the size of the tumor, but the ultrasound tech eventually found the embryonic sack which proved that this was a miracle. I was about four weeks pregnant.

I went in to see my doctor a few weeks later and she listened to determine if we could hear a heartbeat. When she heard the beat, we both gasped! She said, *You must have a direct line to God!* This was my last appointment with her because she was referring me to a high-risk pregnancy specialist due to my age and situation.

Dr. Montgomery, the specialist, was very concerned about my situation. He was afraid I would not live through the pregnancy. I told him, *Don't worry, I'm not going to die.* He said, *I heard you are a woman of faith.* I said, *I am.* He said, *Then you are the perfect person to go through a pregnancy like this because faith's what's going to be required to get you through this.*

The tumor continued to grow. When I was six-months pregnant I was admitted to the hospital because the tumor was compressing my right kidney. Upon admission, I asked if I could have my very painful right leg checked. They sent me for an ultrasound on my leg. The next morning my specialist came into my room and said, *You have a blood clot from your knee to your groin. It could be past the groin but we can't see how far because the tumor is blocking our view of far it goes. This blood clot is like a bullet in a gun ready to go off…* then he broke down and started to cry. When he could continue, he told me that before he came in to tell me this news, he'd had a meeting with over thirty doctors in their hospital concerning my case—not one of them wanted to take me as a patient. Not one of them felt I would survive. He called UCLA and USC to see if they would take my case and they asked what he thought they could do that he couldn't. He called other Kaiser doctors to see if anyone would take me. He found one doctor who said she would take me on. So he said that he was sending me right now to the Kaiser Hospital on Sunset Blvd. in L.A. He teared-up again and gave me hug and said, *I don't want you to die.* I assured him, *Dr. Montgomery, I'm not going to die. The next time you see me, you will see me holding my baby.* He replied, *I really hope that happens. Look at you! You're as cool as a cucumber!* I then said, *Dr. Montgomery, I know God didn't bring me this far for me to die in the end.* To which he responded, *I wish I had your faith.*

Immediately after that conversation, I was sent to the Kaiser in L.A. by ambulance. I was admitted to the ICU where I was watched carefully. When I arrived in my room, I got a call from Dr. Montgomery. He hadn't thought I'd survive the ambulance ride. My new doctor, Dr. Friedrich, put me on a light blood thinner because I was pregnant. She told me the medication was only going to keep the blockage from getting bigger, but wouldn't dissolve the blood clot.

I was in ICU for two weeks under close watch. After two weeks, the doctor wanted to do an ultrasound on my leg to see how the blood clot was doing. I had the ultrasound done and the blood clot was nowhere to be found! I asked the doctor what she thought happened and she said she didn't know, but that maybe the blood thinner worked more effectively that she'd expected. I reminded her of what she said about the blood thinner originally. She said she knew but didn't know how else to explain the absence of the clot. I told her that we had a lot of people praying and I stated, *This is a miracle.* She said, *Well, this will definitely make your delivery a little less complicated.*

A week later, they did surgery to deliver my baby who was born two months before her due date. This life-threatening surgery/delivery ended up going as perfectly as anyone could have hoped.

Natalie and Paul's baby girl, Heaven Faith Valcarcel, was born on October 19, 2011, and weighed three pounds and seven ounces.

The tumor was not removed at the time of Heaven's birth for fear of Natalie losing too much blood and not surviving the surgery. The surgery to remove the tumor was scheduled two and a half months later. During the surgery, they removed the eighteen-pound tumor and her uterus. What they thought would be a four-hour surgery took only an hour and a half.

Today both the mother and baby are completely healthy. They are a miraculous testimony of God's fulfilling His promises and giving us the faith we need to persevere and see a matter through to His perfect end. But for the Valcarcel's, this is just the beginning. For God had told them they would have three children.

When I interviewed Natalie she expressed:

> God was developing our faith in the process over the five and half long years. We had enough faith to start the journey, but He clearly built our faith during that time. For years and years, I prayed for a miracle and nothing happened except the growing threat of the tumor. But I was convinced that God can do anything and usually not the way I expect Him to work. So whenever I had thoughts of doubt or fear or unbelief, I intentionally threw the thoughts out and didn't give them any credence. The Lord showed me many things in the five years—not the least of which is to be bold and press on expecting God to fulfill His promises. Some of the things God told me to do didn't make sense with the limited information we had, but I did them anyway confident I was hearing Him. I was committed to trust and obey Him. During the times when I really struggled the most, I sought the Lord. I would

literally force myself on the floor to pray. If I prayed while sitting, I'd find myself multitasking and becoming distracted. For me to be completely focused, I had to be on the floor.

Having experienced all we have with God with the birth of our daughter, Heaven, we don't doubt God's promise that we will have three children. How He chooses to fulfill His Word is entirely up to Him.

I chose not to edit out elements of her story so that you can understand the constant battle she was in and the continual effort she had to make to intentionally apply to receiving God's blessing. Natalie is an example of what we can endure and how we must persevere through to the end, working hard to fight fears and doubt if we want to receive the fulfillment of God's promises in our life.

Understand, too, that as you hold out in faith—as you stand against opposition to the promise you have from God, you are being a witness for God in the process. The promise fulfillment is not the end of your testimony to His faithfulness—you have a testimony during the process as well.

What I want you to clearly grasp from the Valcarcel's story is that they refused to believe any report other than God's, confident that He could and will fulfill His Word. By following Jesus' example of listening to God the Father and cooperating with Him and His plan, even though Natalie's very life was at risk, they experienced the miraculous. They received according to what God said, because of their belief, against all earthly odds. Hebrews 11:6 reads, "And without faith it is impossible to please him, for whoever would draw near to God must believe that he exists and that he rewards those who seek him."[6]

Faith Pleases God

To understand faith (our belief system), we need to realize that faith can be impacted for better or worse by what we believe to be truth, whether or not what we believe actually is true. Faith can be increased with added knowledge of God's truth and experience. Faith can also be decreased with thoughts, ideas, and conclusions contrary to the Word of God.

The enemy of God does not want Believers to have effective faith, so he is continually at work to cause us to question and doubt God and His Word, character, will, and intentions. By trying to keep Christians ignorant about God and faith, Satan renders our faith impotent, which directly impacts the results and power of Christ at work in and through our lives. Faith is measurable in terms of size, purity, ability, and *commendability*.

God Commends Believing Faith

In Matthew 8:5-13, we can read the story of the Roman Centurion living in Capernaum whose faith impressed Jesus so much that He turned to the crowd that was following Him and said, "Truly, I tell you, with no one in Israel have I found such faith."[7] Highly important to note here is Jesus was not commending faith in and of itself. Rather, He was commending the Centurion's faith *in Jesus* as the promised Savior/Deliverer, also referred to as the *Christ* or *Messiah*. *Christ* is the Greek word for the Hebrew word, *Messiah*, which means Anointed One.

Perhaps Jesus' declaration that if His followers had faith the size of a mustard seed, they would be able to move mountains[8] is comforting for you. It most definitely is for me. We don't need to have the great quantity of faith in Christ required to *move mountains*, but what faith we have must be pure and undefiled to be pleasing to God.

The hope and breakthroughs you need at this point in your life, whether as dramatic as the Valcarcel's or not, are something you can expect to have, if you properly understand and apply your faith correctly—if you effectively battle the enemy's relentless attempts against you.

Belief is Essential to Faith

Belief is essential to faith. To believe is to be convinced through mental processes. Faith is having enough belief to act even though the fullness of what is believed is not yet manifest. The Bible states, "Now faith is the assurance of things hoped for, the conviction of things not seen," Hebrews 11:1.[9]

Scriptural belief, as Jesus demonstrated, demands that we act in faith before God acts in reality based on what God reveals He will do. God initiates and we respond. By stepping out according to our belief in God's Word, character, will, and intent, we demonstrate our faith. Our belief is what releases God's promises in our lives. We demonstrate to both worlds in which we live—the physical and the spiritual—that we believe God is who He says He is and He will do what He's said He will do. This is faith that God commends.

Understand however, that much of what we call faith in our postmodern culture is merely a mental assent. A mental assent, or belief, is not *acting* by faith. "Our spiritual lives depend upon our constant affirmation of what God has declared, what God is in Christ, and what we are to the Father in Christ. *Confession* is faith's confirmation."[10] Correspondingly, action is faith's fulfillment. By acting on our faith, stepping out expecting God to fulfill His Word before He has done so, we affirm His Word. This is the kind of faith that pleases God—faith that He rewards. For anyone to be able to do this, especially in the face of opposition and potential harm, they must be utterly convinced, without a shred of doubt, that they are acting according to God's revealed will.

Effective Faith Positively Influences the World

Through faith in Christ, we are saved *from* the world, but for a time we must still live *in* the world. Why? Because God equips Believers for works of service on earth, in partnership with Him, to draw all men who will come unto Him. Believers have the privilege of partnering with God to help others discover the same personal salvation we've found. The blessed gift of salvation through faith in Christ is not just for our personal redemption, but to also demonstrate power over the ravages of this world, thereby helping to bring others to the saving knowledge and the overcoming power of faith in Christ. Effective faith is *others-focused*—by that I mean effective faith seeks the good for others over and above the self. Philippians 2:3 reads, "Do nothing from selfish ambition or conceit, but in humility count others more significant than yourselves."[11] Notice in the Scriptures how the many miracles, signs, and wonders done were always for the benefit of others and the glory of God. Faith that seeks to serve the self will fail. James 4:3 explains, "You ask and do not receive, because you ask wrongly, to spend it on your passions."[12] We are encouraged in Scripture to present our personal requests before God, and we are also encouraged to let others know of our needs that they may pray for us—that we pray for one another. Every one of God's promises to answer prayer is a conditional promise. The secret to receiving answers to prayer is satisfying the conditions, which is not difficult. We are simply required to become disciples of Jesus and learn His ways. We can do nothing. What's important is that we *become*.

Jesus spent much time explaining that He must leave this world in order to fulfill God's promise of redemption. However, He added that He wouldn't leave His followers without power. The Bible is very clear that in the last days, the evil and wickedness that is in this world will increase. Jesus firmly instructed His followers to remember that even though we will have troubles in this world, we are to take heart, for He has overcome the world.[13] So by not leaving us without power, He has left us with the ability to tap into God's demonstrated supernatural victory over this physical world. Jesus demonstrated and taught His early disciples not only about saving faith, but also how to wield effective faith, and to instruct others to do likewise.

In the next chapter, we'll explore the ways we can prepare ourselves in order to take hold of all that Christ died to provide those who sincerely profess and embrace the Christian faith.

CHAPTER THREE

Faith Personalized

Identify with Christ

Identity theft is a raging problem in this age of technology and global connectedness. But such theft is far from a new crime. The enemy of God has been working since Adam and Eve to cause people to give up their rightful God-given identity and corresponding authority. Because of our adversary's work, that we understand God's character, will, and intentions for us in context with His many promises is vitally important.

As discussed in Chapter One, once we resolutely determine to believe in and receive Jesus as our Lord and Savior, we are spiritually made into entirely new creations. From this new position, we are no longer identified with the enemy of God, but instead with God Himself through faith in Jesus. As such, we have a complete new identity and authority. The Scriptures declare that we are now kings and priests able to reign and rule with Christ. Believers are part of the royal family of the King of kings. We are joint heirs with Jesus in all that God owns and does. What a shame that so few of us thoroughly understand our new identity—that so many of us have been deceived.

What we believe is determined by our individual *free-will*. *We believe only that which we are willing to believe.* With this reality, the strategy of the enemy is to prevent us from being willing to believe the truth, especially about our new identity in Christ. He uses doubts and lies in various attacks to keep us from being willing to believe the truth. This is how he robs, steals, kills, and destroys.

We Must Know God's Promises to Claim Them

Don Gossett, co-author of *Words that Move Mountains,* shared his story of an extended time of financial lack. He wrote, "I asked God many questions. "Why are we in such desperate need financially?" "Why did we lose our home by repossession?" Asking questions when we are suffering is natural. But what Gossett reveals is how we must take hold of the supernatural when we need personal breakthroughs. He wrote:

> During that time, I read a wonderful book by Vernon Howard called *Word Power*. God used the message of that book to help me freshly understand the power of my words, and He gave me this Scripture: *"Can two walk together, except they be agreed?"* (Amos 3:3) God was asking me, "Do you want to walk with Me? Then you must agree with Me. You agree with Me by saying what My Word says. You have disagreed with Me by speaking lack, sickness, fear, defeat, and inability. If you want to walk with Me, you must agree with Me." As this truth became real to me, I asked His forgiveness for my failure to agree with Him and His Word.
>
> I must not hasten away from the truth of Amos 3:3. It's [in] the heart of all sincere Christians to walk closely with the Lord. The Bible records the testimony of Enoch: "[He] *walked with God."* (Genesis 5:24) Enoch wasn't the only person who could walk with God; you and I also can walk with Him. Hebrews 11:5 says that Enoch *pleased God* by agreeing in faith with God. We can walk just as closely with God as Enoch did if we choose to agree with Him in faith. How do we agree with God? We agree by saying what God says while disagreeing with the wicked, lying devil.[1]

We need to learn everything we can from Jesus, beginning with His confidence in God the Father's character, will, and intentions toward Him and all humanity. Additionally, we need to learn about Jesus' calling forth God's plans and purposes by faith as demonstrated through miracles, signs, and wonders as He walked this earth. We need to study and understand that Christ taught His disciples how to perform miracles, signs, and wonders, before He left this earth. The same power to overcome that Jesus and His disciples appropriated is available to the Christian Believer today as we work in partnership with God and His plan.

Christians are the Temple of the Holy Spirit

Christ did not leave us as helpless orphans. Just as He promised, His departure ushered in the coming of the Holy Spirit, the Third Person of the Trinity, to *indwell* every Christ-Believer, without limitation, as a *guarantee* of our ability to have victory in this life.[2]

Christ never relied on His deity to live His sinless life. Rather, He called on the wisdom of God the Father, then obeyed the Father to bring forth the power of the Holy Spirit, for the benefit of humanity in His sphere of earthly influence. Through prayer and earnest communion, Christ called on the Father who dispatched His Holy Spirit to help Christ live in victory and produce amazing miracles.

With our faith in Christ, as our Savior, Lord, and Intercessor,[3] we are to appropriate the victory life Christ died to secure for us in the same way. Through earnest prayer communion, calling on the Father, and obeying His instructions (that will always be consistent with His *Written Word*—the Bible), we can realize victory in this fallen world in many ways including miracles that defy the physical laws of this world. By seeking to live in the fullness of what Christ offers, as Christ's disciples, we partner with God to usher in His kingdom. Christians are ambassadors for Christ able to do not only what He did, but even greater things, for our own benefit and the benefit of others, according to the will of the Father.[4]

Grasping Your New Identity in Christ is Essential for Victory

I shared earlier that essential or *saving* faith is the faith required for a person to genuinely believe in and receive Jesus as his/her personal Savior and Lord. As explained in 2 Corinthians 5:17, once a person genuinely places his or her faith in Christ, the old is passed away and all things become new. With our faith placed in Christ, we are made *newly* alive through Christ. The old naturally-born spirit *is* passed away and the new super-naturally-born spirit *is* birthed. By your faith in believing and agreeing with God, He is moved to recreate your eternal spirit. Your spirit is newly born of the Holy Spirit's power—just as miraculous as Christ's virgin birth. This transforming miracle is known as *justification*, which means to be declared righteous or blameless unto God.

This new sinless spirit within you never existed before. Understand that your spirit-man is the real you. Your new spirit does not strive or work at becoming anything different, but is already created entirely perfect.

Now, your soul (mind, will, emotions, and unique personality) and body are, for the first time, *potentially* subject to your new spirit. *Potentially*, because your new spirit affects your life depending upon which aspect of your three-part being you allow to lead. If your soul and/or body are given priority over your new spirit, then your new spirit is not leading. The opportunity for *salvation* (redemption) and *sanctification* (the process of being transformed soul and body) are both reliant upon your will. Our willful response to God's promises is what allows us to take hold of all that God offers, or not. The human will is amazingly powerful.

If you want to live in the fullness of all that Christ offers you in this life, then you must determine to make your soul and body *subject* to your new spirit. If you allow your body and/or soul to lead, your born-again spirit remains but you will live and enjoy life no differently from one who has not placed their faith in Christ. This is the how the Cultural and Congregational Christians referenced earlier live. The Christian who demonstrates effective faith is the one who has allowed his/her new spirit to be master of both soul and body. Only when the new spirit is the control-center for the soul and body can we expect to see and experience the transformed life Christ offers. The new spirit requires that we learn how to *be* our newly-created selves. Intentional retraining of our mental and emotional processes and ordering our mind and body to comply is how we give our new spirit the helm. As we learn more of the truths from God's Word and apply the principles by which effective Christians must live, then we will experience our new spirit's impact in our soul, body, and physical world. We enter into this process daily and can grow and develop more and more our entire life.

We can settle for a renewed spirit or salvation alone, which many people do. These are the ones who needlessly suffer the ravages of this world and feel hopeless, even in their Christian faith. I know, I lived that way for many years. But as I've learned, to intentionally work with the Holy Spirit to bring our mind, body, soul, and strength into agreement with our new spirit is so much better! The beginning starts with a full and proper understanding of the new creatures we are in Christ. Without a full and proper understanding of our regeneration, our faith and its effectiveness will be crippled.

Coming to a proper understanding of who I am with faith in Christ took me a while. And until I did, I experienced seasons, some long seasons in the earlier days of my Christian faith, when my thoughts were influenced by doubt, anxiety, and fear. I thought things such as *I'm second-rate. I always come in second place. Others are better than me. I'll never be good enough—I should just accept my 'less than' status.* Oftentimes external circumstances contributed to the enemy's success to infiltrate my mind with such thoughts. The human mind—which contains the will—is amazingly vulnerable and therefore a primary battleground of the enemy where he infiltrates our thoughts.

But once I realized that my mind was *unsettled* about who I am in Christ, and I willfully replaced the damaging deceitful thoughts with the truth from God's Word, my countenance and outlook was immediately changed. My ability to better hear God's leading was improved and in short order I could see the path to take for breakthroughs in my circumstances.

With my mind properly functioning on the truth of who I *am* in Christ, nothing could adversely impact my confidence in my Christ-given identity and authority. During these times I've seen incredible answers to prayer and miraculous breakthroughs (some included in the following pages of this book). Breakthroughs such as mine you can also have if you are willing to operate in your new identify in Christ. You accomplish this by learning to replace every thought that sets itself up against the truth of God's Word about who you are in Christ, and focusing on the authority you now have.

Consider the authority given to the Apostle Peter as recorded in Matthew 16:13-19 once he identified himself with Christ:

> Now when Jesus came into the district of Caesarea Philippi, he asked his disciples, "Who do people say that the Son of Man is?" And they said, "Some say John the Baptist, others say Elijah, and others Jeremiah or one of the prophets." He said to them, "But who do you say that I am?" Simon Peter replied, "You are the Christ, the Son of the living God." And Jesus answered him, "Blessed are you, Simon Bar-Jonah! For flesh and blood has not revealed this to you, but my Father who is in heaven. And I tell you, you are Peter,

and on this rock I will build my church, and the gates of hell shall not prevail against it. I will give you the keys of the kingdom of heaven, and whatever you bind on earth shall be bound in heaven, and whatever you loose on earth shall be loosed in heaven.[5]

Peter's belief in Jesus as the Christ, the anointed One—the promised Redeemer sent by God—allowed him to enter into Christ's authority. Christ's authority came from listening to the Father and obeying Him. Christ imparts His authority to Believers who will properly receive that authority.

One of Peter's early experiences of faith in God's Word and power is revealed in Matthew 14:22-33. Peter stepped out of the boat and walked on water toward Jesus who was walking on the water toward Peter. By faith in Jesus' invitation to *come* Peter miraculously defied the laws of this physical world. In fact, noting that Jesus did not operate His earthly existence in any portion of His divinity, but entirely in humanity, they both defied the laws of gravity by faith in obedience to God. Peter simply acted on the command and authority of Jesus expecting God's power to do the rest. He acted in agreement with God. Only when Peter became fearful, (vs. 30), did he *begin* to sink. Clearly God's power was still at work even as Peter became fearful. The passage reveals that Peter *began* to sink. Without God's power, according to the natural laws of this world, he simply would have *immediately sunk*.

Tapping into God's power is the very same for each and every one of us. When we respond to the invitations and instructions of the Father, overcoming fear and doubt, we will do amazing things. However, like Peter, we can be in the midst of doing something miraculous, take our eyes off Jesus and begin to fail. If we, at that moment, recognize that fear has replaced our faith-focus, we can regroup and continue to defy even the natural laws of this world.

If we do not understand the realities of the new creations we are in Christ, we will not be able to withstand the attacks of the enemy. He will be able to wound us greatly, through fear, doubt, condemnation, and the like, preventing us from breakthrough victory. Without a firm and fixed mind-set on who we are in Christ and what God has promised, we are unable to wield the authority that is rightfully, legally, and completely ours.

1 John 4:17 reads: "By this is love perfected with us, so that we may have confidence for the day of judgment, *because as he is so also are we in this world.*"[6] [Emphasis added] Let that sink in. In our newly-regenerated state, we are like Him in this world; we are able to do as He did, overcome as He did, and bless others as He did.

2 Peter 1:1-4 continues:

> To those who have obtained a faith of equal standing with ours by the righteousness of our God and Savior Jesus Christ: May grace and peace be multiplied to you in the knowledge of God and of Jesus our Lord. His divine power has granted to us all things that pertain to life and godliness, through the knowledge of him who called us to his own glory and excellence, by which he has granted to us his precious and very great promises, so that through them you may become partakers of the divine nature, having escaped from the corruption that is in the world because of sinful desire.[7]

That we understand we are entirely new creatures in Christ, able to do great and mighty things by God's power as He directs us, is vital so that He will powerfully bless us and those around us.

Below is a partial list of Bible verses that can help you to thoroughly understand your new self—your new identity in Christ. If you are interested in realizing hope and victorious breakthroughs in your life, don't treat this as a list to skim over. Look up the verses and read them in context. Understand that these professions come from the Word of God and they personally concern you. Meditate on them and get them deep within your heart and mind. Inscribe them within your soul to be readily and confidently called upon at times of need.

Agree with God by declaring these realities aloud as often as possible. I recommend starting each day in prayer before the Lord asking Him to remind you of who you are in Christ. Throughout the day when your mind becomes doubtful or anxious or you've lost your confidence in any way, take time to be reminded of who you are in Christ. This is how we train up the soul and subject the body to the new spirit we receive through faith in Christ.

I am accepted…

John 1:12	I am God's child
John 15:15	I am Christ's friend
Romans 5:1	I have been justified
1 Cor 6:17	I am united with the Lord, and I am one spirit with Him
1 Cor 6:19	I am indwelled by the Holy Spirit
1 Cor 6:20	I have been bought with a price, I belong to God
1 Cor 12:27	I am a member of Christ's body
Eph 1:1	I am a saint
Eph 1:5	I have been adopted as God's child
Eph 2:18	I have direct access to God through the Holy Spirit
Col 1:14	I have been redeemed and forgiven of all my sins
Col 2:10	I am complete in Christ, lacking nothing

I am secure…

Rom 8:1, 2	I am free forever from condemnation
Rom 8:28	I am assured that all things work together for good
Rom 8:31	I am free from any condemning charges against me
Rom 8:35	I cannot be separated from the love of God
1 Cor 1:21, 22	I have been established, anointed and sealed by God
Phil 1:6	I am confident that the good work that God has begun in me will be perfected
Phil 3:20	I am a citizen of heaven
Col 3:3	I am hidden with Christ in God, my old spirit is dead
2 Tim 1:7	I have not been given a spirit of fear but of power, love and a sound mind
Heb 4:16	I can find grace and mercy in time of need
1 John 5:18	I am born of God and the evil one cannot truly harm me

I am significant…

Matt 5:13, 14	I am the salt and light of the earth
John 15:5	I am a branch of the true vine, a channel of His life.
John 15:16	I have been chosen and appointed to bear fruit
Acts 1:8	I am a personal witness of Christ's by the power of the Holy Spirit
1 Cor 3:16	I am God's temple where the Holy Spirit resides
2 Cor 5:19	I am a minister of reconciliation for God
2 Cor 6:1	I am a co-worker with God (1 Cor 3:9)
Eph 2:6	I am seated with Christ in the heavenly realm
Eph 2:10	I am God's workmanship created for good works
Eph 3:12	I may approach God with freedom and confidence
Phil 4:13	I can do all things through Christ who strengthens me

The list above is not exhaustive. As you study Scriptures, make a point to record additional verses that reveal who you are in Christ. Meditate on all the Scriptures you find that inform you of your new identity and lock them in your heart and mind. These disciplines are essential for you to be able to refute the enemy's false accusations especially as you encounter life's trials that test your faith.

You may *feel* the very same as you did before you prayed to invite Jesus to be your personal Savior and Lord. But don't let the enemy of God use that to make you *think* you are the same. Feelings are subjective and often unreliable as they are impacted by many influences. What we think is what matters, and in fact, what we think either propels us forward in a victorious, effective faith, or renders us wounded and ineffective in our faith. When what we think lines up with God's truth, we can tap into His power and authority bringing us to the hope and results we desire, according to God's will.

The enemy of God is the adversary of all humanity simply because we were created by God in His image. In the Garden of Eden Satan won a major battle with Adam and Eve and all people born ever since. And once a person receives God's promise of Redemption, that person becomes *yet again* a target of the enemy. But don't let that concern you! He who is in you [the Holy Spirit] is greater than he [Satan] who is in the world.[8]

Be Utterly Convinced of Your New Identity

Your new identity and authority in Christ as a Believer by faith is what you must fully grasp and *put on*. You can't do anything to earn anything from God. All He offers is a gift that you simply need to 1. Understand; 2. Accept; 3. Believe; and 4. Receive. Be aware that the spirit of religion is the enemy of the Spirit of faith. The spirit of religion tries to make you do what only God can do through striving and works, that is performance. Yet this mind-set will quickly take you out of your rightful spirit-man leadership. Living and moving in the new spirit is not hard, but is, conversely, very easy. We simply accept and step into the new spirit. The fact that the new spirit mind-set is easy is why a lot of people struggle. Understand your new spirit is a gift. There is nothing you can or need to do to qualify, earn points, or improve upon that spirit. Once you have placed your faith in Christ, your new spirit and fullness of potential in Christ is guaranteed.

Some of God's promises are absolute. They will happen whether or not we believe. An example is the Old Testament promise of sending the Deliverer/Redeemer. The New Testament promise of Jesus' return is another example of a promise of God that requires no action on our part. Other promises are made available to us by our active response—by our satisfying the condition. Salvation is one such promise—we must believe in and receive Jesus as our Personal Savor. Sanctification is another—we must willingly cooperate with the Holy Spirit's instructions.

As stated previously, sanctification is the transforming process of God at work in and through us. For this to happen, we must agree with God's will for us.

Charles H. Kraft, Ph.D., president of Deep Healing Ministries, professor of forty years at the School of Intercultural Studies at Fuller Theological Seminary, helps us understand. In his book *I Give You Authority: Practicing the Authority Jesus Gave Us*, (2012), he writes about our authority in Christ using the story of his own son asking to use his credit card:

> "Dad, would you put my name on your credit card?" This request came from my son Rick, who was driving off to college fifteen hundred miles away in an older car. He was concerned lest the car break down and he not have the money to get it back on the road. "You wouldn't want me

to be stranded somewhere without being able to pay the bill, would you?" he continued. "I promise I won't misuse it."

His reasoning made sense...though [his mother and I] were a bit apprehensive about whether he would keep his word not to misuse the card... But he is *our son,* our own flesh and blood. And since we were very much in favor of his going to college, we knew that, in addition to paying his tuition, our granting him the use of a credit card made sense. Our names would appear first on the credit card as the ones with the ultimate responsibility. But Rick's name would appear immediately under our names, giving him authority to spend whatever the credit card company would allow us by way of credit.

When Jesus came to earth, it was as if He carried a credit card from His Father with the Father's name at the top and His own name under it. Like my son, *Jesus came with all the authority His Father's name would bring.* He had full authority to spend whatever was in the Father's account, so long as He kept on good terms with the Father and spent it for purposes of which the Father approved.

As He stated in John 5:30, "I can do nothing on my own authority...I am not trying to do what I want, but only what He who sent me wants."

Jesus' power came from being filled with the Holy Spirit, not from His own *Godness.* [He willingly gave up operating entirely from His deity to live the human existence.] The source of His authority, then, was His intimacy with the Father. [His intentional communion with and obedience to the Father]

Both Jesus and my son Rick knew who they were in relation to the one granting them authority. If we are to operate properly in Jesus' authority, we, too, need to understand who we are in the universe. We need to understand our [new] identity.

Through years of working in inner healing deliverance, I have become convinced that the enemy's primary area of attack is our self-image. *He does not want us to discover who we are.*[9]

We Must Learn to Guard our Mind and Heart

In Hebrews 12:2, we learn that Jesus is the author and finisher of our faith. And in Philippians 1:6 we are assured, "And I am sure of this, that he who began a good work in you will bring it to completion at the day of Jesus Christ."[10] The day of Jesus Christ refers to His second coming. This is yet another promise from God to assure you what you can expect.

Scriptures also tell us that God is no respecter of persons,[11] that each individual is unique with his/her own distinct purpose in God's plan. Therefore, each is endowed with the natural talents and spiritual gifts necessary to accomplish their God-created purpose. Ephesians 2:10 explains, "For we are his workmanship, created in Christ Jesus for good works, which God prepared beforehand, that we should walk in them."[12]

Isaiah 30:18 explains: "Therefore the Lord [earnestly] waits [expecting, looking, and longing] to be gracious to you; and therefore He lifts Himself up, that He may have mercy on you and show loving-kindness to you.... Blessed (happy, fortunate, to be envied) are all those who [earnestly] wait for Him, who expect and look and long for Him...." (AMP)

So why don't we see more Christians operating in the fullness of Christ, demonstrating great hope and enjoying personal breakthroughs? Because they have failed to guard their hearts and minds concerning who they truly are in Christ. They have allowed things of this carnal world to infiltrate their thinking, and/or have accepted lies of the enemy, thereby convoluting their faith and rendering their new-creation possibilities ineffective.

We Receive According to What We Believe

As stated earlier, we will receive according to what God finds in our hearts/*leb*, which includes our minds. We will conduct our lives according to what we maintain in our heart and mind. Some claim that those of the *Charismatic* persuasion (a form of Christianity that emphasizes the work of the Holy Spirit, spiritual gifts, and modern-day miracles) operate with emphasis on emotion and that non-Charismatics operate with emphasis on intellect. However, if we fully understand the way God created us and operate consistent with His will, we will operate utilizing both our mind (intellect) and heart (emotions), with wisdom. There are times we cannot trust our heart just as there are times we cannot trust our emotions. Wisdom is the key.

If we are unforgiving, unkind, unloving, or bitter toward others we will receive that which is in our hearts. If we entertain unwholesome thoughts, prideful or inferior thoughts, and the like, we will limit our own progress in the sanctification process. Jeremiah 17:10 reads:

> The heart is deceitful above all things, and desperately sick; who can understand it? "I the Lord search the heart and test the mind, to give every man according to his ways, according to the fruit of his deeds.[13]

Again, the heart/*leb* refers to the soul—the very essence of a person. Remember the soul and the body will follow whatever is most influential. If you live primarily from your earthly desires, your soul and body will follow. If on the other hand you focus on new spiritual desires, your soul and body will follow those.

I shared earlier that I have so struggled with thoughts of being inferior they actually immobilized me and left me floundering under my circumstances. But once I put on my identity and authority in Christ and became more proficient at training my mind by replacing every negative, crippling thought with the life-giving truth of God's Word, I began to go beyond my self-imposed limitations. Intentional effort is required to first recognize a negative and oppressive thought that is planted in our mind. And deliberate effort is required to cooperate with the Holy Spirit to examine and help us guard our hearts—our *leb*.

Gratefully, we have another promise from God in Ezekiel 11:19:
> I will give them one heart [a new heart] and I will put a new spirit within them; and I will take the stony [unnaturally hardened] heart out of their flesh, and will give them a heart of flesh [sensitive and responsive to the touch of their God]. (AMP)

The Three Realms of our Being

To best take hold of the new identity and authority we have in Christ, we need to understand the realms of our being. As Terri Fivash, author of *Spiritual Toolbox* explains, there are three realms in which humans interact. There are the physical, the mental, and the spiritual realm:

> **The physical realm** is what is normally thought of as the real world. It is the space and things around is, governed

by laws of physics such as gravity, friction and velocity. Anything which can be perceived by sight, hearing, small, taste and touch is part of this realm.

The mental realm is usually referred to as "mind" in the Bible. It consists of everything that goes on in the mind or that which is part of the mind. This includes thoughts, emotions/feelings, decisions, and the human will. This is also what is called the "soul" by many people.

The spiritual realm is third. The Bible often calls this realm the "heart." The apostle Paul calls it "the things which are not seen." He also tells us in 2 Corinthians 4:18 that this realm is the highest reality. "For the things that are seen are temporal, but the things which are not seen are eternal." The unseen is eternal because it emanates directly from God. His simple existence creates this realm. "for God is a spirit," John 4:24.

The heart can be thought of as that part of you which perceives and communicates with the spiritual realm. If we didn't have a heart we could not know this part of reality. "even so the things of God knoweth no man, but the Spirit of God. Now we have received, not the spirit of the world, but the spirit which is of God; that we might know the things that are freely given to us of God."[14] (1 Corinthians 2:11-12 KJV)

The Laws of the Realms

Each realm is governed by law. The laws are in continual operation, whether we are aware of their existence or not. We are acquainted with many of the laws of the physical realm, gravity being one. However, we likely seldom think about them, and yet we use them every day. Science has helped us discover these laws and how to use them to our advantage.

The human brain or the mental realm, also operates by law. Psychology, psychiatry, and neurology are providing a much broader and richer understanding of *mental law*. They are showing how the brain works and what thoughts and memories are.

The ability to spiritually discern matters was given to man at creation. Mankind was created by God in three parts: body, soul, and spirit. Our spirit being is that which allows us to discern spirits and communicate with God. The laws governing the spiritual realm, like all the other realms, operate all the time whether we know or are aware of them or not. Unless we understand the laws of the spiritual realm, we may cause *blessing* or *cursing* upon ourselves. *Blessing* is giving God permission to work in your life. Cursing is giving Satan permission to work in your life.[15]

As we walk this earth, we cannot avoid operating in all three of these realms and the laws that govern them. When we are ignorant of the laws of the realms, we can be violating laws and bringing harm upon our selves and others without realizing it. Learning about the laws and how to use them is key.

The Connection Among the Realms

The human brain connects all three realms. The electrical processes of the brain can be measured with an electroencephalograph, or EEG machine. There are five major types of brain waves identified by Greek letters: *Gamma, Beta, Alpha, Delta,* and *Theta*. Each type is associated with some part of the body's functions. Since what we think directly impacts us physically we should have some understanding of how the thinking process works.

Gamma waves are the fastest, and the most recently discovered. They signal intensive hyper-activity, such as crisis situations. During this state the brain processes information at an incredible rate, which is why what's happening around the person appears to happen in slow motion. This hyper-mental and physical state is normally entered into only at extreme survival need.

Beta waves are slower than Gamma, [waves] and are dominant when the brain is engaged in an activity that requires attention. We spend most of our waking hours in Beta state. The mind is mentally engaged, whether or not there is physical activity associated with the mental part.

Alpha waves, which are slower than Beta [waves] occur when the brain is relaxed and quite, but not asleep. Repetitive physical activity which does not require thought will often produce Alpha state. It is often described as being "zoned out."

The slowest brain waves are **Delta waves**, and they are associated with deep sleep/dreaming, and the autonomic systems that keep your body alive. They signal minimal mental and physical activity.

The last type of brain waves are the **Theta waves**. They are slower than Alpha waves, but faster than Delta, and they are associated with the boundary between the conscious and the sub-conscious, that time when you have almost fallen asleep, but not quite. In the Theta state, ideas can flow freely in the mind, inspiration strikes, and the imagination can take over.[16]

I've found that very often during this Theta state, I seem to hear the *still small voice* from the Lord best. Perhaps because I'm a type-A personality that is otherwise mentally preoccupied, making hearing the Lord throughout the day more difficult for me. Realizing this is my clue to intentionally take times through the day to quiet my mind and seek the Lord, either with a specific question for Him to answer or just to worship Him. During times of quietude seeking the Lord's presence, I often hear Him speak loving, affirming words, and provide me direction I need.

Terri Fivash continues:

> Theta waves beat four times per second in a special rhythm. Anything which beats at this same speed and rhythm will access this part of the mind directly, and the brain will begin to move toward Theta state. You will not have a choice about this. Humans have known of this phenomenon for thousands of years, and the beat is also known as the *Shaman's* beat.[17]

A shaman is someone who is believed in some cultures to be able to use magic to cure people who are sick, to control future events, and so on. Some refer to "shamans as medicine men or witch doctors who routinely use this beat to induce trances and hypnotic states. Why? Because this level of brain wave is the door in your mind to the spiritual realm."[18] In reality shamans practice hypnosis. Hypnosis, in my considered opinion, can be very dangerous allowing unwanted spirits access to our thought life. Many claim benefits of hypnotherapy, but I offer stern caution.

Steady beats such as we hear in music impact not only the Theta state—but other brain states are impacted. When we listen to music, the tempo—the number of beats per second, impacts us more than the melody. This reveals yet another principle that we use regularly without any thought.

Consider the low soft beats common to baby's lullabies that are useful in helping to lull children toward Delta state and sleep.

> Because Theta waves are the door into your mind from the spiritual realm, both God and Satan can use it. It is the only way in. Any thoughts that come to you *from the spiritual realm* will enter on Theta waves. Alpha, Beta, and of course Gamma waves are faster and "louder" than Theta waves. This means they can easily block perception of the Theta waves.[19]

The Spirit, Mind, Body Connection

In a functioning brain, brainwaves including Theta are always present, meaning that the connection to the spiritual realm is always open, regardless of whether we are aware of that connection or not. The *Hypothalamus gland* (a small gland that connects the nervous system with the endocrine system), according to science, is responsible for the mind-body connection.

The hypothalamus operates automatically and will order a response to thoughts we may have ignored. The hypothalamus gland is busy at work with any thought, at any time. The gland makes no judgments about the thought being good or bad, true or false, but will simply respond, instruct the endocrine system, and influence or control every system in the body. Therefore, whoever controls the thoughts in your mind, literally controls you. The job of the hypothalamus gland is to bring the body into agreement with the thought that triggered the action.

> If the thought is, "Oh, it's so peaceful out here in the hammock," the hypothalamus will try to bring the body into a state of peace. If the thought is, "I wish I were dead!" the hypothalamus will try to bring the body into a

> state of death.
>
> Satan and his kingdom understand this very well, and they know just what thoughts to send to produce any desired effect.
>
> Satan is part of the spiritual realm, and the only way he can connect with the physical realm is through a human mind. Proverbs 23:7 (NKJ) states, "As a man thinks in his heart so is he.[20]

Because of the connection between the three realms: spirit, mind, and body; Proverbs 23:7 takes on greater meaning. While we don't need to understand all the scientific information about our brain waves to effectively live our spiritual life in Christ, understanding how the spiritual realm impacts us through our *mind gate* is essential. The Apostle Paul took a great bit of time and effort explaining that the battle is in our mind.

As stated earlier, Believers in Christ have the potential to overcome the ravages of this world providing we have our new spirit leading our life. Terri Fivash explains the progress of the spirit, mind, and body connection:

> In summary, the connection between the three realms begins in the spiritual. Through Theta waves, it moves into the mental realm, and through the hypothalamus gland, it stretches into the physical realm.[21]

Can Satan and Demons Read Our Minds or Implant Thoughts?

The Bible never says directly that Satan cannot know our thoughts or read our minds, but Scripture never shows him reading minds and seems to imply that he can't. Believers hold differing opinions about how Satan influences our thoughts.

That Satan and his demons would only be able to read our minds and directly implant thoughts if this was an ability God created angels with, makes sense. Remember, Satan and his demons are fallen *angels*. Angels, whether fallen or God-honoring, can wield tremendous power in the physical realm.

While demons can possess the bodies of unbelievers and even speak audibly through them (a physical manifestation), that does not necessarily mean they possess the person's mind, only their physical bodies. Angels exist in the spirit realm and are limited in power and reach in the physical world according to God's instruction and our receptivity.

Certainly, even as Believers, we continue to be influenced by our fallen nature and the schemes of the enemy and his dominions. I believe that Satan hears our words, observes our actions, and always accuses Believers of unrighteousness with the intent of indirectly infiltrating our thought life. Scripture teach that even God does not want control of our thoughts. Rather, He wants us free to choose for ourselves.

In my opinion, every satanic attack and temptation is intended to cause us to reject God. We are responsible for our own thought-life and what we choose to accept and entertain or reject and replace with the truth of God's Word. Following Christ yields abundant life. Succumbing to Satan produces bondage and misery.

Our Thoughts Impact our Physical Existence

Matthew 12:35-37, in the words of Jesus, reads,

> A good man out of the good treasure of his heart brings forth good; and an evil man out of the evil treasure of his heart brings forth evil. For out of the abundance of the heart his mouth speaks. But I say to you that for every idle

word men may speak, they will give account of it in the day of judgment. For by your words you will be justified, and by your words you will be condemned.

Thoughts within our hearts/minds are in reality words that we automatically respond to physically. The words we speak reveal what is in our hearts/mind. By deliberately choosing to speak life-giving words, our own *ear gate* hears our words which in turn impacts our heart/mind and spirit. This is why proactively confessing the truth of God's Word both mentally and audibly is important.

Referring again to the book co-authored by Don Gossett previously cited:

> The law of [effective] faith [or the Law of Speaking] is that you confess to yourself that what God says about you is true. We have been instructed in God's Word to "hold fast the profession of our faith without wavering; (for He is faithful that promised)," Hebrews 10:23. As we hold fast to the confession of the Word, we are to "affirm constantly" (Titus 3:8) those things that God has revealed to us.
>
> To hold fast to our confession is to say what God has said over and over again until the thing desired in our hearts and promised in the Word is fully manifested. There is no such thing as possession without confession. When we discover the rights we have in Christ, which are given throughout the Bible, we are to affirm them constantly, testify to them, and witness to these tremendous Bible facts. Therefore, our faith will be effective only as we confess with our mouths all the good things that are ours because we belong to Jesus.

We know that in Jesus Christ we have been given salvation, not just for our souls, but for our bodies—in our health, our finances, our peace of mind, and our freedom from bondage and fear. There are hundreds of powerful affirmations to make constantly as we speak the language of Scripture. For example:

God is who He says He is.
I am who God says I am.
God can do what He says He can do.
I can do what God says I can do.
God has what He says He has.
I have what God says I have.[22]

God is the giver of all good and perfect gifts. He longs to lavish upon us more than we can hope or imagine. Praying to ask and thank God for what He has already planned to give us is not wrong. We are asking according to His will, as we're instructed to do in 1 John 5:14-15. Because the enemy is ever roaming about seeking whom he can devour, we need to intentionally maintain life-giving thoughts in our hearts/mind and then they will flow from our lips. Psalm 37:4 instructs us to delight ourselves in the Lord and then He will give us the desires of our heart. If our delight is first and foremost in the Lord then He will give us more of Him. From this we can enjoy the promise of Matthew 6:33. When we seek first the Kingdom of God, God is pleased to give us more than what He already knows we need. He enjoys giving to us in abundance.

Effective Faith Transcends Salvation

The Bible is clear that Jesus did much more than bring people to saving faith in Him as their Redeemer. He also taught them to live in what I call effective faith. Jesus demonstrated that He was and is the Deliverer whose power and authority makes victory over all that sin brought upon this world possible for us. The intention of the Holy Trinity was that Jesus' life, death, and resurrection would provide a way for humanity to be restored to God *and* have His supernatural victory to enjoy His abundance, beginning in this life, while we live out our earthly existence. God has assured us certain hope and prominent breakthroughs.

Once we learn to make our primary focus our new spirit-self, and we work in cooperation with the Holy Spirit to transform us from the inside out—that is to have our new spirit dictate the transformations that take place in our soul and spirit and into our physical world—we will go beyond salvation to sanctification and begin to see the manifestations of the Spirit in and through us. In short, if we conduct ourselves like Jesus we can expect *Jesus results*.

With a better understanding that our hope is in Christ, that resolute belief in God and His Word are essential, and that we must intentionally operate according to our new identity in Christ, let's next consider how we can progress within both the physical and spiritual worlds.

CHAPTER FOUR

Faith Materialized

Operate in the Spiritual

My father was a policeman. He taught me from a young age that *ignorance of the law is no excuse*. Whether I know the laws of the land or not, I will still be held accountable to them. That means if I violate a law, even if I am completely unaware that the law exists, I would still be punished according to the law. I didn't require a high I.Q. to realize that I'd better do all I can to know the law! That principle is no different for us living in the natural and spiritual worlds.

There are laws that govern the existence of our physical world. You are aware of many of them. There are the laws of gravity, the laws of thermodynamics, the laws of aerodynamics, the laws of motion, and so on. Most don't know all the laws of the physical world, but that doesn't make us exempt from them.

Did you know that there are also laws that govern the spiritual world? As a new creation in Christ, your new spirit has access to the holy, spiritual world of God. However, our original bodies and souls remain part of physical world until the last day of our earthly existence. This means that as new creations in Christ we live in two worlds. That we learn the laws of both worlds makes sense, especially in light of our desire for confident hope and personal breakthroughs.

Grasping the Spiritual Laws

In modern day Christian circles, the term *Spiritual Laws* generally refers to what's become known as *The Four Spiritual Laws*. These are the laws or principles that govern our relationship with God. They are:

1. God loves you and offers a wonderful plan for your life. (John 3:16, John 10:10)
2. Man is sinful and separated from God. Therefore, he cannot know and experience God's love and plan for his life. (Romans 3:23, Romans 6:23)
3. Jesus Christ is God's only provision for man's sin. Through Him you can know and experience God's love and plan for your life. (Romans 5:8, 1 Corinthians 15:3-6, John 14:6)
4. We must individually receive Jesus Christ as Savior and Lord; then we can know and experience God's love and plan for our lives. (John 1:12, Ephesians 2:8,9, John 3:1-8, Revelation 3:20)

These laws are essential for one's salvation and the ability to live the victorious life that Christ wants us to live in relationship with Him. From the very beginning, God's will for humanity was for us to have complete authority over all that exists. Genesis 1:26-31 reveals God's plan for mankind. But as we already explored, the free-will choice of the first man and woman ushered sin, and all sin represents, into the world. In response, God gave us His promised Redeemer through the person of Jesus Christ. Because of Jesus, Believers now have access to God the Father, Son, and Holy Spirit in ways unavailable during the Old Testament era.

Understanding the Governing Laws of Both Worlds

The physical things of this world were created by God as patterns to help us discover the spiritual realm. The laws of this physical world, such as gravity or motion, are ever at work. They never cease and they never change. They are constantly affecting what we do and the results that we experience, regardless of whether we think of, or are even aware of, the laws.

All the laws of this physical world are actually scientific systems that we rely upon. God created these physical systems so that we could depend upon and have confidence in them every day. You may or may not understand how these laws work, but you can have faith in them and use them to your advantage or your harm, depending on your actions. For example, if you want to travel from California to New York you can choose to fly on a commercial plane. You board the plane with confidence that the laws of aerodynamics will allow the pilot to override the laws of gravity and, with the laws of thrust and motion, power the plane to take off so that you land in New York within a few hours. You may not consciously consider the use of the physical laws, but you rely on them just the same. Conversely, if you jump off a cliff without the aid of a glider or a parachute, because of the law of gravity, you will soon find yourself hitting the ground hard, likely with a great deal of bodily harm if not death.

The law of gravity never ceases to exist. Yet when other laws are utilized, gravity is overcome sufficiently to allow planes to take off, then later safely land. As individuals we may not know or even think about all the laws at work allowing us to board a plane and fly to our destination. Rather, we count on the education and efforts of others who have studied the laws, while we enjoy the benefits of their application of those physical laws.

We can rely upon the physical laws of this world without *personally* understanding them, and expect them to bring us benefit. Simultaneously, there are actions we could take that can bring us harm because we are personally ignorant of, or we willfully defy, the physical laws. Ignorance of the law is no excuse.

The same is true of spiritual laws. The laws exist and continue to operate whether we are aware of them or not. They can bring us benefit or harm depending upon our actions and the specific combination or use of the laws.

We can't expect God to bless and protect us if we abuse His physical laws. When Satan suggested that Jesus throw Himself down from the precipice to demonstrate He was in the care of God the Father, Jesus replied, "Again it is written, 'You shall not put the Lord your God to the test.'"[1] Jesus' response demonstrated awareness and wisdom to not abuse God's physical laws.

The laws of this physical world govern us in the physical realm only. However, the laws of the spiritual world govern us and have impact on both the spiritual and the physical worlds. Again, the physical and spiritual worlds co-exist. This brings us to next consider the sovereignty of God.

God's Sovereign Control

Although God is all powerful, He has chosen to impose limitations and constraints upon Himself. One such self-imposed limitation is *free-will*. God gave His created beings free-will decision-making capabilities. Both His created angelic beings and human beings were given free-will. A more complete discussion of free-will is provided in the first book in this series, *Examine Your Faith! Finding Truth in a World of Lies*. But the shorter consideration for the purposes of this book's chapter is, that by angels and humanity having free-will, we have complete control over the decision to worship God or not. God does not impose Himself or His ways on anyone.

As previously discussed, there is an enemy of God, but understand there is no equal to God. The struggle of good and evil we see playing out in this world is not evidence of two entities equal in power striving with each other. If that were the case the fight would continue forever. However, God is the supreme power over all and, as such, He is working His plan to ultimately completely overcome evil.

People ask "If God is sovereign over all, why doesn't He either remove us from this fallen world when we embrace Christ as our Savior, or eliminate from this world all the vile sicknesses, death, suffering, and evil?" Naturally no one wants to suffer. With that in mind the question is understandable. However the question is asked without an understanding of God's plan that is already in motion to eradicate evil.

First, God is sovereign over all, but that does not make Him responsible for all. The free-will that angels and humans have—that is the power of independent reason and will—allows choice regarding relationship with God or not. Because of the free-will of mankind, Adam and Eve were able to reject God's authority and usher into this world all the ravages of sin.

Second, God is in the process of eradicating all sin from this world, one person's free-will choice at a time. God does not desire that anyone should perish. 2 Peter 3:9 reads, "The Lord is not slow to fulfill his promise as some count slowness, but is patient toward you, not wishing that any should perish, but that all should reach repentance."[2] Clearly through God's personal sacrifice in the person of Jesus, He has demonstrated His great love and desire for all to be reconciled to Himself; and by Christ's bodily resurrection, He has won the victory over all sin and death. What we are living out is the *fullness of time*, predetermined by God, allowing for all of His creation, including those not yet physically born, to have the chance of reconciliation through faith in Christ.

Third, we who willfully receive Christ remain on this earth with the privilege of partnering with God to overcome evil. We are to partner with Him to bring His kingdom authority to reign and rule on earth as He does in heaven. This is God's plan. If His plan is not apparent to us now, God still has not failed to do His part. Rather, Christians have failed in understanding and doing our part. This provides yet another reason for us to better understand spiritual laws so that we can impact the physical world in cooperation with God, for our benefit and the benefit of many!

Application of Spiritual Laws

Spiritual laws and principles, like physical laws and principles, operate continuously. Spiritual laws and principles are used by both God and Satan. People have access to these laws; however, due to ignorance and deception, we have failed to make full use of them.

From their new spirit, Believers in Christ have the authority to call on God's holy, spiritual laws to impact the physical world and bring God's kingdom rule on earth. Conversely, those who are not redeemed through faith in Christ, whose natural-born spirit is at enmity with God, can (and automatically do from ignorance and apathy), partner with Satan and his demons to further his cause.

As we live in this physical world, even as Believers, we easily allow this physical life to be our focus. This, sadly, is how many Believers live. As a new Creature in Christ living carnally—that is, with our primary emphasis on the things of this world—we set up a conflict and tension between the spirit, soul, and body. Carnal Believers have not learned how to live out of their new spirit-self. As a result they look, act, and experience life as an unbeliever, but with even more internal tension since the new spirit and the ways of this world are in opposition to one another.

Believers who seek to learn how to live according to their new spirit-self are those who are able to appropriate God's promises for victorious living even in this fallen world. Believers who understand that learning about God's kingdom is a life-long process, as opposed to a single lesson, are the ones who enjoy confident hope and demonstrate effective faith in ever increasing measure.

If we understand that the spiritual realm is the highest eternal reality, and that that realm has power to impact the physical world, then we would be smart to have a solid understanding of the laws of the spiritual world. As previously discussed, God has made all that exists. Everything we see and experience in the natural is intended by God to help us discover and understand the spiritual.

God's Spiritual Laws

First, let's consider the *Law of Sin and Death*. After God created the first man, Adam, from the dust of the earth, He clearly told Adam that if Adam chose his own way instead of the way of God, he would die. In Genesis 2:16-17, God told Adam that he could eat from all the trees in the garden, except the tree of the knowledge of good and evil. God clearly stated that if he ate from the tree of the knowledge of good and evil, he would surely die. Despite God's warning, Adam and Eve disobeyed God. Immediately the spirit within them became estranged from God. Their rejection of God's commandment resulted in every human being born after them inheriting the same spiritually dead condition. This is the Law of Sin and Death and an explanation of how the law entered the world. The power of free-will clearly has ability to bring about life or death.

Next, let's consider the *Law of Life*. Immediately upon Adam's acknowledgement of his rebellion, God promised to send a Redeemer, Whom we know came in the person of Jesus. Through Jesus' sinless life, sacrificial death, and resurrection, God offers the only way for life to be restored to anyone who wants to be restored unto Him. Romans 8:2 reads, "For the law of the Spirit of life has set you free in Christ Jesus from the law of sin and death."[3]

In order for the Law of Life to produce new life, the old life must die and be done away with. Christ's death makes this possible for us by faith. In John 12:23-26, Jesus proclaimed the Law of Life from His own death:

> And Jesus answered them, "The hour has come for the Son of Man to be glorified. Truly, truly, I say to you, unless a grain of wheat falls into the earth and dies, it remains alone; but if it dies, it bears much fruit. Whoever loves his life loses it, and whoever hates his life in this world will keep it for eternal life. If anyone serves me, he must follow me; and where I am, there will my servant be also. If anyone serves me, the Father will honor him.[4]

This brings us to the *Law of Faith*, with its history in another set of laws often referred to as *the Law of Moses* or simply *the Law*. Both terms refer to the compilation of decrees found in the first five books of the Old Testament, summed up in the *Ten Commandments*. Because of the sacrifice of Jesus, those who apply the Law of Faith are set free from the Old Testament Law because that law was *fulfilled* in the life, death, and resurrection of Jesus. In Matthew 5:17, Jesus declares, "Do not think that I have come to abolish the Law or the Prophets; I have not come to abolish them but to fulfill them."[5] Because Christ fulfilled the Law of Sin and Death, we are no longer bound by the Law of the Old Testament. Instead, by faith, we enter into God's grace allowing us to be *justified*, as though we personally fulfilled the Law, because our faith is in Christ—the only one to ever fulfill the Law.

Romans 3:27 explains, "Then what becomes of our boasting? It is excluded. By what kind of law? By a law of works? No, but by the law of faith."[6] By faith in Christ, we are set free from the Law of Sin and Death, whereby we enter into truth and God's grace. In John 1:17 we learn, "For the law was given through Moses; grace and truth came through Jesus Christ."[7]

The *Law of Permission* or *Authority* is our next consideration. The first book of the Old Testament explains that God gave this world to man to rule. Genesis 1:26 explains, "Then God said, 'Let us make man in our image, after our likeness. And let them have dominion over the fish of the sea and over the birds of the heavens and over the livestock and over all the earth and over every creeping thing that creeps on the earth.'"[8] Recall that Satan had been banned to this earth at some point in time.

When God gave this world to Adam and Eve to rule, they were also intended to rule over Satan. This is the Law of Permission or Authority. But when Adam and Eve chose to be influenced by Satan rather than God, they, in effect, obeyed Satan. By abdicating their God-given authority, and rejecting God's authority, they positioned Satan as ruler of this world. However, Christ's death on the cross redeemed those who believe, restoring access of authority to humanity in keeping with God's original intent. Again gleaning from Terri Fivash, author of *Spiritual Toolbox*:

> Because He knew that "the gifts and the calling of God are irrevocable" (Romans 11:29 NIV), Jesus gave the world and the [God-given] responsibility [to rule over it] back to us. He assigned us a task when He returned to heaven (Mark 13:34)—the job of reconciling the world to Him

> again, (2 Corinthians 5:18-20). [We are equipped for this] job here on earth, and God is not going to do it for us. We are to further the interests of God's kingdom in this earth. Because of the Law of Authority, when we see Satan and his kingdom working on earth, we can shut the door on him, and open it to God."[9]

Next, let's consider the *Law of Sowing and Reaping,* also referred to as the *Law of Multiplication.* Galatians 6:7-8 informs us, "Do not be deceived: God is not mocked, for whatever one sows, that will he also reap. For the one who sows to his own flesh will from the flesh reap corruption, but the one who sows to the Spirit will from the Spirit reap eternal life."[10] This law explains how a person who may have a new spirit through faith in Christ can still reap corruption by conduct that *feeds the flesh* instead feeding the spirit.

With the Parable of the Sower in Matthew 13, Jesus explains the *heart of man.* The heart of man, as intended in this passage, is derived from the Hebrew perspective of the heart. As considered in Chapter One, the Hebrew word for heart is *leb. Leb* means the unique essence of the individual soul (mind/intellect/will, heart/emotions, and distinct personality).

Matthew 13:23 reads:
> As for what was sown on good soil, this is the one who hears the word and understands it. He indeed bears fruit and yields, in one case a hundredfold, in another sixty, and in another thirty.[11]

In the very next parable, Jesus says the same thing but adds the sly activity of the enemy when we're not tending or guarding our hearts:

> The kingdom of heaven may be compared to a man who sowed good seed in his field, but while his men were sleeping, his enemy came and sowed weeds among the wheat and went away. So when the plants came up and bore grain, then the weeds appeared also. And the servants of the master of the house came and said to him, 'Master, did you not sow good seed in your field? How then does it have weeds?' He said to them, 'An enemy has done this.' So the servants said to him, 'Then do you want us to go and gather them?'[12]

What we need to understand here is that the Law of Reaping and Sowing means that whatever is placed in the ground/heart will increase and multiply whether the insertion is good or bad. Whatever is sown in a person's heart, if allowed to remain and grow, will find expression in the actions of that person. Who put the seeds there doesn't matter, or whether the person wanted them there. If they are not intentionally removed, they will eventually manifest in that person in a physical way. The only way a harvest is reaped, good or bad, is after sowing and growing are done.

God's first command to mankind was to be fruitful and multiply. (Genesis 1:28) Once Adam and Eve chose their own way instead of God's way, sin was planted in their hearts. Sin is the *fruit* that grew and multiplied in the human race and this world as a result.

Lastly, concerning the Law of Sowing and Reaping, consider that God loves a cheerful giver. "The point is this: whoever sows sparingly will also reap sparingly, and whoever sows bountifully will also reap bountifully."[13]

The *Law of Speaking* is another law we need to know. Spoken words are the way the physical and spiritual realms interact. Romans 10:17 states: "So faith comes from hearing, and hearing through the word of Christ."[14] *The word of Christ*, implies the whole counsel of God. While I've been very familiar with that passage for many years, the phrase *by the word of God* took on more powerful meaning once I understood that words, either spoken or written, *not just God's, but ours too*, are the way the spiritual realm interacts with the physical realm. How important that everything we speak is in alignment with the Word of God!

Consider again Christ's temptation by the Devil. Immediately after Jesus was declared the Son of God and Savior of the World,[15] Jesus was tempted for forty days. Remember that Jesus, Who was wholly God and wholly Man, did not operate His earthly existence with any measure of His divinity. He laid that down entirely to live the human experience. Each time the enemy tried to entice Jesus to reject God, Jesus responded by quoting the very Word of God—the very same Scriptures that we have today as confirmed by the Dead Sea Scrolls. Christ's awareness of God's Word, and faith in God Himself, allowed Him to overcome the temptation of the enemy. And the same principle applies for us.

Proverbs 18:21, from the Amplified Bible, states that "Death and life are in the power of the tongue, and they who indulge in it shall eat the fruit of it [for death or life]." God takes the power of our words very seriously. Matthew 12:36 reveals that we will be required to give account for every careless word we speak.

Now, let's consider what some have called the *Law of Supply*. This law operates very differently in God's kingdom than in the physical world. Again quoting Terri Fivash from her book *Spiritual Toolbox:*

> In God's kingdom, the more you use, the more you have. The less you use, the less you have. If you use it all, you've used none of it, and if you don't use any of it, you've used it all. The Law of Supply is based on the limitless, inexhaustible resources of God. With God, there will

always be more. The story of the poor widow in 2 Kings 4:1-7 illustrates the way God's supply works. The widow's sons were about to be sold to pay the debt she owed a creditor, and all she had in the house was a cruse [earthen pot] of oil. The prophet Elisha told her to gather a lot of empty pots and start pouring oil. [As she did] the oil ceased flowing only when the widow ceased pouring. As long as the widow poured, the oil flowed. There was always more.[16]

The Supreme Laws Are Found in the Attributes of God

One of the most influential studies I've ever done was learning the attributes of God. These are His absolute and unparalleled characteristics. Because God is Spirit and the Creator of all that exists, all creation is subject to His being. Like the laws of the physical world or the laws of the spiritual world, whether we know about Him or not, He still exists, continually operates, and we are subject to His realities.

The single most important attribute of God, in my estimation, is the fact that He is *immutable.* That is, He cannot change. As Believers in Christ, when we understand the magnificent attributes of God and realize that in *all His ways* He cannot ever change, we can possess a confidence and a peace that is otherwise not available—not anywhere or from any other source. Although this list is not exhaustive, consider and allow yourself to meditate on the attributes of God listed here. God is:

A personal Spirit: I can have intimate fellowship with Him: "I reach out for You. I thirst for You as parched land thirsts for rain." (Psalm 143:6 NLT)

Omnipotent—All powerful: He can help me with anything: "O Sovereign

LORD! You have made the heavens and earth by Your great power. Nothing is too hard for you!" (Jeremiah 32:17 NLT)

Omnipresent—Everywhere present: He is always with me: "Where can I go from Your Spirit? Where can I flee from your presence? If I go up to the heavens, You are there; if I make my bed in the depths, You are there. If I rise on the wings of the dawn, if I settle on the far side of the sea, even there Your hand will guide me, Your right hand will hold me fast. If I say, 'Surely the darkness will hide me and the light become night around me,' even the darkness will not be dark to You; the night will shine like day, for darkness is as light to You." (Psalms 139:1-12 NLT)

Omniscient—All knowing: I will go with Him with all my questions and concerns: "He determines the course of the world events; He removes kings and sets others on the throne. He gives wisdom to the wise and knowledge to the scholars." (Daniel 2:21 NLT)

Sovereign—In control over all: I can count on His will being done: "All the people of the earth are nothing compared to Him. He has the power to do as He pleases among the angels of heaven and with those who live on earth No one can stop Him or challenge Him, saying, 'What do You mean by doing these things?'" (Daniel 4:35 NLT)

Holy—Total purity—incorruptible and separate from all the rest of creation: As His child, I can draw from His moral purity: "So obey God because you are His children. Don't slip back into your old ways of doing evil; you didn't know any better then. But now you must be holy in everything you do, just as God—who chose you to be His children—is holy. For He Himself has said, *You must be holy because I am holy.*" (1 Peter 1:14-16 NLT)

All Righteous—His goodness and holiness are demonstrated by His works: I will live by His standards: "Throw off your old evil nature and your former way of life, which is rotten through and through, full of lust and deception. Instead, there must be a spiritual renewal of your thoughts and attitudes.

You must display a new nature because you are a new person created in God's likeness—righteous, holy, and true." (Ephesians 4:2-24 NLT)

All Just—The ultimate judge over the lives and actions of all beings: He will always treat me fairly: "For we must all stand before Christ to be judged. We will each receive whatever we deserve for the good or evil we have done in our bodies." (2 Corinthians 5:10 NLT)

All Love—Unconditional true love, extended to all: He is unconditionally committed to my well-being: "Can anything ever separate us from Christ's love? Does it mean [H]e no longer loves us if we have trouble or calamity, or are persecuted, or hungry, or destitute, or in danger, or threatened with death? No, despite all these things, overwhelming victory is ours through Christ, who loved us. And I am convinced that nothing can ever separate us from God's love. Neither death nor life, neither angels nor demons, neither our fears for today nor our worries about tomorrow—not even the powers of hell can separate us from God's love. No power in the sky above or in the earth below—indeed, nothing in all creation will ever be able to separate us from the love of God that is revealed in Christ Jesus our Lord." (Romans 8:35, 37-39 NLT)

All Merciful—Forgiving, compassionate, forbearing, withholding judgment to extend His benefit: He forgives me of my sins when I sincerely confess them. "Have mercy on me O God, because of Your unfailing love. Because or Your great compassion, blot out the stain of my sins. Create in me a clean heart, O God. Renew a right spirit within me. Do not banish me from Your presence, and don't take Your Holy Spirit from me. Restore to me again the joy of Your salvation, and make me willing to obey You." (Psalm 51:1-12 NLT condensed)

Ever Faithful—Consistently at work to fulfill His plan: I will trust Him always to keep His promises. "Remember that the temptations that come into your life are no different from what others experience. And God is faithful. He will keep the temptation from becoming so strong that you can't stand up against it. When you are tempted, He will show you a way out so that you will not give in to it." (1 Corinthians 10:13 NLT)

All Truth—Utterly unable to lie: As He is the source of all truth, I can trust God alone implicitly: "Sanctify them by Your truth. Your word is truth." (John 17:17 NLT)

Imminent—Ever at hand: I have confidence that God is continually at work in my life: "He is not far from each one of us; for in Him we live and move and have our being." (Acts 17:27-28 NLT)

Immutable—Unable to change His mind, His characteristics, His plan: My future is secure and eternal. "Every good gift and every perfect gift is from above, and comes down from the Father of lights with whom there is no variation or shadow of turning." (James 1:17 NLT)[17]

There is no other like Him.

Relating with God

Hopefully you've realized that Believers are uniquely able to operate in the physical world and to tap into all the benefits of God's spiritual world. In order to do this, you must first become a Believer in Jesus by faith. Then, you can enter into personal relationship with God. As with any relationship, you need to get acquainted first, and then grow and mature your relationship. As you build relationship, you become more intimately involved with God, and the level of trust and commitment is increased. Relationships are established and built based on heart to heart communications.

Dr. Charles Stanley of In Touch Ministries explains:

> Communication that builds relationships is dialogue. Genuine prayer has all of the qualities and characteristics of

a deeply meaningful conversation between two people. God said to the prophet Isaiah, "Come now, and let us reason together." (Isaiah 1:18) This image of God and man sitting down together for a good talk is our best image of prayer.

When we have a deep and heartfelt conversation with another person, we very often come away from that experience saying, "I have a much better understanding of him and his problems, needs, and concerns.

The same is true when we communicate intentionally with God. We know Him more fully, understand Him better, feel more at home in His presence, find cause to praise Him more, and have a deeper relationship with Him.

Prayer is the key to a relationship with God. Intentional dialogue with God ultimately establishes and deepens our relationship with Him. The purpose of prayer is that we might know God better, experience more of His love, and have an abiding awareness of His work in our lives. Talking to God doesn't build relationship. Communicating with God does—both speaking and listening.

Because prayer is intensely personal, there are no universal formulas. The specifics of your prayer relationship with God are as distinctive as any other aspect of your life and your ability to communicate.[18]

We are assured from God's Written Word that if we ask anything according to His will, we will receive our requests. A key point then is to know God's general will as expressed in the Bible as well as His specific will for our individual lives. We learn His specific will through communing and relationship with Him, just as Jesus exemplified.

With the character, will, and intentions of God and His attributes known, you can confidently know that He will never fail you. He has only your best in mind at all times. This doesn't mean you will never suffer. As long as we live in this fallen world, we are subject to the ravages of sin. However, when you suffer, you have the distinct ability to call on God and His promises to be manifest in your life.

Remember, to access anything involves a four-step process:
1. Understanding – to learn and gain knowledge/vision.
2. Accepting – to personally acknowledge as truth.
3. Believing – to stand, rely upon, trust and expect.
4. Receiving – to personally obtain.

We will grow in our understanding according to the effort we make to know God. As defined in Chapter One, the Hebrew word *yada* means to know God intimately and experientially. We express our acceptance of God by first acknowledging Him, then believing in Him, which is to trust Him. Once we've accomplished those three things, we are in position to receive from Him.

Receiving From God

With all conditions met to receive God's promises, we can enter into *prayers of supplication*, which is the effort of asking Him earnestly, humbly, and expectantly. When we have a situation where we want or need God's intervention, we go to Him in prayer and present the problem or desire. Then we listen, watch, and wait. God may reveal His solution to the matter during your prayer time or afterwards. He may impress you Spirit to spirit, He may reveal His answer through the unfolding of circumstances or through interactions with other people, or in some other way. God is continually communicating with us in a variety of ways. We must train our spirit to discern and hear from God's Spirit.

Once we understand or *see* what God has revealed as the solution, then we need to thank Him for His response and by faith believe for His answer as though our request has already been fully established. This is precisely what Natalie Valcarcel did, as revealed in her testimony in Chapter Two. This is entirely different from what has been called the *Word Faith* or *Name it Claim It* movement. We do not identify what we want then expect God to always give our desires to us. This expectation woefully displaces God and is a gross abuse of faith. Faith must be in Christ, not in faith itself. Faith is not a force as some believe. On the contrary, following Jesus' example, we commune with God to learn what He wants to do in any given situation. I explain His actions this way, "When God names it, we are foolish not to claim it." When we are in personal relationship with God, then He reveals His plans—His will.

Proverbs 29:18 reads, "Where there is no prophetic vision the people cast off restraint" [or the people are discouraged].[19] *Prophetic vision* speaks of God-inspired vision. Hosea 4:6 reads, "My people are destroyed for lack of *knowledge*; because you have rejected *knowledge*, I reject you from being a priest to me."[20] [Emphasis added] Knowledge refers to knowledge about and from God. When we are confident about God's will for any matter, believing His will is as good as done demonstrates faith. Hebrews 1:1 states, "Now faith is the assurance of things hoped for, the conviction of things not seen."[21] Trusting God for His Word—His promises—to be fulfilled before they are, is acting on faith.

Some teach that visualizing a matter is essential *in order* for what we're believing for to come to fruition. This concept is taught in the Word Faith movement, New Age teaching, secular leadership (i.e. Napoleon Hill, author of *Think and Grow Rich*), and many occult practices and has found its way into the church. I urge great caution here.

While to imagine a thing like an artist imagines his finished painting before his work is completed is within proper realms of visualization, attempting to give power for the existence of something by our own visualization is not. Depending upon how one is using imagination or visualization, we can move into dangerous territory. If visualization is taught as a technique for creating an image in your mind and using that [image as] an effort to *create or control* reality through mind-powers, you enter the realm of sorcery and divination.[22] Jeremiah 23:16-18 states: "Thus says the LORD of hosts: "Do not listen to the words of the prophets who prophesy to you, filling you with vain hopes. They speak visions of their own minds, not from the mouth of the LORD.""[23]

If a vision is given by the Lord, that's another matter. The Lord can give us a vision. But a vision is not something we create on our own. We can ask the Lord to give us a vision concerning a particular matter to help us *see* what He wants us to receive. By envisioning those things God has revealed or that God says is true, we align our soul (mind, will, emotions) with our spirit that is being led by the Holy Spirit. This kind of imagination or visualizing can actually be exceedingly helpful in attaining what God wants us to have. Remember the process is 1. Understand; 2. Accept; 3. Believe; then 4. Receive. Imagining a matter that God has promised *as being done* before it is fulfilled, is faith that pleases God. When we confidently proclaim that God will do what He says He will do, or that we are who God says we are, we are in agreement with God's truth, which removes hindrances from God's working power.

Again we need to carefully choose the thoughts we think, whether in words or mental images, and the words we speak. We want to refrain from any perspective that negates the promises and provisions of God. If we are operating from fear and doubt or any measure of unbelief in God's revealed truth, we negate fulfillment of His promises. When we think, *God is not near me*, or *God doesn't care*, or other such thoughts that oppose God's revealed truth, we harbor deception in our heart, which will prevent our receiving what God wants us to have.

If God provides a promise for a particular outcome, keeping that promise in your mind's-eye, envisioning the outcome in the same way you envision a goal you want to accomplish—imagining what things will be like when the goal's met—this is healthy and can actually help you persevere through opposition. Understand, however, that when God fulfills His promise the fulfillment is often not as we imagined, but can be far greater. According to Ephesians 3:20, God is able to do far more than we could ever ask or imagine.

Hebrews 11:6 assures us that when we come to God believing that He is, meaning that He is who He claims to be and He can do what He says He will do, that we will receive what we ask for when we ask according to His will—not our own imaginations. 1 John. 5:14-15, "And this is the confidence that we have toward him, that if we as anything according to his will he hears us. And if we know that he hears us in whatever we ask, we know that we have the requests that we have asked of him."[24]

Now that we've established a basic understanding of the Conditions of Faith, we'll move into how to Develop our Faith in the chapters of the next Section.

PART TWO

DEVELOPING FAITH

Faith is a gift from God likened to a mustard seed—among the tiniest of seeds but able to grow to enormous proportions and provide benefit for many creatures. As a seed must be nurtured and maintained under proper conditions to grow, so must our faith in order to mature and become enormously effective. Our response in times of opposition will either develop or diminish our faith. This section helps you learn how to best develop your faith.

CHAPTER FIVE

Faith Exercised

Growing Through Opposition

The Christian faith is not for sissies! For most of us, life's difficulties actually increase from the moment we place our faith in Christ. Again, that's because Believers become the primary target for Satan. Satan doesn't need to spend time wreaking havoc on unbelievers. He's already got them in his clutches. What Satan wants to do is rob God of His glory, so he does all he can to defeat Believers and ruin our testimony. We must have a great deal of spiritual tenacity to stay the course.

I've completely worn out my copy of Oswald Chambers' devotional book, *My Utmost for His Highest*. I've found much of what he wrote to wonderfully challenge me in my Christian growth. Here is what he says about spiritual tenacity:

> Tenacity is more than endurance, it is endurance combined with the absolute certainty that what we are looking for is going to transpire. Tenacity is more than hanging on, which may be but the weakness of being too afraid to fall off. Tenacity is the supreme effort of a man refusing to believe that his hero is going to be conquered. The greatest fear a man has is not that he will be damned, but that Jesus Christ will be worsted, that the things He stood for—love

and justice and forgiveness and kindness among men—will not win out in the end. Then comes the call to spiritual tenacity, not to hang on and do nothing, but to work deliberately on the certainty that God is not going to be worsted.

If our hopes are being disappointed just now, it means that they are being purified. There is nothing the human mind has ever hoped for or dreamed of that will not be fulfilled. Our greatest strain in life is the strain of waiting for God. "Because thou has kept the word of my patience." [1]

I couldn't begin to count the number of times I willed myself to remain firm in the faith, choosing to believe that God would not let me down. To stand firm on the character, will, and intent of God as revealed in His Word, when seemingly everything is opposing what we're believing God for, takes fierce courage, steely determination, and an unwavering faith.

Learning a matter to the point of fiercely knowing the truth is not accomplished from reading books. Experience is the best teacher. To illustrate: Likely your parents told you not to touch the stove because you would get burned. Yet, you no doubt learned that the stove was hot by ignoring their instructions and touching anyway. Faith is developed similarly.

Persisting Through Trials Develops Faith

Ironically, by faith we realize our breakthroughs, and in the process of getting our breakthroughs our faith is developed. But that's faith's developmental method. My husband, David, and I learned this one a number of years ago.

David was hired to rescue a master-planned community at the development stages. He worked for the managing partner and was paid a handsome six-figure income for the job. We were elated with this prospect, even though accepting the position meant we had to move to a brand new community, away from all family and friends. Our plans were to rent out the home we purchased when we were first married and buy another. We thought that would be a great way for us to build our financial portfolio, especially considering the loss we suffered with the sale of my property-management company.

Even though the sale of my business was overseen by expert attorneys, the man who bought my company was a crook. He paid the down payment and only one month on the four-year note. Then he ran the business into the ground, filed bankruptcy, and sued for divorce leaving me no way to collect. I sold the business to be a work-from-home mom. We were counting on the four-year income. But David's new position seemed an answer to our prayers.

Everything went well in our efforts to find tenants for our Huntington Beach home and to purchase a new home in Temecula. However, just about a year later, David discovered why the project he was hired to rescue was failing. The financial partner was functioning illegally. In short order, the project was seized by the federal government and the owners sued on seven counts of fraud. Everyone associated with the project was let go. Here we were, a young family, our daughter about five years old and our son two years old, in a new community away from family and friends, with no income and the responsibility for two mortgages. David's company car was taken from him, leaving us with only one car. We had scraped every possible penny together to make the down-payment on our new home, which meant we had no savings or financial fall-back position. All this occurred in the early 1990s when the economy seriously tanked. Selling our rental home made sense, but actually selling during that particular market was not easy.

We exhausted all our resources in a very short period of time. Our families did what they could, but no one was in a position to rescue us. If you've experienced loss of employment then you know the loss comes with much more than simply the loss of income. The trial tested our marriage, our health, our hope, and even our faith. The only way I could function each and every day was to pore over God's Word to find His precious promises to buoy my resolve. Ephesians 6:10-18 instructs Believers to put on the full armor of God to be able to combat the devil and stand firm, believing God to work on our behalf. I imagined myself actually putting on the armor and wielding the weapons of warfare prayerfully engaged in the battle. I sought prayers from family and friends whose support fortified me to persevere until our breakthrough came.

Within months, we had no money for food or utilities, neither could we make our house payment, so the process of foreclosure on our new home began. Friends and church family members brought us groceries, gave us checks, and money orders. Our first response was to thank them and return the gifts. But as the months continued on, we humbly accepted their abundant kindness, praying for them to be blessed as the givers.

I worked part-time on weekends so that David could be free to look for gainful employment during the week. With our small children and no family nearby, the cost for child-care outweighed the benefits of me working full-time. At one point David worked three part-time jobs: a school crossing guard, a graveyard-shift tow-truck driver, and a flower delivery man— sometimes delivering flowers to people who had worked for him.

The economy was so bad that the new community of Temecula became a ghost town. Business owners that stayed cut out upper management to personally do the work they had once hired people like David to do. Foreclosures in the county where we lived were the highest in the nation. We were forced out of our house with foreclosure and faced the real prospect of being homeless. Who would rent to an unemployed family of four?

We found a couple who rented to us. We were so grateful! But within a year, we learned why they allowed us to live there. Their home was in foreclosure and had been all along, but they didn't bother to tell us. Once again, we had nowhere to go. Banks owned the majority of homes in the community. This time, the bank offered to allow us to rent a different home from them.

We had excellent credit, just no cash. To file bankruptcy didn't make sense. So by necessity, we had to use our credit cards for basic living expenses. Each time I charged something, I felt like another shovel of dirt was being put on top of us, burying us alive. During that entire period, we racked up over $30,000 in credit-card debt. There is much more to this story of suffering intensely for what turned out to be four long years. But God did a tremendous amount of work in both me and my husband in the process.

You have to know that receiving groceries and charity was humbling! But we were placed in a tender and cherished connection with the Lord and His people that we would otherwise not have known. Proverbs 3:34 states that God opposes the proud, but gives grace to the humble. Were David and I proud when he was hired to manage the project? Apparently! But I assure you that going through all we did, for as long as we did, has helped prevent us from being pride-filled ever since.

Truly, David and I saw God work in many miraculous ways during those years and the many that followed. In fact, David continued to be unemployed or to work part-time for a total of about nineteen years.

Although our losses have been significant, David and I both agree that by going through the trying times and not giving up on God, we have gained far more than we ever lost.

The Impact of Doubt or Presuming upon God's Word

No suffering is ever pleasant at the time! But with persevering faith, reliance on the Word and power of God, and the community of Believers, we will see breakthroughs—you will see the promises of God fulfilled if you believe. James, the brother of Jesus encourages us:

> Count it all joy, my brothers, when you meet trials of various kinds, for you know that the testing of your faith produces steadfastness. And let steadfastness have its full effect, that you may be perfect and complete, lacking in nothing.
>
> If any of you lacks wisdom, let him ask God, who gives generously to all without reproach, and it will be given him. But let him ask in faith, with no doubting, for the one who doubts is like a wave of the sea that is driven and tossed by the wind. For that person must not suppose that he will receive anything from the Lord; he is a double-minded man, unstable in all his ways.[2]

When we are enduring an especially difficult time, we easily find fears and doubts crowding in on our thoughts. We need to follow Christ's example and persevere with resolute confidence in God and His Word. Jeremiah 29:11, Romans 8:28, and Hebrews 11:6 became my Scriptures of promise for hope to help fight the demons of doubt:

> For I know the plans I have for you, declares the Lord, plans for welfare and not for evil, to give you a future and a hope.[3]
>
> And we know that for those who love God all things work together for good, for those who are called according to his purpose.[4]
>
> And without faith it is impossible to please him, for whoever would draw near to God must believe that he exists and that he rewards those who seek him.[5]

Perhaps the most crucial Biblical accounts to help us understand the application of faith are the two temptation stories: one about Adam, the first man, and one about the *Second Adam*—a term for Jesus. The issue in the two temptation stories is identical and applies to us today: *Do I gain power by obeying God's Words or by following my own carnal desires?*[6]

In the Garden of Eden, Satan caused Adam to doubt God's character, will, and intentions in the words God *spoke* to Adam. Satan tempted Adam to follow his own [carnal] principles in the belief that he could be in control of his own life and independent of God. Adam's choice was, in reality, a choice for Satan over God.

Satan's temptation of Jesus was to turn the *written* word of God against the *spoken* Word of God, to get the *Word of God* made flesh (Jesus) to reject God and worship Satan. Essentially Satan was asking Jesus to pre-apply or misapply Scriptural promises to His life and ministry. Jesus' response in each temptation is that He will not misapply a Scriptural promise. Rather He waits to hear from the Father directly.

Jon Ruthven's online article does an excellent job explaining the lessons for us in Christ's temptations:

> [Satan speaks directly to Jesus, basically saying:] "Step out

> in faith upon the holy, authoritative Word of God. Doesn't the Word promise: 'He will command His angels about You, and they will lift You up in their hands, so that You will not strike Your foot against a stone? Can't You Say, 'God said it! I believe it! That settles it!'?"
>
> Jesus interpreted this as trying to arrogantly bully God into action by misapplying the promises of His [God's] Word.
>
> Finally, Satan took Jesus to a "very high mountain" with the perfectly scriptural proposal that all nations should be His, as was scripturally due Him as Messiah.
>
> But this was to pre-apply a Scripture—Jesus must first be obedient and endure rejection at the cross. Misapplying or pre-applying Scripture, then, is the equivalent of falling down and worshipping Satan, as was Adam's act of seeking knowledge apart from God. [7]

This great test for Jesus was also intended as a test for every Christian. By independently *claiming the promises* do we sometimes ignore God? Do we seek to manipulate God in the way we want to interpret Scripture? Or might we at times even abandon God to follow the tempter?

Jesus never acted independently. He knew the Scriptures, yet He didn't act on God's Written Word without confirmation through God's Spoken Word. When Jesus spoke or when He performed miracles, signs, and wonders, He acted only according to the instructions of God the Father.[8] An unwavering faith in God and His Word—His Spoken Word as confirmed in His Written Word—will produce personal breakthroughs, every single time, *in God's time*. When we act independently or contrary to the fullness of God's Word (according to our own will and way), we stumble and fall. Additionally, when we expect matters to happen according to our timetable we falter.

Unwavering Faith is Established in Knowing God's Will

One key to confidently holding out for God to respond to our prayers is being certain we are praying according to *His* will. As our example, Jesus clearly and repeatedly explained that He sought to only do the Father's will. He took time to get alone and pray, which is to converse, with the Father in order to hear His specific instructions. When Jesus taught, when He healed the sick, or delivered people from demons, whatever He did was always done according to the Father's will. When we are convinced that God's character, will, and intentions toward us are ever and only to provide good for us, then deferring our will to His is easy. Besides, since God can the see the future, consulting Him makes perfect sense!

The only way a person can stand firm in the faith in the midst of opposition is by having a confident faith, firmly rooted, and already established in knowing God's will, along with having a vital personal relationship with Him.

Trials Today Strengthen Us for Tomorrow's Troubles

About fifteen years into my Christian life, having worked hard to persevere through various trials, I had the advantage of experience. Looking back over my years as a Believer, what I realized is that my faith had continued to be strengthened with each trial I successfully endured. This is a good thing! I saw a pattern of how each trial today is intended by God to strengthen us for the trials of tomorrow. I see this truth in the lives of the Old Testament Patriarchs and New Testament Apostles. If we understand that God never intends for our trials to defeat us, but instead to be an opportunity for us to grow, influence others for Christ, and glorify God, this perspective alone will help us better persevere until our breakthrough comes.

Faith is like a muscle that needs to be regularly exercised to stay in the best shape. When we over-exert a muscle, we actually tear down the tissue. Then, as the tissue repairs itself, the muscle is made larger and stronger than before. With the realization that our faith is strengthened to the degree we cooperate with God, how willing cooperation behooves us! And, as cannot be over-stressed, we must firmly deal with unbelief. I want you to experience the fullness of all God has for you, so let's get belief firmly established, for without strong belief we cannot persevere.

Unbelief Prevents the Miraculous

There are three passages that instruct us about unbelief: Matthew 17:14-21, Mark 9:14-29 and Luke 9:37-42. These are three accounts of the same event. By overlaying all three we get the broadest understanding possible. A father brought his son to Jesus' disciples requesting that they heal him.

The story reveals a father's relentless faith in the authority of Jesus, in contrast to unbelief on the part of Jesus' own disciples. Charles H. Spurgeon, a British Particular Baptist preacher who remains highly influential among Christians of various denominations, lived in the mid to late 1800s. The first point he makes in teaching from these passages is "We may be the servants of God and yet we may be occasionally defeated."[9]

The passages of this story reveal that the disciples were bewildered as to why they could not deliver the boy. When they inquired of Jesus, He replied, "Because of your little faith. For truly, I say to you, if you have faith like a grain of mustard seed, you will say to this mountain, 'Move from here to there,' and it will move, and nothing will be impossible for you."[10]

The very reason Jesus did not perform miracles in His own hometown was because of the unbelief of the people. Matthew, Chapter 13, verses 54-58, reveals that Jesus traveled to His own country where He spoke and taught in the synagogue as He'd done elsewhere. The people who'd known Him as a young boy growing up in His Father's home—a lad who'd learned the trade of carpentry—were amazed at His teachings. They asked, "Where did this man get this wisdom and these mighty works? Is not this the carpenter's son? Is not his mother called Mary? And are not his brothers James and Joseph and Simon and Judas? And are not all his sisters with us? Where then did this man get all these things?"[11] The people greatly offended Him so He did not do many mighty works there, because of their unbelief. Understand that the unbelief of the people did not produce some sort of power that rendered Jesus impotent. Rather God doesn't reward unbelief. Just as we are not inclined to give good gifts to people who won't appreciate them, neither is God.

There will be times in our Christian life when we are faced with something that reveals a limit to our faith. To experience the personal breakthrough and press beyond the limitation, we need to know what is hindering us. There are many possibilities, all of which have their root in a form of unbelief. Doubt, worry, fear, and anxiety can be evidences of a lack of belief in God—His character, His will, His intent, and His ability. Pride is an elevated belief in oneself that displaces proper belief in God.

Each of us deals with belief and unbelief in varying measures. The Apostle Thomas, who had been a disciple of Jesus for approximately three years, and who was among the disciples performing signs and wonders, when faced with the prospect of Jesus being raised from the dead, struggled. John 20:27-28 records this dialog with the risen Lord:

> Then he said to Thomas, "Put your finger here, and see my hands; and put out your hand, and place it in my side. Do

not disbelieve, but believe." Thomas answered him, "My Lord and my God!

When you suspect that you are being hindered by a form of unbelief, make a point to go to God in prayer and pore over His Written Word. I have found that having some books that list God's promises found in Scripture by topic very helpful. If I'm needing a breakthrough in a matter of health, for example, I could look up God's promises for *healing*. By focusing on His specific promises, and prayerfully seeking God to help your unbelief, you will be on the right path for your breakthrough.

We Must Walk Before We Can Run in the Faith

Consider the first twelve disciples of Jesus. As we read about the approximately three years they spent with Jesus learning from Him directly, we observe them acquiring knowledge, weighing what they learn against what they previously understood, doubting, questioning, sometimes even challenging Jesus' statements. Many times Jesus rebuked His disciples for being slow to accept His teachings, even questioning how long He would have to contend with them. We read about times they successfully stepped out in faith and performed signs and wonders, and we read about times when they didn't succeed.

Matthew 14:30, Matthew 17:21, and Mark 4:38 provide evidence of times they failed in their attempts to demonstrate faith. Mark 9:38 reveals when they tried to prevent others from performing miracles. Other times they were amazed (and understandably so!) at the great and mighty works the Spirit did through them (Matthew 21:20).

The disciples demonstrated the very same human tendencies we all have. Scriptures reveal that they struggled with faith and kingdom effectiveness. I can't help but wonder about the likely existence of some competition among these rugged disciples. John 20:4 tells of Peter and John running to the tomb of Jesus after the women declared the tomb was empty. In Scripture, John makes the point of recording that he outran Peter. John refers to himself five times in the Gospel of John as the disciple whom Jesus loved, or the most beloved disciple. This same reference is not made anywhere else in the New Testament. I wonder how this made the others feel. Maybe John's attitude was part of what prompted Peter, after learning from Jesus about how his final days on earth would be, to ask Jesus about John's final days. Jesus' response to Peter was to basically mind his own business, saying, "What difference does that make to you? You follow Me. (John 21:22)

Distinctly Unique, Yet Equally Valued

Like each of the Apostles, God had a purpose in mind for you before you were conceived. Psalm 139:15-16 reveals that our unique existence was carefully planned by God before we were conceived. Scriptures clarify that although we are each unique, and each yet another aspect of the image of God, we are all equal. There is no difference in value among us. We are all equal. Regardless of a person's lofty or lowly state in life, there is no difference in status in God's eyes. In Acts 10:34, Peter is given a vision to cause him to understand there is no difference between Jew and Gentile, therefore there is to be no distinction or discrimination among mankind. Romans 2:11 clearly states that God is no respecter of persons. Galatians 3:26-28 explains that we are all children of God through faith in Jesus. All who believe and are baptized into Christ are equal and one in Christ. There is neither Jew nor Greek, slave nor free, male or female, we are all one in Christ.

As humans, we are each unique in personality and purpose, and because we are each unique, we are equally-valued by the Father in the same way. Certain abilities, callings, and stations in life are not to be esteemed greater than any other. Ephesians, Chapter Four, explains we've each been created for specific works of service—that is, kingdom-ministry work.

The *Epistles* (letters) of Romans and Ephesians, both written by the Apostle Paul, use a lot of papyrus stressing the importance of operating with the premise that we are each unique, yet equally-valued. I want you to clearly understand this principle so that you are able to withstand the enemy when he tries to convince you that you are not worthy to receive your breakthroughs, or that you are not in position for hope.

Disobedience, Not Failures, Brings Consequences

As we step out in an effort to exercise our faith, we will encounter some times of failure, just as the disciples did. Drawing from Spurgeon's instruction, let's realize:

- Failures should serve as a means of causing us to want to learn what is preventing us from advancing. The father, the boy, and the disciples all went to Jesus to inquire of Him.
- Failures should cause us to examine our heart attitudes. Could the disciples have become complacent, thereby reducing their expectations to more of a mechanical or rote expression? Such would displace a proper expectant belief.
- Realization that we have lack and need assistance reminds us of the superiority of our Master and turns our focus to Him. Our recognized inadequacies should drive us to want more of Christ, learn more, press in and get hold of the more we need.
- When we are baffled, as the disciples were about why we are

unsuccessful to do a certain thing by faith, we must go to the Father to learn why. It may be that we've acquired a measure of doubt or fear or unbelief.[12]

God knows that we will encounter serious challenges in our faith while we live in this fallen world. He knows there will be times we experience failures in our faith. Unbelief is the enemy's goal for us, which he attempts to impose upon us through doubts and fears that he implants in our minds. Learning from failure is something we understand. When we rebel, we suffer the consequences. But when we attempt to step out in faith and we fail because of fear and doubt, there are no consequences *per se*, just an opportunity to re-group and try again.

Matthew 17:14-21 records the story of Christ's disciples who were unable to cast out the demon from the boy brought to the disciples by the boy's father. The disciples couldn't cast out the demon because of their unbelief—they were stepping out in faith they really did not have. There was no consequence or discipline that Jesus administered. Rather He expressed His desire that they should be further along in their faith, then helped them understand what they lacked so that they could have success moving forward.

Do not let the enemy beat you down in effort to defeat or immobilize you when you fail. Instead, refocus your mind on the truth of God's Word and His promises, and boldly step out in faith commanding any fears or doubts to leave you according to the authority of Christ in you. Use Scripture promises such as "Submit yourselves to God. Resist the devil, and he will flee from you" to help you overcome fear and doubt. (James 4:7 NIV)

Expect the Unexpected

As we study the many miraculous healings and deliverances that Jesus and His disciples performed, we will find no formula, no three-step plan, and no specific map of directions to take. In every instance, the method and the miracle were uniquely performed. I'm confident this is by God's design to keep us working together and ever alert to Him.

Not all the accounts of Jesus healing blind men recorded in the Gospels reveal specifically what Jesus did. In some instances we only read, "He healed them." But we do have three examples of Jesus healing blind men, each in a distinct manner.

Matthew 20:34 states Jesus touched the blind man and he was healed. Mark 8:23 records that Jesus spat on the man, then after only a partial healing, He next laid His hands on him. John 9:6 explains that Jesus spit on the ground and made a mud clay that was placed on the blind man's eyes, who was then told to go wash and then he would see. With just these few examples of the thirty-seven documented miracles performed by Jesus in the New Testament (He performed many more that were not recorded according to John 21:25.), we see that each method was different.

Warnings About Counterfeits Mean the Authentic Exists

My intentions in writing my book series are to help people realize the victorious life that we can and should be living in Christ. Many have commented that my writing and ministry work is guided by love. If we do not agree, let's do so in love so that we don't fracture the unity that enables us to make an impact on this world. My hope, however, is to win more people to the perspective that the supernatural gifts demonstrated by the early disciples (not just the Apostles), which are recorded in Scripture, are available for disciples (Christ-followers) today. Applied, open-minded study is necessary, as is belief. Without belief that a spiritual matter is true, manifestation of the matter will not be granted. Consider again the reason Jesus would not perform miracles in His own home town.

One of the simplest evidences that the supernatural gifts are available today and up to the end of the Church age are the many warnings in Scripture to beware of the counterfeit. There would be no reason to be on guard for a fake if the authentic wasn't also available. Yet, the Bible warns Believers to be cautious and not to be deceived.

A list of claims made by those who do not believe the supernatural gifts are available today state that every true miracle always had all the following characteristics:

- There was conclusive evidence that the event really occurred.
- The event occurred instantaneously (or in exactly the limited time period God specified).
- There were never any failures when miracles were attempted (by Jesus or by His apostles after they received Holy Spirit baptism).
- The results always completely and perfectly accomplished the intended purpose.
- The event was clearly impossible by natural law.

Let's simply use the reality of a person's salvation today in response to the above claims. I will use my own experience as the example:

- Ask anyone who knew me twenty years ago if I'm the same woman and they will tell you I am not.
- Ask my roommate and my closest friends at the time that I asked Jesus to be my Savior and Lord about their shock concerning me from one day to the very next literal day they saw me.

- My spiritual transformation is so evident and has continued without fail (failure differs from perfection) to this very day.
- The results have and continue to be completed to perfectly accomplish the intended purpose. Salvation was instant and sanctification is a process.
- My spiritual transformation is clearly impossible by natural law.

Salvation is one eternally-amazing miracle—a statement that even Cessationists agree upon. For clarity, Cessationists believe that the miracle of salvation and that God answers prayer are the only supernatural events available today. They claim that the miraculous gifts have ceased, including tongues, prophecy, healing, and presumably also the gift of miracles, which the Apostle Paul distinguishes from the gift of healing in 1 Corinthians 12. As I wrote previously, I have a very difficult time believing that with Scriptures being so clear that the end times would be the worst of all, that God would withdraw from us the power we need to have victory. I discuss this in more in Chapter Seven.

Unrelenting Belief and Perseverance

While I love Oswald Chamber's explanation of spiritual tenacity, I believe there are two essential elements: *unrelenting belief* and *perseverance*. These two elements can be easily supported by one passage from the book of Hebrews: "And without faith it is impossible to please him, for whoever would draw near to God must believe that he exists and that he rewards those who seek him." (Hebrews 11:6)

Clearly, as Christ and His disciples demonstrated, the rewards God wants us to have go beyond salvation and include other blessings in this earthly life. Psalm 27:13 reads, "*I would have lost heart, unless I had believed that I would see the goodness of the Lord in the land of the living.*"[13] (NKJ)

Through our long years of part-time work and unemployment, living below the poverty level for several years, I found great comfort in Matthew 5:1-12, a section of Scripture known as the *Beatitudes*. The term beatitudes comes from the Latin noun *beātitūdō* that means *happiness*. I've heard preachers claim that Jesus isn't as concerned about our comfort as He is our character. While that may be technically true, I think people may inappropriately discount their very real, emotional, mental, and practical needs because of that premise.

The deep compassion of our Lord for His people who are contending in this fallen world is evident. Within the Beatitudes, He encourages Believers who suffer being poor in spirit, who mourn, who are meek, who hunger and thirst for righteousness, those who are merciful, pure in heart, peacemakers, and who are persecuted for righteousness sake, that each will be blessed, comforted, established, and see their reward—some rewards will be experienced in this life and some in heaven.

In Matthew 6:25-34, where Jesus is still speaking to the multitudes, He lovingly admonishes Believers not to worry:

> Therefore I tell you, do not be anxious about your life, what you will eat or what you will drink, nor about your body, what you will put on. Is not life more than food, and the body more than clothing? Look at the birds of the air: they neither sow nor reap nor gather into barns, and yet your heavenly Father feeds them. Are you not of more value than they?[14]
>
> But if God so clothes the grass of the field, which today is alive and tomorrow is thrown into the oven, will he not

> much more clothe you, O you of little faith? Therefore do not be anxious, saying, 'What shall we eat?' or 'What shall we drink?' or 'What shall we wear?' For the Gentiles [unbelievers] seek after all these things, and your heavenly Father knows that you need them all. But seek first the kingdom of God and his righteousness, and all these things will be added to you.[15]

God is concerned with every thing that concerns you. Scriptures tell us that your name is written in the palm of His hand, (Isaiah 49:16) and that He knows the very number of the hairs on your head, (Luke 12:7).

Let me lovingly challenge you with what I often ask my audiences in person:

> Understanding the unfathomable lengths God has already gone through, with Him personally taking on human form, to live this earthly existence, to suffer and be mercilessly tortured, even to die the most agonizing death ever known to man, crucifixion, to secure your eternal relationship with Him, beginning now and for all eternity, do you really think He's going to bail on you in this matter you are presently suffering?
>
> With all that God has already done to secure our eternal future, why do we have difficulty trusting Him to work in our temporal lives?

The Deception of Denial

When I talk with people about how they are managing in the trial they are suffering, I find that many, if not most, draw on the power of denial instead of the power of the Lord. Denial is a powerful tool we use to avoid reality—a coping mechanism that offers enough relief that we conclude denial is working, when in reality the opposite is true.

You've probably heard the popular definition of insanity: attempting to do the same thing the same way while expecting different results. This describes insanity, and to that I'll add *denial*.

Many have learned how to stop the pain caused by life's disappointments and sufferings—not by changing our circumstances, but by pretending our circumstances are something other than what they are. Yet nowhere in Scripture or in real life did Jesus or any of his Disciples ever suggest we live in denial. Denial is yet another demonstration of unbelief, for if we truly believed, we'd confidently take our life's disappointments and sufferings to the Father knowing He will answer our prayers.

To the uninitiated, when a Believer stands firm in the faith, believing God for His Word—His very promises—the action *appears* like denial. However, when a Believer has a confident faith, a clear direction from the Lord, and the tenacity to press in and wait no matter how long the answer takes, as crazy as that practice may look to outsiders, when the answered prayer comes, unbelievers are astonished. At this point your joy and testimony becomes a calling card for Christ. Think about that and let the thought sink in. Your daily life can be a witness for Christ that draws others unto Him simply by the way you demonstrate your faith.

God's Provisions Includes Community

Of course there will be times when remaining strong and steady is difficult. I had plenty of those times in my darkest seasons! But that's when we call on fellow brothers and sisters in the faith to pray with us according to James 5:13-16:

> Is anyone among you suffering? Let him pray. Is anyone cheerful? Let him sing praise. Is anyone among you sick? Let him call for the elders of the church, and let them pray over him, anointing him with oil in the name of the Lord. And the prayer of faith will save the one who is sick, and the Lord will raise him up. And if he has committed sins, he will be forgiven. Therefore, confess your sins to one another and pray for one another, that you may be healed. The prayer of a righteous person has great power as it is working.[16]

Additionally, it is God's plan that we practically provide for one another:

> By this we know love, that he laid down his life for us, and we ought to lay down our lives for the brothers. But if anyone has the world's goods and sees his brother in need, yet closes his heart against him, how does God's love abide in him? Little children, let us not love in word or talk but in deed and in truth.[17]

When my family suffered the four long years of unemployment and part-time work, I'm convinced there would have been no way for us to endure our trial to the end, unto the reward we received, (which I shared some about in Chapter Five), without the prayers and support of our brothers and sisters in the faith on our behalf. The precious women and men from the Bible study and our church were instruments of God who helped us practically, mentally, emotionally, spiritually, and beyond.

God never intended us to live this life purely in our own strength and ability or outside the community of Believers. God, as three-Persons in

One, is a community in and of Himself. We who are made in His image are created by design with the need for community. *Unity* in community among Believers is what can produce the greatest good.

Put on the Whole Armor of God

Ephesians 6:10-18 implores us to put on the full armor of God that we may be able to stand against the wiles of the enemy. This passage reminds us that we do not battle with flesh and blood—*fellow man*—we battle with powers and principalities and wicked rulers of dark places. With the whole armor of God in place we:

- Have confidence in the truth of God's Word,
- Are righteous because our faith is in Jesus,
- Are prepared with the gospel of peace,
- Display our faith as a protective shield,
- Are fitted with the helmet of salvation to guard our minds,
- Wield the sword of the Spirit, which is the Word of God,
- Persevere in prayer and watchfulness *together with all the saints*,
- Will see the goodness of the Lord in the land of the living.

As we don the full armor of God, operate according to the leading of the Holy Spirit, and maintain proper fellowship with other Believers, the victory is easier won. While the fact that God can and does zap miracle solutions into existence is true, more often He chooses to work through His people. As Scriptures reveal, to give is better than to receive. No one likes being in a position of need where we must receive. But learning to receive is an essential aspect of experiencing breakthroughs.

In the next chapter we'll learn of the actual experiences people have had while daring to hold out for God, and expecting Him to deliver according to His Word.

CHAPTER SIX

Faith Exemplified

Encouraging Examples of Faith

Scriptures tell us that with God nothing is impossible.[1] Do you believe that? Do you really believe that? No, I mean do you emphatically, implicitly, radically believe that?

One Christian adage I've always appreciated states, "Christians are like tea bags. You can't really know what they're made of until you put them in hot water." There's nothing like a *test of hot water* to reveal who we really are. Do we claim to be Christian, but fall apart when our life circumstances do? How is faith demonstrated in that? We may say we'd never give up on God. But only in the face of the greatest opposition can we know this with certainty.

Consider Luke 1:37 from this perspective: Since nothing is impossible with God, we must acknowledge that any time we give up on anything good, we're giving up on God. Are there situations or expectations in your life that you've given up on? If God has indicated that He will do a thing, He will do it—so long as we believe Him. Remember, unbelief kept God from wanting to operate supernaturally through Jesus when He was in His in His home town, (Mark 6:4-5).

Don't Ever Give Up on God!

We have tremendous true-life stories in the Bible where men and women have been put to extreme tests without giving up on God. In addition to

Jesus personally enduring torture and crucifixion unto death, nearly all the first Apostles were martyred for their faith, as well as many of the first century followers. Even unto our present day, Christians have displayed incredible faith, even unto death. Only those utterly convinced of the object of their faith or the significance of their cause can willingly face death without denouncing their belief.

Daniel of the Old Testament was such a man, (Daniel Chapter Six). In approximately 605 B.C., the Babylonians conquered Israel, taking many promising young men into captivity. Daniel was one of those men.

Through a life of hard work and obedience to God, he had risen through the political ranks as an administrator of the pagan kingdom of Babylon. Daniel's reputation was so outstanding that other government officials became jealous of him and wanted to have him removed from office. They could find nothing to charge against him, so they sought to use Daniel's faith in God against him. They tricked King Darius into passing a decree that during a thirty-day period, anyone who prayed to another god or man besides the king would be thrown into the lions' den.

Daniel learned of the decree, but did not change his habit. Just as he had done all his life, he went home, knelt down, faced Jerusalem, and prayed to God. Lying in wait, the wicked officials observed him and told the king. King Darius, who loved Daniel, tried to save him, but the decree could not be revoked.

At sundown, Daniel was thrown into the den of ravenous lions. Scriptures reveal that the king could not eat or sleep all night. At dawn the king ran to the lions' den, hoping to hear a response before he could see, asking "Daniel, has your God protected you?" The king indeed hear Daniel's reply: "My God sent His angel, and He shut the mouths of the lions. They have not hurt me, because I was found innocent in His sight. Nor have I ever done any wrong before you, O king." (Daniel 6:22, NIV)

Scripture says the king was overjoyed. Daniel was brought out, unharmed, "...because he had trusted in his God." (Daniel 6:23, NIV)

King Darius had the men who falsely accused Daniel arrested, and along with their wives and children, they were all thrown into the lions' den, where they were immediately killed by the beasts.

Daniel was an ordinary person just like you and like me. Was he perfect? No, Jesus is the only one to ever live a perfect life. What Daniel was, and what we can be, is completely and radically sold-out to God, no matter what. Daniel didn't get to the place of sold-out faith a few moments before he was thrown into the lions' den. He made a deliberate effort, day upon day, throughout his life, to increase his knowledge of God. Daniel is believed to have been nearly eighty years old when he was thrown to the lions. He'd clearly built on every life experience in the light of truth about God and His Word, so that when he faced a horrendous reality, he relied on God.

Job was another righteous man who had been tremendously blessed by God. He most unexpectedly suffered great loss as we read in the Old Testament book of Job. Regardless of his extreme loss and unimaginable pain, Job proclaimed, "Though He may slay me, yet will I trust Him." Daniel no doubt resolutely maintained the same confident devotion.

Job and Daniel are but two of the countless men and women who through the ages have possessed the faith of Abraham. Abraham was asked to sacrifice his long-awaited son of promise in obedience to God. Abraham was willing to obey God, believing that God redeems what appears to us to be hopeless.

Revelation 12:11, speaking of the Believers who were martyred for their faith, reads, "And they have conquered him by the blood of the Lamb and by the word of their testimony, for they loved not their lives even unto death."[2] Naturally none of us wants to be faced with such extreme tests of faith, but as Believers, we should always be working on increasing our faith so that our faith can sustain us in any situation.

As written before, there is great power in free-will. Our prayers will not overcome another person's will—even God, by His own design, has chosen to limit Himself concerning free-will. However, we can ask God to orchestrate circumstances and events to cause another to question and to be troubled to the point that they are willing to reconsider a matter. In fact, this is the loving thing to do when a person is clearly outside God's will.

Whether we are praying for something because we know our prayer is consistent with God's general will, such as the salvation of a loved one, or restoration of relationships, or if we are praying a specific Word of promise from God, we must be persistent and pray until the answer or new direction is provided by the Lord, no matter how hopeless things look in the process.

God always redeems evil—whether by ushering the righteous from our earthly dwelling into our heavenly home, or by dealing with evil and suffering on the earth. We can count on God to always redeem, and with that knowledge we must never give up. According to Romans 12:3, God gives to all a measure of faith. But developing our faith, strengthening that faith, and acquiring the kind of confidence to be persistent in prayer until the answer comes is up to us.

- What if Moses gave up as he reached the Red Sea?
- What if Joshua gave up when he heard the exaggerated report of giants in the Promised Land?
- What if you give up before realizing the promises God has for you?

The Confidence of Abraham Is Our Goal

The stories of the Bible reveal real people of all types: some with strong confident faith in God; some weak and fearful; some who lived upright; some who lived wickedly; some who lived as enemies of God until a particular encounter caused them to repent and seek God; still others who knew God, but when pressed through opposition, turned away from God.

Luke 22:54-62 reveals that the Apostle Peter denied knowing Jesus *three times* after Christ was arrested. Peter was entirely void of faith in the face of his Lord's arrest. But he was later greeted by the risen Christ, recorded in John 21:1-19, and Christ lovingly restored Peter who then went on to be a mighty man of God. Yet at a point before Jesus' crucifixion, Jesus said of Peter, "Blessed are you, Simon Bar-Jonah! For flesh and blood has not revealed this [that Jesus is the Promised Redeemer] to you, but my Father who is in heaven. And I tell you, you are Peter, and on this rock I will build my church, and the gates of hell shall not prevail against it."[3]

The name Peter (*Petros* in Greek) means "rock" or "rock-man." Christ used *petra* (upon this rock), a feminine form for "rock," not a name. Christ used a play on words. He did not say "upon you, Peter" or "upon your successors," but "upon this rock"—upon this divine revelation and profession of faith in Christ.

Like Peter, we may have a strong profession of faith, but when faced with adverse circumstances we find that our faith is beyond weak. Even apart from adversity, we may realize that our faith is weak concerning certain desirable promises from God.

Consider that both Abraham and Sarah had a tough time believing God's promise that they could conceive a son in their advanced years. Sarah laughed at the prospect. After years waiting for the fulfillment of the promise, Abraham agreed with Sarah to *help God out* by having a child (hopefully a son) with Hagar, Sarah's handmaiden. At this point Abraham's faith was not what it would become.

Indeed, Hagar did bear a son who was named Ishmael. But he wasn't the *son of promise*. As a result, Ishmael's very existence brought much turmoil to the extended family. Not until Sarah and Abraham miraculously conceived *the son of promise*, whom they named Isaac in obedience to God, was their faith was solidified. So much so that when God asked Abraham to sacrifice the very life of Isaac, he willingly sought to comply, now able to believe God for His promise regardless of natural realities.

Scriptures speak of Abraham's faith as it was ultimately developed:

> No unbelief made him [Abraham] waver concerning the promise of God, but he grew strong in his faith as he gave glory to God, fully convinced that God was able to do what he had promised. That is why his faith was "counted to him as righteousness." But the words "it was counted to him" were not written for his sake alone, but for ours also. It will be counted to us who believe in him who raised from the dead Jesus our Lord, who was delivered up for our trespasses and raised for our justification.[4]

Clearly Abraham's and Sarah's faith was developed as they held out hope, even with an occasional lapse in faith. There are many other stories of men and women in the Bible and in real life who find there are times their faith is weak. Experiencing occasions, or even seasons, of weak faith will never disqualify you from God lovingly working in your life. However, when we find ourselves weak in our faith we must intentionally do everything possible to strengthen our faith without delay. Because in seasons of weakness, the enemy of God seeks to overcome us, just as he tempted Jesus after His forty days in the wilderness (Matthew 4:1-11).

Pour over Scriptures, seek prayer and counsel from mature Believers, review your previously answered prayers, and find strength from the testimonies of others, such as recorded in this book. Do all that you can to fortify your faith.

Faith is Developed Through Obedience

You know some about my husband's years of part-time work and unemployment. In actuality, we suffered the effects of that for over twenty years. Only once he decided to become self-employed were we established on a path of recovery. I'd always found operating from an entrepreneurial spirit easy. Self-employment wasn't frightening to me. But as head of a family of four, David found the consideration of self-employment an entirely different matter. I recall lovingly encouraging David to go out on his own (he might say I nagged…), because I sensed God was directing him to do so. After four consecutive hard-core years of part-time work and unemployment that ended in 1996, David found jobs within his experience and education, but they were all short-lived with many months between them. We still suffered greatly with underemployment. I clearly saw these times as God orchestrating circumstances to bring David to decide for himself. Finally in 2005, by pressing through his fears, David heard the Lord clearly directing him and he established Christian Development Company. After the first five years of operation, we have been blessed with a steady rebuild from year to year. With all the losses and debt we accumulated, we are still a way from financial comfort. But, I'm confident we would not have made the progress we have had David not intentionally pressed past his fears to finally hear and obey God.

Like my husband, and countless other Believers, I, too, have had to push through my fears in order to obey God. Of the many ideas I had for my own life work, I never dreamed of doing some of the things I have done. Serving as Teaching Director for the Community Bible Study (CBS) class, working as a national keynote speaker, hosting live radio talk shows, doing commercial television, and writing books were all God's ideas. With each of these God clearly downloaded a thought into my spirit that I couldn't deny. Each time I initially resisted, and reasoned (argued) with Him until I knew I had to act or be outside God's will for me.

The first time I experienced God's clear leading was about teaching the CBS class. Admittedly, I reluctantly obeyed. I had only been a Christian for five years when He revealed His will for me! I took three days arguing with Him, because I didn't think I was the right candidate. I finally stepped out and, honestly, I attempted to establish the class in my own strength, because that was where I had experience and a measure of confidence. So, when my efforts fell flat and produced nothing good, I regrouped. I submitted the entire effort to God, relied on Him and His abilities, and then I saw Him do the impossible. The class was established and grew strong. By the end of my nearly seven-year effort, we had not only the class I started, but an evening and a men's and a home-schooling class as offshoots.

The same way our trials test and strengthen us for the troubles ahead, the guidance we willingly receive from God brings us to accomplish the impossible. This process also increases our trust in Him to do even more in the future—renewing our hope and providing remedies for personal breakthroughs.

Obedience Produces Blessings

In my progression of faith built upon obedience, I have many amazing testimonies, including how I came to host live Christian radio.

I'll never forget driving in my car listening to the same teaching and talk Christian radio station I had for years. I heard an announcement that the station was looking for a female host. Upon hearing those words, I felt a physical reaction similar to butterflies in my stomach. I dismissed them as nothing until I heard the same announcement three additional times with each time generating a stronger physical reaction. I asked, *Lord is this You? Really God? How could I possibly apply for a position with absolutely no training or experience?* I was actually a little irritated...

Within a few days, I got an email from a dear friend of mine, June Naslund, who had heard the same announcement. She wrote to tell me that she thought I should apply for the position. I sat at my desk incredulous because June is the very same woman God used to confirm the speaking ministry that followed my years of teaching CBS. I remember saying aloud, "Oh, that's good God, but that's not good enough. You'll have to do better than that." Yeah, I really said that.

Thereafter, each time I heard the announcement, I had a stronger reaction, so believing God was more than nudging me, I decided I would call Rich Buhler. Rich had not only worked for the same station, he has been accredited as the Dean of Christian talk radio. I'd had the privilege of meeting him a few years prior. He knew my background and abilities. I called him and asked without taking a breath, "Rich, you worked for the station, you know me, do you think I should apply for the position?" There was a long pause, then I heard him say with his deep booming voice, "Absolutely!" I thought, *Oh, no*... as I physically slumped in my chair.

Now understand, I know the importance of being positive when applying for a position, but in this case I reluctantly picked up the phone and called the station. When the phone was answered, I intentionally said, "You're not still looking to fill the female host position are you?" The reply came, "Why, yes, we are." Again, I thought *Oh, no*... They asked me to

FAX my résumé to the station and told me I should expect to hear back by the end of the week should they want to interview me. I sent my résumé, then thought, *Okay, now I've been obedient. That should be the end of it.* I got a call the very next day that they wanted to interview me. *Oh, no...*

I arrived at the station from my home after a half-hour drive with no traffic. I interviewed with the station manager. The next thing I know, he wants to put me on air within the hour. *What! I've never been on air before. I have to do well or the whole world will hear me bomb!* I thought *I want my own Bible so I can easily find passages I will likely need on air.* But I didn't have time to drive home and back, especially now during peak traffic. I called my husband and he battled the traffic and arrived on time with my Bible. I went on air, I don't remember a thing, but when I was done they said they wanted me back to host a half-hour program as part of my audition. *Oh, no...*

I was completely in charge of the program. I called Rich Buhler who gave me a few pointers to help me plan the program. I decided to have a guest expert in the studio and that we'd raise a topic and take questions and comments from callers. I must admit by this stage about two months into the interview process, I was no longer reluctant. There were others also vying for the same position, but I now *wanted* the job. I remember that program. Everything went exceptionally well and I was sure I got the job! I went home and waited expectantly. After all, hadn't God been the one who downloaded the idea for me on radio in the first place?

Some days later I got a letter in the mail that read, "We have decided to go another direction for the 2:00 p.m. program and not hire you. The reasons are proprietary, but know that it was not an easy decision. You were the runner-up, so I definitely think it was worth something. Hopefully you do, too." (I am looking at the letter as I write this. I had my rejection framed and the letter hangs on my office wall to this very day.)

What? The runner-up? Who wants to be the runner-up? I couldn't believe what I was reading and I cried and cried and cried. Clearly God had led me every step of the way. I was not only obedient, but no longer reluctant. My rejection made no sense to me whatsoever. I cried some more.

A few months later, I called Rich again. "Rich, you know that I came in as the runner-up for that host position. And with my audition so clearly being God's leading, I'm believing I have some aptitude for hosting radio in His plan. Which of these three broadcast training schools do you recommend?" His reply was "None of them. But if you're wanting to be trained to host radio, I'll train you." I couldn't believe my ears! Rich Buhler *offered* to train *me*? This means he believes in me. He later told me that he had trained others for radio, but I was the only one he ever offered to train. What a blessing!

After being trained from behind the desk, there was nothing to do except to get me on air. The same station at which I had auditioned picked up extra hours during the three summer months which meant they had program times to fill. I called the station requesting a one-hour weekly time slot. They would only sell me a two-hour slot, for a cost of more than $20,000—much more than the one-hour program expense I expected. We sure didn't have that kind of cash, not to mention the other costs that would be required. I prayed asking for the Lord's guidance.

I then called a very conservative Certified Public Accountant (CPA) who had also been an elder at our church. I explained the situation and asked if he thought I should purchase the slot. My husband was willing to go into debt if so. The reply was, "Yes, I absolutely think you should do it. In fact, I have several people in mind who may be willing to support the effort since you'll be on Christian talk radio." With that inspiration, I then called a friend who owns an educational non-profit organization. I asked if I could work under her corporation so anyone making contributions could get a tax deduction. She said her attorney (who is always impossible to get through to) would have to approve. I had a deadline from the station to confirm purchase of the air-time or not. Amazingly, the attorney was immediately available, and the idea was approved.

I then called three of the people the CPAt recommended. After I explained what the program would be, they each offered to make a donation. With just the first three calls, I had enough income promised to cover a full month of broadcasting! Encouraged by those circumstances, I stepped out in faith.

Rich had cautioned me that the most I should expect to recover was about half of all my costs. But by the end of the three months, I had not only raised enough money to pay for the entire broadcast time, but also enough to pay my producer, make a donation to the 501c3 that supported me, and pocket $2,000 for my labor. You can imagine how grateful I was to the Lord for continuing to nudge me every step of the way, even though I resisted. But imagine how utterly delighted I was when I was then hired by Salem Communications to host their evening drive-time talk show in San Francisco! And, based on outside ratings evaluations I have in my files, the program ratings were significantly increased in the single year I hosted the show.

With my all my *God experiences* up to this point, when a delightful Pastor by the name of Saeed Awad was my in-studio guest and prophetically spoke to me during a break stating, "I see you on television," I didn't flinch. I've seen what God can do with a person who is willing to obey him, even without any training or experience. I knew that if this was God, He would bless my efforts. Based on God's miraculous work in my life in the past, on the chance the prophetic word was true, I enrolled in classes to be trained in television production and hosting.

Not long after that, through another amazing story and succession of events that had to do with my surviving sudden cardiac arrest, (yes, I died and was revived… I tell you about that later), I was selected as the principal talent for a national Proctor and Gamble television commercial. The ad ran for a couple of years, handsomely paid me, and made possible our being able to have medical insurance during a season when we wouldn't have otherwise been covered.

Testimonies are most definitely encouraging. Even reconsidering our own God-experiences can fortify our faith. With that in mind, allow the testimonies that follow to be used by God to encourage you.

Modern Day Family Miracle

Kim Phillips is a special friend that I get the pleasure of meeting on most Mondays at a prayer group we jointly attend. She and her husband, Todd, and family have been a tremendous inspiration to countless numbers of people in their faith-walk. Here in her own words is their story of the Lord's inspiration for them to adopt a child and His provision to make the adoption possible:

"The Lord made it compellingly clear that He wanted us to adopt a little blind girl from China. When we started the adoption process, we had only $50.00 in our bank account, but needed about $30,000 to complete the process. We knew of absolutely no way to earn the additional money, but we boldly moved forward in obedience to God.

"Every single step was a testament to the miracle provision of God, and how when He calls His own to act in faith in any matter, He provides. Random people we didn't even know heard about our effort and would inquire what they could do to help. The Lord led several people to donate large amounts of money. On more than one occasion, we were amazed to see the Lord speak to individuals to give. And what they'd hand us would turn out to be the exact amount for whatever fee was due at the particular time.

"The day before our family was scheduled to fly to China to pick up our daughter, we needed at least $4000. We were supposed to have this money in cash and it had to be in new hundred dollar bills. We were told that the China adoption coordinator would not accept any old bills. We needed to pay $3,000 towards adoption fees and we needed about another $1,000 for food and expenses during the required two week stay as a family. We were about an hour away from getting in the car to leave with literally zero dollars in our bank account.

"We've heard many stories of God coming through at the last minute for people going on missions trips, etc., and He had been right-on time every step of the way for us so far, so we determined to expect that He would do something. It was not at all easy. We didn't want to be foolish. But, neither could we disregard the unrelenting unction from the Lord to simply take the next step.

"I sat with my 9-year-old daughter, Abigail, on our bed. She looked at me and asked knowingly, "Mom, we don't have all the money we need, do we?" Looking at her I said, "Either God is real, or He's not, and since He is, and has brought us this far, get ready to see a miracle!" I hoped beyond hope that the words I dared to speak would be honored for everyone's sake!

"Our friends who live near the airport were set to watch our dog and were also having a little going-away party for us before our 1:00 a.m. departure, so we went to the their home. Everyone gathered around us for prayer and someone asked me specifically if we had all the money we needed. I explained our situation and confessed that we weren't sure how to proceed because we didn't want to be foolish by traveling to China with our kids without the funds, but also wanted to walk in faith.

"Moments later one of our friends walked up to us and handed us a big wad of cash! He then told us how a tenant who rents a property of his had paid him the monthly rent *a week early—in cash!* He was really tripping out because that normally didn't happen. There before us was $3000 in brand new hundred-dollar bills! It was such a beautiful moment, I couldn't stop crying.

"Every step of the way God had been making sure we had the money we needed, and here He was again right on time! I was worried about our friend giving us so much money, but he kept insisting, and even slipped us another thousand, knowing that we needed it for expenses. I was completely aware that our friend needed the money to pay the mortgage on his house. I felt so badly about him giving us so much money, but he said that he really felt the Lord prompting him.

"When we arrived home from China overjoyed with the successful adoption of our precious *China daughter*, our generous friend told us that he ended up getting two random checks in the mail *the very next day*, and that God had covered what he needed to pay his mortgage. Both checks were from work he had done a long time ago, that he wasn't expecting. One was for $3,200 and the other was for $800, the exact amount they had given us! We were so thankful because we knew he needed that money.

"God impressed upon us the idea of adopting this precious girl. He knew He'd placed a desire deep inside my heart to bring our daughter home from China, even though we didn't have the financial resources. We believe that God waited until the very last minute so we would have the opportunity to trust Him, especially in the face of the impossible, and so we could see that He was going to make this adoption happen—we didn't have to strive.

"I admit it was extremely agonizing to get that close to the brink of the time of need, and see nothing possible. But, true to His character, God did not fail us! I consider the events of knowing how close we came to not going to our friend's house, believing that it didn't make sense to go to China without the money we needed. But based on the encouragement of the *smaller* miracles we'd seen God do in the overall process, we stepped out with radical-believing faith that somehow God would come through. I know He honored our faith (even though it was with some fear and trembling), and we not only have our daughter but increased faith we would not have had if we acted based on the realties."

The Phillip's story has so many nuances where God worked in many people's lives throughout the adoption process. Their *China daughter's* eyesight has been failing. But with their daughter believing and proclaiming she will be healed, and the rest of us joining them in expectant prayer, I look forward to writing another testimony of the Phillips family in the future.

A Modern Day Occupation Miracle

I have met so many amazing people who are my brothers or sisters in Christ. Kristine Noelle is no exception. She is a highly-educated woman who has lived an amazing life of stepping out in faith, wanting ever and only to do what she hears the Father instruct. But that doesn't mean when she steps out in faith that it's not without degrees of anxiety. Here's one of her amazing stories of God's clearly leading and providing the fulfillment of His direction:

"I worked at Saddleback Church for five years and had a good salary, office, and benefits and thoroughly enjoyed my work. Then after several encounters with the Lord over a three-month period, I sensed He wanted me to put my job on the altar to follow Him on a journey deeper into His heart and to pursue my calling as an *intercessory missionary* on a full-time basis. This required a giant leap of faith. I'd been raised to be independent and self-sufficient and *living on faith* financially was terrifying—I had no grid for it. Yet I knew it was God and I needed to trust Him. So, in early 2010, I launched forty days of night and day prayer at Saddleback and resigned my position as a member of the church staff.

"Right after that I went to Kansas City, Missouri, for six months of training in the convergence of the global prayer and missions' movement, healing prayer, prophetic ministry, and Bible study. It amazed me how God provided for my housing and personal needs the entire six months. I never collected unemployment insurance or did any fund-raisers. My own savings and the non-tax deductible donations from generous donors met my needs.

"At the end of that time, I found myself at another precipice with God. I had prayed and asked Him where He wanted me to launch my new house of prayer ministry when I returned to Orange County, California. I sensed Him say Ladera Ranch, a small city I knew very little about. Soon after that I learned that an intercessor friend had prayer-walked the city to prepare for a church plant launch that ended up planting elsewhere. She knew of a perfect *watchman on the wall* place on a hill in Ladera Ranch to launch the ministry.

"It was an apartment complex in a wealthy area. When we stepped out of the car and I saw the view of the city, I felt the presence of the Lord and teared-up. He was already stirring my heart for Ladera Ranch. Yet I didn't have faith that the Lord would provide rent money for a two-bedroom apartment in this upscale area. I told my friend I couldn't afford it and we needed to move on. She obliged and we tried another place, but there was no life on it in the Spirit. After driving around, I finally agreed to go back to the first place once more to see what would happen. When we got out of the car, I felt the presence of God with us again. Still, my unbelief persisted about the cost of rent and I expressed this to my friend. She gently rebuked me and said I couldn't afford even a much less expensive place in my own strength, reminding me that I was living by faith. She said I was focused on the wrong thing. The question I needed to ask was, *what is God's will?*

"So we called it a day, and I wrestled with God about it. Another friend suggested putting out a fleece to God to discern if this was indeed where He wanted me to live and launch the house of prayer. I figured I had nothing to lose, so I wrote in my journal and asked God for $10,000 by a certain date to confirm if I should plant the house of prayer there. I asked specifically for two checks for $5,000 and wrote this detail in my journal, too. After that, I was reading the Bible and sensed that God was going to give me an answer in three days, which was ahead of my requested deadline.

"Unexpectedly, a couple who'd heard me share the vision for the house of prayer decided to give me a gift three days after I wrote out the *fleece* to God in my journal. They told me they wanted to bless me with $5,000 right away and another $5,000 after it launched! I burst into tears and later showed them what I'd written in my journal. It was faith-building for all of us to know God was speaking and we were listening. And it was heart-healing for me to realize my Abba Father would provide, and I didn't have to be afraid. I just needed to obey."

I've said before, God can speak anything into existence He desires. But most often, He prefers to work through His people. You may be in need of a miracle-blessing. You might be put in a position to be a miracle-blessing for someone else. Either way you are in His care.

Modern Day Relationship Miracle

Anita Agers-Brooks is a gentle power-house for God who generously encourages others in all she does. Because of her life experiences, she is wonderfully qualified to help others in many areas. One very personal area is that of her marriage. She has graciously agreed for her story to be shared here. In her own words:

"It was my greatest fear. More than death, disease, or some other disaster, I worried about adultery.

"Affairs come in many forms, long-term sexual encounters, short trysts, overnight dalliances, emotional connections, phone sex, pornographic fantasies, online meet-ups, sexting—but it's all adultery. Cheating takes what we believed about our most intimate relationship and rips it to shards. The night I found out my husband had betrayed me, a part of me wanted to die.

"There's nothing worse than answering a late night telephone call to hear a strange man say, *Ma'am, I'm sorry to tell you this, but your husband is having an affair with my wife.*

"I felt as if my husband had torn my heart from my chest, thrown it onto the ground, and jumped up and down on top of it, shattering it into millions of pieces. And in those moments of fresh, raw rage, I wanted a divorce—except somewhere deep inside of me, I really didn't. What I really wanted was to wake up from the nightmare, so my pain would go away.

"Those first weeks were the worst. I wrestled with conflicting thoughts. I believed the Bible gave me permission to divorce my husband because of adultery. But I also knew, just because I could didn't mean I should. And it was clear, in my case, God wasn't releasing me. At least not yet.

"Repeatedly, 1 Corinthians 7:13-16 popped up into my life. On the radio, in books, at church, even during conversations with friends. In my grief, particularly when circling back through the stage of anger, I didn't want to hear what God was saying to me about my marriage—but He forced me to listen anyway.

> And if a believing woman has a husband who is not a believer and he is willing to continue living with her, she must not leave him. For the believing wife brings holiness to her marriage, and the believing husband brings holiness to his marriage. Otherwise, your children would not be holy, but now they are holy. (But if the husband or wife who isn't a believer insists on leaving, let them go. In such cases the believing husband or wife is no longer bound to the other, for God has called you to live in peace.) Don't you wives realize that your husbands might be saved because of you? And don't you husbands realize that your wives might be saved because of you? 1 Corinthians 7:13-16 (NLT)

"I must admit, in my emotional state at that time, I was more concerned for my hurt feelings than my husband's soul. I wanted God's revenge more than Jesus' mercy for my husband and his mistress's actions.

"One night, alone in my home, I lay on my floor and wrestled with God, crying out in the silence. 'I know you say I need to forgive in order to be forgiven, but I have to be honest. I don't want to. You'll have to do it in my place until you can change my desires. Please rip the roots of bitterness out of my heart, and plant flowers of forgiveness in their place.'

"There were moments when I almost gave up, even to the point of packing my suitcases. I lived out of them from the closet where they rested, waiting for God to release me from my painful relationship. But instead, God gave me a mission out of the misery.

"Today, because of God's merciful persistence, I know what it's like to live-out love from a place of sheer resolve. Love is not a warm fuzzy noun in wait—it is an active verb requiring forward action. To do what you should, versus what you could. To say, *I love you*, as a decision more than a feeling.

"At my lowest points, I had to refuse to listen to the lies of Satan or my emotions. I had to hang on through many long and excruciating months, when glimmers of hope were hard to come by. I had to believe God when He said His promises were reliable. But the victory is worth it all.

"My husband and I will soon celebrate our thirty-second anniversary. By faith, believing God when appearances said it was futile, we now know happiness. I often tell my husband, *I don't just love you—I adore you*. And I mean it.

"In my experience, faith in Christ kills our greatest fears and awakens true love."

And I'll add that faith in Christ produces miraculous hope and breakthroughs. Anita Agers-Brooks is a fellow author, International Speaker, and Co-Host of Engaging Life and Leadership, an on-demand radio podcast. You can learn more about her and her work at www.anitabrooks.com.

Modern Day Resurrection Miracle

A very close friend and respected colleague of my pastor is Pastor Andrew Womack, an American Conservative Evangelical Christian faith teacher and healer, and founder of Andrew Womack Ministries (1978), and

Charis Bible College (1994) out of Colorado Springs, CO. He has presented at our church on several occasions. What follows is a miraculous story demonstrating what faith in God's promises can produce used with permission. As Andrew shared:

"Some of you have heard me mention before, that on March the 4th, 2001, my youngest son, Peter, died. And he was dead for five hours.

"I got a call after about four hours of him being dead. My oldest son, Joshua, told me that Peter was dead. I asked him what happened [I listened] and then I said, *Well, the first report's not the last report.* I said *"Don't let anybody touch or do anything until we get there.* And then my wife and I had to get up and get dressed [to drive to be with our sons].

"It took us an hour and fifteen minutes to drive into Colorado Springs and during this period of time, our cell phones didn't work. There was no way to get an update to find out what was going on. And during that drive in, just like anybody else, I began to start having feelings of sadness, grief, sorrow…thoughts of how could this happen…feelings of condemnation like *God, you know, I failed you somehow or another* and I had all of these negative things going on the inside of me. But you know what? I knew that some of these thoughts that I was having…and I was beginning to feel like *God, how could you have let this happen?* But see, I knew that God doesn't [cause] things like that. Nonetheless, even though I knew what the truth was, here's how my feelings were [heading].

"Some of you will be able to relate to what I'm talking about. You know the truth, but you just feel a certain way, and if you feel it, well then your feelings empower it and that becomes [your] reality whether it's truth or not. But, because of the way I thought—because of the way that the Word of God has influenced me, you know what, I was able just to start…I just started out of my innermost being praising God and saying, *God, you are not my problem. You did not kill my son. This is not your judgment upon him or upon me.*

And I just stated saying you're a faithful God. And I started praising Him. And you know what I started doing was going back to my relationship with God. And as I just started fellowshipping with God and saying, *God, I want you to know that regardless of whether my son comes back to life or not, that you're a good God and that I'm going to serve you.*

"And as I just started focusing on my relationship with God, the Lord started bringing Scriptures back to me. He brought prophesies back to me about my son that hadn't been fulfilled yet, and just a number of different things. And within a very short period of time, I mean I had such an assurance in my heart that my son would live and not die, that I was praising God. I was shouting. My wife wondered what had happened to me…if I had lost it. But I told her, I said, *this is going to be the greatest testimony you've ever seen.* And when we finally got into the Springs…it's a long story…but my son, Joshua, came out and he said *Dad…five or ten minutes after I called you, Peter just sat up. He was in a cooler…stripped naked with a toe-tag on him.*

"They don't do that to people who are alive. He had been dead for nearly five hours. And he just sat up and we went in and talked to him. He was totally coherent. God raised him from the dead! And praise God, today he's working for me…he's working here in the ministry. I've got a granddaughter who's three years old now. And you know what, praise God for what happened. It all came out of relationship. I was able to overcome the sorrow, the grief, the fear…all of these negative things that all of us fight against and you know how I did it? I went back to my relationship with God and I just started thanking Him and loving Him."[5]

Andrew Womack teaches about the importance of learning what God wants by hearing the Word of God, "So faith comes from hearing, and hearing through the word of Christ." (Romans 10:17)[6]

Our faith is acquired by hearing the Word of God. Then we need to establish vision for what God reveals. Andrew Womack was able to stand firm on God's promises because he *saw with his mind's-eye* the fulfillment of what God had promised concerning his son. He believed God, so as one who has a firm goal in mind, he envisioned the promise as fulfilled. 2 Corinthians 5:7 states, "For we walk by faith, not by sight."[7] With confidence in the character, will, and intentions of God, believing as though His promise already exists, we are to expect God to fulfill His promises. God declares in Isaiah 55:11 "...so shall My word be that goes forth from my mouth; it shall not return to me empty, but it shall accomplish that which I purpose, and shall succeed in the thing for which I sent it."[8]

God's Timing and Purpose

One of the arguments people use to discount miracles today is that they don't occur instantly. Given the above stories revealing the truly miraculous taking place over a period of time, and those found in Scripture, I don't accept that argument. Even some miracles recorded in the Bible were not instant. In Mark 8:22-25, Jesus worked to heal a man who was blind. Initially the man had only partial sight restored. But when Jesus touched him a second time, the blind man could see.

There are many reasons why the healing or redemption we pray for is delayed. One is that God has in mind a specific timing for the miracle to occur for the greatest impact possible. Remember that when God acts miraculously, He always acts for the benefit of many, not just one individual.

Another reason for delay could be the condition of the heart or will of those involved. If the heart has set up a desire that has not come from the Lord, to protect the individual God will often refuse to fulfill the prayer. However, if the person persists and the particular heart desire interferes with a work God wants to do, there are times He will give us over to the desires of our heart. The story of the Prodigal Son found in Luke 15:11-32 is a perfect example. In this story the son decides in his heart to rebel and go his own way. He secured his inheritance from his father in advance then lived wildly until he'd squandered all the money and found himself literally in a pig pen. Only then did he come to his senses and return to his father. Circumstances can be the same for us or people we know, that we must come to the end of ourselves before we turn our heart to God and begin to experience His loving work in our life. God will give people up to their own pride and lusts when they persist in exchanging the truth for a lie. Let us be diligent to always guard our hearts.

The chapters within this section are devoted to developing our faith. In the next chapter we will consider specific ways to guard our hearts.

CHAPTER SEVEN

Faith Jeopardized

Claim Your Authority

As stated in the Introduction, effective faith that renews our hope and ushers in personal breakthroughs is a matter of *becoming* rather than *doing*. There is nothing we can do to make God love us more. There is nothing we can do to make God want to give us more. He has already done everything necessary for us to have everything we need for a victorious life, even in this fallen world. Christ has completed the work.

Since Christ has done everything necessary for our victory, why aren't we seeing more effective faith demonstrated? I believe we have not seen because we have not become what we are fully able to be in Christ. Besides ignorance and misunderstanding, there is a spirit of intimidation that is excellent at evoking fear and doubt. Previously we've talked about how fear and doubt hinder us. Now let's talk about how to get the upper hand and claim our authority.

A Testimony of Exercising Authority

During the trial of part-time work and unemployment that my family suffered you can imagine, or perhaps you can relate from personal experience, my husband and I fought depression daily. We did not want the enemy to have any more victories in our life than he already had so for that reason we fought back. Fighting was hard. Depression was very hard. I didn't win the battle every day. Some days I was stronger than others and then I experienced victory. One day my husband came to me, fighting tears. Bringing my husband to that point of emotion takes a lot. He was feeling utterly defeated and responsible for letting down his family. We'd already spent all available cash, sold everything we could, and had lost our home to foreclosure. At this point, we were renting a bank-owned property. With his head down, David spoke, "Pam, I am so sorry. I know that rent is due and nearly past due, but I have no idea where we're going to get the money." In response I said, "I don't know either, but God does and He'll provide." No sooner did those words leave my mouth than did fear try to set in. I hoped I was right, and I decided to square off the fear with the literal promises of God's Word. At this point I knew many Scriptures where God promises to take care of those who belong to Him, so I proclaimed them, aloud and repeatedly.

Later that day, David came to me again with an expression I couldn't fathom. In his hand was the daily mail we'd just received. He handed me an envelope he'd opened. Without any exchange of words, I read the letter only to learn that the man who had purchased my property management company several years prior, had divorced his wife. Somehow through their property settlement, she owed me $2000! Our rent was only $1000. Looking at one another, we both broke down in tears.

I wasn't one-hundred-percent confident when I made the proclamation that God would provide. But with *mustard seed* faith I determined to act in hopes God would come through, based on Psalm 37:25, which reads: "I have been young and now am old, yet have I not seen the [uncompromisingly] righteous forsaken or their seed begging bread." (AMP) By faith I spoke in all the authority in Christ I could muster, and believed. God would not fail us. I pushed past fear and walked into victory.

God Rewards Preference not Performance

One of my favorite verses (if you haven't noticed) is Hebrews 11:6: "And without faith it is impossible to please him, for whoever would draw near to God must believe that he exists and that he rewards those who seek him."[1]

Faith is a gift from God. Faith is not something for which we can take any credit,[2] but, once we have faith, we must work with the Holy Spirit to keep our faith pure and increasing, in order to be strengthened and prepared for the battles ahead. Fear and doubt distort our faith rendering us ineffective.

James 1:5-8 helps us further, "If any of you lacks wisdom, let him ask of God, who gives to all liberally and without reproach, and it will be given to him. But let him ask in faith with no doubting, for he who doubts is like a wave of the sea driven and tossed by the wind. For let not that man suppose that he will receive anything from the Lord; *he is* a double-minded man, unstable in all his ways."[3] Doubt, unbelief, and fear are enemies of faith and authority.

God wants us to enjoy all the benefits of all His promises. Psalm 84:11 reads, "For the LORD God is a sun and shield; the LORD bestows favor and honor. No good thing does he withhold from those who walk uprightly.[4] Grace is something that has been taught through the years of church history in many different ways. Dr. Tom Barkey, Pastor of Church of Grace, has devoted his life to understanding what grace means as God intends. With over thirty years in ministry and study, he has deduced that "Grace is God's favor and ability to do His will, His way."

From a purely physical-world perspective, we tend to think that performance is the measure for reward. In the workplace, where we exchange our time and abilities for the currency of the world-system, that is generally true. But that's not how the economy of God's spiritual world works.

Faith, believing, trusting, pursuing, and expecting God to act is the currency of God's kingdom. *Expectant faith* was easier for me to possess once I learned that God rewards us for our preferences for Him, not our performance. Certainly by my deeds, I do not deserve any reward! But gratefully, God rewards us according to our faith and pursuit of Him.

God will not be harsh with us when we are attempting to *walk by faith* any more than a parent would be harsh with their toddler who falls taking his or her first steps. God knows what we know, what we don't know, and what we should know, based on what He's revealed. He will hold us accountable accordingly. Whenever you find yourself in a position to wield authority by faith, simply make sure you step out in the fullness of the faith you genuinely have, and God will honor and encourage you as you learn to walk by faith.

Put on the Full Armor of God

There are no kinks in God's armor! His armor is impenetrable and allows us to replace fear with courage. The Apostle Paul writes in Ephesians 6:10-18:

> Finally, be strong in the Lord and in the strength of his might. Put on the whole armor of God, that you may be able to stand against the schemes of the devil. For we do not wrestle against flesh and blood, but against the rulers, against the authorities, against the cosmic powers over this present darkness, against the spiritual forces of evil in the heavenly places. Therefore take up the whole armor of God, that you may be able to withstand in the evil day, and having done all, to stand firm. Stand therefore, having

fastened on the belt of truth, and having put on the breastplate of righteousness, and, as shoes for your feet, having put on the readiness given by the gospel of peace. In all circumstances take up the shield of faith, with which you can extinguish all the flaming darts of the evil one; and take the helmet of salvation, and the sword of the Spirit, which is the word of God, praying at all times in the Spirit, with all prayer and supplication. To that end keep alert with all perseverance, making supplication for all the saints…[5]

I have on more than one occasion imagined myself actually putting on this suit of armor and taking up my weapons then taking my position on the battle field. Feet firmly planted unable to be moved, because greater is He who is in me than he who is in the world. (1 John 4:4)

Operating in our new identity and authority in Christ is an area of weakness for many Believers. To overcome this weakness, to face off the spirit of intimidation, requires that we act contrary to what we see. This is walking by faith. Until we overcome our weakness in this area, the enemy will continue to defeat us.

In the words of Dr. Charles H. Kraft, the president of Deep Healing Ministries and a seminary professor for over forty years, "You're already on Satan's hit list by virtue of being a Christian. And if you're not fighting, you're losing every time."[6]

Whether we like the reality or not, we are in a battle against a real enemy. We have responsibility for the appropriation of the victory Christ died to provide us. The victory's not automatic. This is why faith must be guarded and consciously developed.

Pamela Christian

The Exchange of Authority

From the very beginning God intended that His created humanity would co-rule and reign over the earth with Him. Genesis 1:27-28 reads, "So God created man in his own image, in the image of God he created him; male and female he created them. And God blessed them. And God said to them, "Be fruitful and multiply and fill the earth and subdue it, and have dominion over the fish of the sea and over the birds of the heavens and over every living thing that moves on the earth.""[7] The authority that God gave to humanity is a primary, if not *the* primary reality that Satan does not want us to understand. If we were to completely grasp and operate in our full God-given authority, Satan would be subject to us. I found especially interesting to note that with a proper rendering of Psalm 8:6, reading from the original Hebrew translation—not the *Septuagint* version, (a Greek translation of the Hebrew Scriptures)—we see clearly that humanity was created just a little lower than God. The passage should read: "You made them [humans] inferior only to Yourself [literally 'a little lower than God']; You crowned them with glory and honor. You appointed them rulers over everything You made; You placed them over all creation." [8]

Clearly, just by our existence we are a target of Satan. So he devised a way to displace us, which we know was accomplished by deceiving Adam and Eve. Genesis Chapter Two reveals that by leading Adam and Eve to doubt the truth of what God said, Satan suggested that they had the ability to know as God knows, enticing them to believe that they could be *equal with God*. They succumbed to the temptation and Satan led them to disobey God. Adam and Eve's rejection of God's authority and His Word was acceptance of Satan. From that moment *until* the resurrection of Jesus, Satan had the upper hand over humans in ruling over this world; however, his rule was still completely under the authority of sovereign God.

Authority Restored But Misunderstood

With the life, death, and resurrection of Jesus, as He declared, "It is finished."[9] (John 19:30) The payment for sin is finished because Jesus satisfied the entire debt of sin for all humanity, for all of time. Satan no longer has the upper-hand in authority over God's creation. What the first Adam gave up in the Garden of Eden, the second Adam, Jesus, redeemed on the cross at Calvary, giving Believers legal authority over earth and all that is within, both physical and spiritual.

Unfortunately, far too many Believers don't understand this and still consider Satan as the "god of this world." In reality, all authority has been restored to those who belong to God the Father through faith in Jesus Christ. This puts us, as Believers in Christ with Christ's authority, in Satan's perpetual cross-hairs.

In his informative article *The Authority of the Believer*, Dr. John E. Russell writes:

> God commanded the believer to do certain things. Along with God's commands, he delegated authority to the believer to accomplish those commands. With this authority comes responsibility. And with responsibility comes accountability. The believer will be held accountable for obeying God's commands on that day when he stands before the Lord Jesus.
>
> In traditional Christianity, some of God's commands have been taught to the exclusion of others. Furthermore, the authority of the believer has not been taught properly.

I agree with Dr. Russell that Believers have not been properly taught about the authority we have in Christ, rendering us impotent and unnecessarily wounded by the enemy. By simply *thinking* that Satan is the god of this world, we relinquish power and authority that we could otherwise wield. If we properly understood that Satan *was* the god of this world and that now because of Jesus, all who belong to Him have full and complete authority, God's will most definitely would be done on earth the same as He rules in heaven. Satan knows this so he works overtime to keep people, especially people who have placed their faith in Christ, deceived.

With the majority of people thinking of Satan as the god of this world, he is *given* power:

> The phrase "god of this world" (or "god of this age") indicates that Satan is the major influence on the ideals, opinions, goals, hopes and views of the majority of people. His influence also encompasses the world's philosophies, education, and commerce. The thoughts, ideas, speculations and false religions of the world are under his control and have sprung from his lies and deceptions. So, when the Bible says that Satan is the "god of this world," it is not saying that he has ultimate authority. It is conveying the idea that Satan rules over the unbelieving world in a specific way. In 2 Corinthians 4:4, the unbeliever follows Satan's agenda: "The god of this world has blinded the minds of unbelievers, so that they cannot see the light of the gospel of the glory of Christ." Satan's scheme includes promoting false philosophies in the world—philosophies that blind the unbeliever to the truth of the Gospel. Satan's philosophies are the fortresses in which people are imprisoned, and they must be set free by Christ.[10]

More than blinding the eyes of the unbelieving world, Satan has successfully *blinded the minds* of Believers. And this is a large reason why we don't see Christians demonstrating effective faith and enjoying the victorious, abundant life that is available through faith in Christ. In reality, Satan only has as much power as human beings give him. Think about that. Gratefully, even in our ignorant ineptitude, God works in our behalf.

Satan's Powers are Limited by God

Why God allows evil to continue at all is a major stumbling block for many people. The question asked is, *If God is a loving and all-powerful God, why does He allow evil to continue to exist?* With all my study of explanations by well-respected scholars, I've concluded the above question a highly legitimate one that we, in our finite abilities, can only answer in part.

As already considered, evil was first revealed by Satan and his follower's with the exercise of their God-given free-will. When Satan and his followers rebelled, they were cast outside of heaven with no hope for redemption.

Later, God created mankind in His image, also bestowing upon humanity the privilege of free-will. Influenced more by Satan than by God, the first-created man and woman also chose to rebel against God.

Considering that God created both the angels and humanity holy and perfect, but with the ability for free-will, God knew the potential for evil depended upon individual choice. God was not surprised when some angels and the first man and woman rebelled against Him.

At this point, some question why God created angels and humanity with free-will. Because, quite simply, only if His creatures had free-will would they be genuinely devoted to Him. Without free-will, God's creatures would simply be *programmed*, which does not equate to authentic devotion. Additionally, people question God's wisdom for allowing Satan to roam the earth only to influence the first man and first woman. As I understand, because of free-will, the existence of the two trees in the Garden of Eden, and God's specific instructions, Adam and Eve were faced with a choice with or without the influence of Satan. They had free-will. Satan rebelled without the influence of another being. Adam and Eve didn't *need* the influence of Satan to rebel. But, because Satan enticed them, he is subject to eternal judgment and justice at the hand of God.

Adam and Eve were told they could freely take of the *Tree of Life* and were sternly warned what would happen if they instead chose to take of the *Tree of Knowledge of Good and Evil*. With their own free-will choice to rebel against God, their eyes were instantly opened to the reality of the existence of good and evil. Authority was lost by their choice and all of Creation was corrupted as a result.

To prevent Adam and Eve from also taking of the Tree of Life, which would forever seal them in a state of rebellion against God, He removed them from the Garden and offered the Promise of Redemption to those who willfully choose God. The same offer for redemption is available to every human being born ever since.

Denial Empowers Satan

Just as dangerous as overemphasizing Satan's power is ignoring or denying his existence. Dr Charles H. Kraft, author of *I Give You Authority Practicing the Authority Jesus Gave Us* wrote:

> This is a fallacy that millions of Western Christians have fallen into. We have allowed the enemy to do his work unchecked by ignoring him. Many sincere Christians even deny his existence, preferring to see the evil of the world totally as a result of humans and/or human structures. They think Jesus was simply accommodating Himself to

> the ideas of His day and to His culture by referring to psychological problems and other unexplained phenomena as demons and by personifying evil and naming it Satan.
>
> Misunderstanding the position of the devil relative to that of the children of God is a misunderstanding of who we are and the authority we are given in our position. Unlike Satan, we bear the image of God and have been both redeemed by God and made co-inheritors with Jesus of the riches of our Father God (Romans 8:17; Galatians 4:7). We carry, by virtue of our position and the fact that God the Holy Spirit lives within us, infinitely more power and authority than the whole satanic kingdom. This we must understand as we probe the various dimensions of [our] spiritual authority.[11]

Disbelief in Satan and his powers is a growing position for many people in our post-modern culture. Rather than believing in him as a literal being, they conclude he is merely a concept. Generally speaking, those who hold to this position also conclude that the Bible need not be taken literally.

By what I've written so far, you should see that I firmly believe the Bible's content is to be taken literally. With all that is written in Scripture about God, angels, Satan, humanity, and the entrance of evil into Creation, along with a cursory look at human history, the Bible is the single document of religious authority that provides the best plausible answers for all that exists. Denying the literal existence of Satan is a first step to denying many other truths contained in the Bible. This progression of denial is, in my considered estimation, another tactic of the enemy to empower himself at our expense.

If you are not convinced of the truth of the Christian faith—if you have doubts, you will not experience the confident, victorious authority Christ desires you to possess.

Confusion About the Supernatural

First, let's understand that Scriptures are clear, that confusion is of the enemy. What better way for the enemy to disarm God's people than to cause division among us about the accessibility of supernatural powers today. By confusing Believers over the existence of the supernatural, he can limit us to the natural. By causing people to believe he doesn't exist, that God doesn't exist, that we have no interaction with the spiritual world, or to bring people into a gross interaction with the dark spiritual world, he can take us way off the mark and render us ineffective.

By convincing Believers that the powers demonstrated by Jesus and His disciples were limited to the days of Jesus' earthly life and that of His Apostles, Satan could (and sadly does) prevent Believers from wielding their God-given authority and power over all that opposes the truth of God. With this, Satan creates confusion and division among us, rending us woefully ineffective.

The Christian and Missionary Alliance, published an article entitled *Spiritual Gifts*, and offers the following in answer to the question, *Have Some Spiritual Gifts Ceased to Exist?*

> No. Because spiritual gifts were given to build up the church, the body of Christ, as long as the church is under construction, spiritual gifts are needed. A day will come when spiritual gifts will no longer be needed (1 Corinthians 13:8). However we do not believe that this day has yet come. It will come when perfection comes (1 Corinthians 13:10). Some [Cessationists] interpret this "perfection" to

be the completion of the canon of Scriptures (the Apostolic Age). However, this is not a good rendering of the Greek text. We believe that this refers to the Second Coming of the Lord Jesus Christ. When the Church, the Bride of Christ is complete and perfect, that is when spiritual gifts will no longer be necessary.[12]

Spiritual gifts are not only discussed in great detail in the New Testament, they are recorded as events that occurred in the lives of many different people through many different methods of application. The Apostle Paul had much to say about spiritual gifts, which we can read in 1 Corinthians, Chapters 12, 13, and 14. If you are not familiar with the spiritual gifts, be sure to read these chapters. I especially appreciate the treatment that Matt Slick with Christian Apologetics and Research Ministry (CARM), gives to this topic.

> There are groups that say that if you do speak in tongues, then you are under demonic control and are not saved. On the other hand, some say that if you do not speak in tongues then you are not saved. What's more, both extremes use Scripture to support their positions.
>
> Fortunately for the Christian church, whether or not the spiritual gifts are for today is not a salvation issue. Therefore, we need to be gracious. Romans 14:5 says, "One man regards one day above another, another regards every day alike. Let each man be fully convinced in his own mind," [NASB]. As you can see, the Bible leaves room for debate and differences of opinion on non-essential doctrines. The issue of whether or not the charismatic gifts are still around is a debatable issue and charity needs to be

granted from both sides of the argument. This is not an issue to divide over as many, unfortunately, have chosen to do.

It is my opinion that the charismatic spiritual gifts are still in effect. I do not believe they ceased with the apostles or with the completion of the Bible. If you disagree, that is fine. But let me give you my reasons here. For simplicity's sake, I will state a standard objection to the continuance of the spiritual gifts and then I will give what I believe is a basic but sufficient refutation for that argument.

Argument 1: *Since we have the Bible we do not need spiritual gifts.*

1 Cor. 13:8-13 is usually quoted as scriptural support for the position: "Love never fails; but if there are gifts of prophecy, they will be done away; if there are tongues, they will cease; if there is knowledge, it will be done away. [9]For we know in part, and we prophesy in part; [10]but when the perfect comes, the partial will be done away. [11]When I was a child, I used to speak as a child, think as a child, reason as a child; when I became a man, I did away with childish things. [12]For now we see in a mirror dimly, but then face to face; now I know in part, but then I shall know fully just as I also have been fully known. [13]But now abide faith, hope, love, these three; but the greatest of these is love."

Some vigorously maintain that the "perfect" is the completed Bible and, therefore, the extraordinary gifts are no longer needed. But I do not think these verses can be used to support cessationism. This is why: verse 12 says, "...then we shall see face to face." The word "then" refers back to the phrase "when the perfect comes." Since the only infallible interpreter of Scripture is Scripture, a quick examination of the way God uses the term "face to face" should help us understand this passage better.

The phrase is used throughout the Bible and always means an encounter with a person. When God uses it in reference to Himself, it means a visual, personal encounter with Him (Gen. 32:30; Ex. 33:11; Num. 12:8; Deut. 5:4; and Jer. 32:4). Likewise in the New Testament it is also used in speaking of personal encounter (2 Cor. 10:1; 2 John 1:12; 3 John 1:14, etc.). "When the perfect comes... then we shall see face to face" seems, most logically, to refer a personal encounter; at least, that seems to be how God uses the phrase.

If the position is taken that the "perfect" is the completed Bible, how then do we encounter God in the manner as the phrase suggests: an encounter with a person? Seeing Christ face to face occurs when He returns. Another "then" is mentioned in verse 12: "then I shall know fully, even as I am fully known." The word "then" again refers back to the phrase "when the perfect comes." Again, we need to look at how the Bible uses words. This time we'll look at the word "know." Scripture says that eternal life is to know God (John 17:3). Only the believer is known by Jesus (John 10:27; Gal. 4:8-9; Rom. 8:29). The unbeliever is not known by Jesus (Matt. 7:21-23). In every verse except for one, God says He only knows believers. This is a *salvific* knowing; that is, it is a kind of knowing that God does of the Christians. He knows them and they are saved. The unbelievers are not known and are, therefore, not saved.

It would seem most consistent with Scripture to say that "...as I am fully known" would refer to a salvation relationship between Jesus and the Christian. At the return of Christ we (the ones known) shall know fully; we shall see face to face the One who is our Savior.

Also, we don't "know" Jesus through the Scripture; we know about Him from the Scripture (John 5:39). Instead, we know Him by personal encounter (John 1:12; 1 Cor. 1:9) through the Holy Spirit's indwelling. We don't know in a full sense right now, even though we have the Bible, because we [our soul and flesh] are still corrupted by our sin nature. In our fallen state we can only see Christ through sin-clouded eyes. We see a reflection of Christ in the Word. When Jesus returns the reflection of the truth will pass to clear understanding (the way childish thoughts give way to mature ones) when we receive our resurrected bodies, no longer have to battle sinful flesh, and can see Him face to face because "we shall be like Him" (1 John 3:2) and then, "...we shall know fully." The context of 1 Cor. 13:8-13 seems, in my opinion, to show that the spiritual gifts will cease when Jesus returns.

Interestingly, 1 Cor. 1:7 may be consulted here as well. It says, "so that you are not lacking in any gift, awaiting eagerly the revelation of our Lord Jesus Christ." The Greek word here for "revealed" is *apokalupsis*. It means the apocalypse, the return of Jesus. In both this verse and 1 Cor. 13:8-13 the gifts, which aren't differentiated as to kind, are connected to the return of Christ, not the completion of the Bible. One more thing, the word gift in the Greek is *charisma*. This is where we get the word 'charismatic.'

Argument 2: *Present day tongues are further revelation and must then be equal to Scripture and should be included in the Bible. But since the Bible is not to have anything added to it, the gift of tongues (and therefore, the rest of the spiritual gifts) must no longer be valid.*

This is a faulty argument because the Scripture itself recognizes inspired revelation that is not to be added to the Bible: "What then shall we say, brothers? When you come together, everyone has a hymn, or a word of instruction, a revelation, a tongue or an interpretation. All of these must be done for the strengthening of the church." (1 Cor. 14:26) Here, in the Corinthian church, revelations were given that were not made part of the Bible. This shows that there were, for a lack of a better word, "different" kinds of revelation: one from the prophets and apostles meant for canonization and another through the Spirit to be used in the church for edification—not canonization. So, in my opinion, for someone to maintain that revelation today is a threat to the Canon does not consider 1 Cor. 14:26, and is not applying Scripture properly.

Argument 3: *There is such misuse of the gifts that they couldn't possibly be real.*

First of all, misuse of the gifts implies their existence. They couldn't be misused if they did not exist. The only real position to be taken here would be that the use of the

> gifts really is no use, but is only fakery and self-deception.
>
> I do not deny that the gifts are misused. I have heard manifestations of tongues, interpretations of tongues, and prophecy that, in my opinion, were not genuine. But I do not discredit the gifts based upon those experiences anymore than I would say that the gift of preaching is gone because I have seen it misused. Experience does not make doctrine, the Bible does.
>
> Second, it is not a sick child that needs discipline and correction, it is the active, energetic, exploring child that needs to be guided. This was so with the Corinthian church. They were using the gifts greatly but improperly and needed to be corrected on their proper use.
>
> 1 Cor. 13 is the main place where the Cessationists go for their position. However, upon looking at the context, I believe 1 Cor. 13 teaches that the gifts will cease when Jesus returns.[13]

I completely agree with the position of CARM and maintain that unless we properly understand, believe, and operate in the authority and power available to us through faith in Christ, we will not be able to take hold of the hope or experience the personal breakthroughs that are our rightful inheritance. My prayer also is that we will mature as the Body of Christ, in unity consistent with Ephesians Chapter 4, to better fulfill the Great Commission we've been given by Christ, according to Matthew 28:18-20.

We should expect God to bring us to all truth according to John 16:13-16:

> When the Spirit of truth comes, he will guide you into all the truth, for he will not speak on his own authority, but

whatever he hears he will speak, and he will declare to you the things that are to come. He will glorify me, for he will take what is mine and declare it to you. All that the Father has is mine; therefore I said that he will take what is mine and declare it to you.[14]

And the Apostle Paul, addressing the Believers in Corinth concerning spiritual gifts said:

Now concerning spiritual gifts, brothers, I do not want you to be uninformed. You know that when you were pagans you were led astray to mute idols, however you were led. Therefore I want you to understand that no one speaking in the Spirit of God ever says "Jesus is accursed!" and no one can say "Jesus is Lord" except in the Holy Spirit. Now there are varieties of gifts, but the same Spirit; and there are varieties of service, but the same Lord; and there are varieties of activities, but it is the same God who empowers them all in everyone. To each is given the manifestation of the Spirit for the common good.[15]

Embracing Signs and Wonders

In a widely-circulated presentation given by Tom Pennington, Pastor-Teacher of Countryside Bible Church in Southlake, Texas, author, and modern day leader for the doctrine of Cessationism, Tom clarifies the position of Cessationists. Cessationism is the belief that the miraculous gifts have ceased, including tongues, prophecy, and healing. Pennington stated: "The New Testament nowhere directly states that the miraculous gifts will cease during the church age." He then states that this is irrelevant "because the New Testament doesn't directly say they'll continue either."[16]

Not a strong argument to start off with, but let's consider three more of the seven arguments he made in support of Cessationism.

1: The Unique Role of Miracles

There were only three primary periods that God worked miracles through gifted men, when God gave human beings miracle working power. The first was that of Moses and Joshua, from the Exodus through the career of Joshua (1445-1380 BC), about 65 years. The second window was during the ministries of Elijah and Elisha (ca. 860-795 BC), again only about 65 years. The third time was with Christ and His Apostles. It began with His ministry, and lasted through the death of the Apostle John, also about 70 years.

2: The End of the Gift of Apostleship

In two places in the New Testament, Paul refers to the apostles as one of the gifts that Christ gave His church. The first is in 1 Corinthians 12:28. He's illustrating the diversity that the [S]pirit has created within the body. Here he includes apostles. Although not all spiritual gifts are offices, all New Testament offices are gifts to Christ's church. He makes this plain in Ephesians 4:7-8. One of the gifts Christ gave His church was the Apostles. But they were a temporary gift. [T]o be a true apostle you had to meet three qualifications: (1) You had to be a witness of the resurrected Christ, Acts 1:22; (2) You had to be personally appointed by Christ, Act 1:2, 24; (3) You had to be able to work miracles, Matthew 10:1-2 and 2 Cor 12:12.

3: The Foundational Nature of the New Testament Apostles and Prophets

The New Testament identifies the Apostles and prophets as the foundation upon which the church was built. Turn to Ephesians 2. Here, Paul lays a foundational understanding of the church—this one new man that has been created in which Jews and Gentiles have been brought together, peace has made individually with God, and between all the differences that distinguished us before but are now brought together in Christ.

If the Spirit were still gifting believers with the miraculous gifts, they would be the same gifts that we find in the New Testament. However, the Charismatic gifts claimed today bear almost no resemblance to their New Testament counterparts.[17]

In response to these claims let's consider the Continuationist's point of view. The basic belief of Continuationists is that none of the supernatural gifts or prospect of miracles have ceased.

1: The Unique Role of Miracles

Continuationists do not agree that there were only three primary periods when God worked miracles through gifted men. We can clearly read recorded miracles in the books of Genesis, Judges, Daniel, Isaiah, Daniel, and Jonah. Additionally, the entirety of Scriptures by definition is filled with the gift of prophecy. There are documented testimonies of many, many people who have been supernaturally healed outside of Scripture.

2: The End of the Gift of Apostleship

First point of clarity is that of Apostles. According to the original Greek language, an apostle is one sent on a mission with delegated authority and a disciple is a student. The original twelve selected by Jesus were the first Apostles. But with Judas Iscariot's suicide before Christ's ascension, there remained only eleven of the original twelve Apostles. The eleven deciding the need for a twelfth, cast lots and appointed Matthias, also referred to as an apostle, (Luke 1:26).

The Apostle Paul, formerly Saul of Tarsus, was radically and supernaturally transformed and declared an apostle by the risen Lord, as we read about in Acts 26:14-18. Further, Barnabas, one who ministered with Paul was also called an apostle, (Acts 13:2 and 14:14). A case could be made for Apollos, Silas, and possibly Timothy also having been called Apostles.

Additionally in Luke 10:1 and 17, there is reference to Jesus sending out seventy or seventy-two others (scholars remain unclear which number is correct) who are referred to as Apostles by Eastern Christians and as disciples by Western Christians. Some have worked to identify the seventy/seventy-two, arriving at a plausible list drawn from extra biblical evidence.[18]

Claiming that the gifts ceased with the conclusion of the *Apostolic Age*, for Cessationists means with the death of the Apostle John, approximately 95-96 AD. But this is problematic for the reality of the Apostles Matthias and Paul at the very least.

Based in part on the above, and the extensive teachings of the Apostle Paul *to common Believers* concerning the proper use of the supernatural gifts, Continuationists believe that the Holy Spirit may bestow the sign gifts to persons other than the original Apostles, at any time in the Church age.

3: The Foundational Nature of the New Testament Apostles and Prophets

Eph 2:20 does not say that the gifts of apostleship and prophecy were "completed" after the church was founded, just as the ministry of Jesus isn't "completed" [until the end of the Church Age]. Pennington has already decided that apostle[ship] is something that only existed in the past, and thus he is unable to see that Paul talked in a contemporary sense about the church's foundation, a foundation that was expanding and thus needed more and more apostles, why the early church appointed quite a lot of them apart from the original twelve.[19]

4: The Nature of the Miraculous Gifts

Regarding the gift of tongues: there are many documented events that occurred at various revivals such as the Azusa Street Revival, 1906 through roughly 1915. During this time "many people spoke in existing languages. Interpreters, immigrants and missionaries went there and identified countless languages: French, Greek, Hindi, Zulu. More examples of [such modern era occurrences] can be found in *Spoken by* *the Spirit* by Ralph W. Harris."[20] Additionally, Paul is very clear in 1 Corinthians 12-14 that languages that are not of this earth, therefore not understandable by men, but only angels and God. Many modern day Christians will attest that speaking in tongues and interpretations are regular occurrences for those who believe.

Regarding the gift of prophesy: Pennington states: Nowhere does the New Testament distinguish Old Testament prophecy from New Testament prophecy. Just as the Old Testament prophets spoke direct, infallible revelation from God, so did the New Testament prophets. And once it was checked against previous revelation and approved, it was added to the Church's revelation.[21]

This logic seems to confuse the prophetic with the *canonization* of Scriptures. The word *canon* originated in reference to a measuring reed or standard by which something is measured. In reference to the Bible, a canon has to do with genuinely-inspired writings. Most definitely prophets living during biblical times spoke prophecies that weren't recorded in Scripture.

Pennington's arguments for Cessationism is also an argument against Continuationism. "To check against previous revelation," is precisely what commendable Continuationists do, consistent with the instruction from 1 Thessalonians 5:19-22. Do not quench the Spirit. Do not despise prophesies. Test all things; hold fast what is good."[22] (NKJ)

Regarding the gift of healing: Pennington takes the position that "when someone with the New Testament gift of healing used his gifts, the results were complete, immediate, permanent, undeniable, every kind of sickness and every kind of illness."

Scripture reveals that Jesus Himself prayed for one blind man twice (Mark 8:23), and He did not perform healings in His home town of Nazareth due to unbelief, as previously discussed Additionally, the Apostle Paul writes *as a New Testament Prophet* with the gift of healing about some who were not healed, he himself being one, (2 Corinthians 12:7-10).

The book of Revelation is a prophetic book written to warn and equip Believers to be able to properly understand and respond to the events of those future days. Revelation is filled with supernatural events, miracles, signs, and wonders including false miracles performed by Satan. This fact alone should, in my considered opinion, cause Cessationists to reconsider their position.

Early and repeatedly in this book, I asked you to be willing to reconsider what you have been taught and have believed, so that you can be confident you are basing your faith on what is true. I pray that you do precisely that. But above all, may we grasp what the Apostle Paul instructed about seeking and using the supernatural gifts and promoting unity of all Believers (1 Corinthians chapters 12, 13, and 14), that in all things we are to abide in faith, hope and love—the greatest of these being love.[23] Let us never allow *non-essential doctrine* (doctrine that does not impact salvation) to divide Believers. Instead let us embrace one another in Christ's love.

CHAPTER EIGHT

Faith Amplified

Overcome with Knowledge

When we find ourselves faced with serious life adversities, one tendency is to ask God, "Why?" In reality we know *why*, we live in a fallen world where Believers and unbelievers alike are subject to the evil contained therein. The difference is that as Believers in Christ, we have access to the power and authority to overcome. However, many professing Christians are unaware or misinformed and therefore unable to fully experience the victory Christ died to provide.

The Old Testament Prophet Hosea, speaking for God declares, "My people are destroyed for lack of knowledge."[1] Other translations use the word *vision* in place of knowledge. This passage in context reveals that the Lord declares that when we reject knowledge, we bring destruction upon ourselves. So rather than asking God *why* we should be asking God *what* What do we need to know to successfully overcome the situation?

Properly Identify the Source of Trouble

Years ago I subscribed to a Christian magazine. A month passed and the magazine never arrived. I called and was told to expect the next month's issue. That issue never came. I called again. Same routine and the third time the magazine was still a no-show. I called again and happened to get connected to the Editor in Chief. I explained the saga to which she replied, "Oh, well. God's in charge." I wanted to explode! Instead I bit my tongue, prayed and commented, "Yes, God's in charge but there is such a thing as human error." God was not responsible for the missing magazine! Yet, that's what her response implied.

The mindset that causes people to ascribe everything that happens—good, bad, or indifferent—to God, is not Biblical. And frankly I suspect the times God is grieved are when we either attribute a destructive or painful happening to Him, or when we fail to appreciate Him for the good and perfect work He does.

There are three potential sources for pain and suffering:

- you brought the circumstances on yourself with a free-will choice
- the pain and suffering were imposed upon you by another's free-will choice
- the enemy is directly attacking you.

Notice that God is not a source of pain, suffering, sickness, disease, or death. Just because God is sovereign over all doesn't make Him responsible for all. Sin and all the evil represented by sin came upon the world by the influence of Satan and the decision of Adam and Eve. Ever since then, God has been actively involved in eradicating the world from sin, as explained in Chapter One. Until this earth is completely void of evil, or your body dies and you exist in heaven, you will suffer pain. However, God promises to use suffering for purposes of refinement according to Romans 8:28.

The first thing to do when faced with adversity is determine the source so you can properly decide your course of action.

If the source is the enemy who is harming you and trying to prevent you from walking in the fullness of God's blessings to destroy your testimony, then your weapon is to wield the Word of God, as Christ did when He was tempted by Satan. The Word of God is your weapon to take authority over the enemy's attacks. Proclaim who you are in Christ and call on God for His power to overcome the enemy attacks in order to properly subdue him. As explained in Chapters Five and Seven, putting on the whole armor of God is vital whenever we must take a stand against the enemy.

If the source of affliction is a choice you made, repent and do all that is possible to make restitution, seek forgiveness from anyone you harmed (your responsibility is to genuinely seek forgiveness regardless of the outcome), and rely on the promises in the Word of God to restore you. Then move on in the confidence of the promises of Romans 8:1-2 that there is no condemnation for those who are in Christ Jesus.

If the source is the choice another made that is adversely impacting you, (e.g., Adam's sin that brought sickness, disease, pain, and suffering), seek God. Stop and prayerfully consider the specific correction or advancement God wishes to produce (yes, we can be spurred to advancement by adversity as I believe my husband was by finally choosing to become self-employed). Then seek to cooperate with God. Submit to both His *rhema* Word that is spoken Spirit to spirit, and His *logos* written Word by earnestly studying Scripture. Remember His spoken Word will never contradict His written Word. If you notice a contradiction, you are not hearing from God.

Be Transformed by the Renewing of Your Mind

As mentioned several times already, the battle for our faith and testimony is in our minds. Roman's 12:2, 2 Corinthians 10:5, and James 4:7 make clear how we are to secure victory:

> Do not be conformed to this world, but be transformed by the renewal of your mind, that by testing you may discern what is the will of God, what is good and acceptable and perfect.

> For the weapons of our warfare are not of the flesh but have divine power to destroy strongholds. We destroy arguments and every lofty opinion raised against the knowledge of God, and take every thought captive to obey Christ…
>
> Submit yourselves therefore to God. Resist the devil and he will flee from you.[2]

Our thought life, part of our *leb*, is what must be guarded and corrected continually.

As was addressed earlier, when you became born-again, you were given a completely new spirit—one that had never before existed. This spirit is in position to influence your soul/*leb* (mind, heart, personality, emotions, intellect, and will) and your body. But the deal is not finished. You must actively *retrain* your mind, which is the control center for your entire being. Through your mind you determined to submit your will to Jesus to become your Savior and Lord. And through your mind with the knowledge of truth is how you can become mature in matters of truth and possess effective faith.

Bruce Yocum, is President of Christ the King Association and a member of the International Executive Council of The Sword of the Spirit. Expanding on Romans 12:2 he wrote:

> The Christian mind doesn't just happen to people. It doesn't arrive at [the point of salvation or] at baptism, and it doesn't come simply because we want it to. In fact, it won't develop without a great deal of effort on our part. Where do we begin? What can we do to transform our mind from a secular stronghold to a place inhabited by the Spirit of God?

We can begin by resolving to view our mind as our servant rather than our master. God gave us a mind so we could think, reason, and know Him. He intended that we use it help establish order in our lives. But because our mind plays such an important role in helping us regulate our activities and because the intellect is so exalted in our day, it's easy to assume that the mind is the master of life. We must dismiss that view and determine that our mind will serve rather than control us.[3]

We make our minds master of our lives by:
1. setting our minds on things of the Spirit (Romans 8:5) and;
2. actively replacing every destructive, deceptive thought with the truth from God's Word.

Our job is to deliberately maintain truthful thoughts. If we are in church listening to a sermon and distracting thoughts come, we must deliberately redirect our attention to the sermon and drown out the distracting thoughts. If we're talking with a friend, our attention belongs with our friend and the conversation at hand. We have the ability to choose our thoughts. When we recognize prideful or lustful thoughts, we need to immediately replace them with truth. If we allow the unwholesome thoughts to remain—if we entertain such thoughts—we are permitting the work of the devil to preoccupy our minds. Negative, critical, suspicious, judgmental, unforgiving, rebellious, self-centered, doubt, and fear are just a few of the divisive mindsets we can have that will bring nothing but destruction. Romans 12:1-2 tells us that the way we are transformed—the way we learn to live Christ's life—is by the renewing of our minds, **by putting off our own negative and fleshly corrupt thinking and putting on**

God's truths. Consider the exercise *thought replacement.*

When we consider our thoughts, there only four forces that can impact them:

1. God or the Holy Spirit
2. our own self-generated thoughts
3. the intrigues of this world, and
4. Satan, the devil

Concerning the devil, understand that he is not omnipresent. Only God is everywhere at once. The devil must rely on his demons to report back to him. Scriptures do not state that the devil or his demons can read our mind. They can hear our words and observe our actions and from that strategize thoughts to cause us to think in a particular matter. We are not held responsible for the fleeting thoughts that enter our mind. But we are responsible for those which we choose to keep and entertain. And a mental preoccupation on any unwholesome thought provides a gateway for the enemy's infiltration.

Again quoting Bruce Yocum:

> A common obstacle to forming a Christian mind is [reluctance] of using our mind, based on a conviction that the intellect hinders the spiritual life. Our mind, however, as a tool given us by God is to be actively used in building His kingdom. An idle, empty mind is of little use to the owner or to God. Moreover, an empty mind, unoccupied by the things of God or other concerns proper to the task at hand, is likely to fall prey to distracting thoughts or thoughts planted by the evil one.
>
> A mind filled with the Word of God is a solid defense against the snares of the world, the flesh, and the evil one.

Formed by God's Word and relying on His promises, the mind is quiet, receptive and open to the promptings of the Holy Spirit. It reaches out to God and welcomes His truth in Scriptures, prophecy, and teaching. The mind that is immersed in Scriptures will easily apprehend the mind of God and is well on its way to becoming a truly Christian mind.[4]

The enemy will meet you in your mind with the plans of defeating, even devouring you. You must learn how to do battle with the confidence that the war has already been won. Be clear that the enemy of God is known as the Father of Lies. He is a master of deception. As I often state, "Unless we examine what we believe and why we believe, so we can be sure our beliefs are based on truth, we could easily be deceived and not know that we are. Because, after all, the very nature of deception means the victim is unaware." This mustn't strike fear or worry in you that you are deceived and don't know you've been misled. Rather, you should strive to be intentional about your thoughts and conclusions in matters of truth and faith—simple!

With every lie and accusation of the enemy, be prepared to counter his attacks with the truth from God's Word. Below are some examples to consider.

Satan's Lie
- You are a sinner because you sometimes sin.
- You get your identity from what you have done.
- You get your identity from what people say about you.
- You behavior tells you what to believe about yourself.

God's Truth
- You are a saint (one declared righteous by God) who sometimes sins.

- You get your identity from what God has done for you.
- You get your identity from what God says about you.
- Your belief about yourself determines your behavior.

Thoughts are words we think. As explained in Chapter Three, we must intentionally reinforce who God says we are, not who Satan accuses us of being, is vital.

Proverbs 23:7a (NKJ) reads, "For as he thinks in his heart, so *is* he." Don't let the enemy of God win any battles against you. Christ has already fully paid the price for you to be redeemed and delivered, beginning with your earthly life. Control your mind by your new spirit and your body and life will follow.

Understand God's Response to Evil and Suffering

We know from Scripture that God hates evil. Psalm 5:4; 45:7; 92:15, 97:10 and Proverbs 8:13 are just a few of the verses that reveal that. So, how do we make sense out of verses such as: Lamentations 1:5, 14; 3:38; Isaiah 30:20; 31:2; 45:7, and Amos 3:6 that clearly state: God afflicts; God delivers people into harm; God speaks both good and evil; God brings distress to eat and suffering to drink; God brings disaster; God creates calamity; God is responsible for disaster on a city. These verses seem to indicate that God *causes* evil. Yet that would be for Him acting inconsistently with His nature. Since there is great danger in concluding a matter of doctrine on a few passages of Scripture, we must be careful.

What can we safely conclude about God's hand in evil? We've actually already covered this. But knowing that when we are presented the same basic question in a different situation we can stumble, let's consider the question again. When seeking to understand Scripture, letting Scripture verify or interpret Scripture is important. By this I mean we need to consult the entire Bible on the particular topic.

Genesis 1:31 records that when God finished His Creation, He saw everything and declared it "very good." Many Scriptures affirm that God is not the author of evil: "God cannot be tempted by evil, and He Himself does not tempt anyone." (James 1:13) "God is light and in Him there is no darkness at all." (1 John 1:5) "God is not the author of confusion." (1 Corinthians 14:33) And if this is true, He cannot in any way be the author of evil.

John MacArthur, an American Calvinist Baptist Pastor, recognized by *Christianity Today* as one of the most influential preachers of his time, helps us better understand with his article entitled *Is God Responsible for Evil?* In it he writes:

> It is helpful, I think, to understand that sin is not itself a thing created. Sin is neither substance, being, spirit, nor matter. So it is technically not proper to think of sin as something that was created. Sin is simply a lack of moral perfection in a fallen creature. Fallen creatures themselves bear full responsibility for their sin. And all evil in the universe emanates from the sins of fallen creatures.
>
> Romans 5:12 says that death entered the world because of sin. Death, pain, disease, stress, exhaustion, calamity, and all the bad things that happen came as a result of the entrance of sin into the universe (see Genesis 3:14-24). All those evil effects of sin continue to work in the world and will be with us as long as sin is.
>
> First Corinthians 10:13 promises us that God will not permit a greater trial than we can bear. And James 1:13 tells us that God will not tempt us with evil.

> God is certainly sovereign over evil. There's a sense in which it is proper even to say that evil is part of His eternal decree. He planned for it. It did not take Him by surprise. It is not an interruption of His eternal plan. He declared the end from the beginning, and He is still working all things for his good pleasure (Isaiah 46:9-10).
>
> But God's role with regard to evil is never as its author. He simply permits evil agents to work, then overrules evil for his own wise and holy ends. Ultimately He is able to make all things-including all the fruits of all the evil of all time-work together for a greater good.[5] (Romans 8:28)

God's permission for evil to exist could be said to have been included with His provision of free-will. He knew the prospect of choice and that a choice to rebel against Him would result in sin entering the world. But He was fully prepared for that. So what do verses such as Isaiah 45:7 which reads, "I form the light and create the darkness, I make peace and create calamity; I, the Lord, do all these *things*," actually convey? Matthew Henry's Concise Commentary specific to Isaiah 45:5-10 explains:

> There is no God beside Jehovah. There is nothing done without him. He makes peace, put here for all good; and creates evil, *not the evil of sin, but the evil of punishment*. He is the Author of all that is true, holy, good, or happy; and evil, error, and misery came into the world by his permission, through the willful apostasy of his creatures, but are restrained and overruled to his righteous purpose. This doctrine is applied, for the comfort of those that earnestly longed, yet quietly waited, for the redemption of Israel. The redemption of sinners by the Son of God, and the

pouring out the Spirit, to give success to the gospel, are chiefly here intended. We must not expect salvation without righteousness; together the Lord hath created them. Let not oppressors oppose God's designs for his people. Let not the poor oppressed murmur, as if God dealt unkindly with them. Men are but earthen pots; they are broken potsherds, and are very much made so by mutual contentions. To contend with Him is as senseless as for clay to find fault with the potter. Let us turn God's promises into prayers, beseeching him that salvation may abound among us, and let us rest assured that the Judge of all the earth will do right.[6] [Emphasis added]

The commentary for Isaiah 45:7, in context with the surrounding verses, helps us discern what God is communicating. However, I think Henry's use of the word *create* in the phrase, "creates evil, not the evil of sin/sufferings, but the evil of punishment," is unfortunate. I think a more accurate statement would be to say that God orchestrates or God directs evil for the purposes of correction or judgment. With this we conclude that God does not create sin/evil, but rather at times He uses sin/evil to bring change for the better.

Evil that God permits is *measured* according to 1 Corinthians 10:13, because He promises that He will never allow us to be tempted into sin without also providing us a way of escape. We always have the choice to obey God and His ways, or cooperate with Satan and his ways. Any calamity that God permits is often intended to cause us to realize our wayward ways, repent, and be fully restored into unhindered fellowship with God the Father. God uses sin to correct unto good. Satan uses sin to destroy unto evil.

Any evil is always under the watchful eye of God. Nothing happens that escapes His knowledge or awareness. This can be difficult for us to accept when we consider such atrocities as the Holocaust. But, we must remember that God is also just. There is nothing—no crime or evil—that will not go unpunished.

J.I. Packer, author of *Knowing God*, a book that has sold over a million copies and has been used in seminaries writes,

> [T]he Bible's proclamation of God's work as Judge is part of its witness to His character. It confirms what is said elsewhere of His moral perfection, His righteousness and justice, His wisdom, omniscience and omnipotence. It shows us also that the heart of the justice which expresses God's nature is retribution, the rendering to persons what they have deserved; for this is the essence of the judge's task. To reward good with good and evil with evil, is natural to God.[7]

We have the assurance in God's character and His word that He will ultimately deal with evil thereby creating a new heaven and earth where no evil exists. In the meantime, think of the reality of the promise of Romans 8:28—that God will cause all things to work together for good. The enemy can do the worst evil possible, and God will use that evil for good. Imagine being an enemy who seeks to cause utter destruction, but no matter what evil is done that evil is turned to good! Consider the frustration, fury, and torment of wanting to cause destruction only to see what he does used for good. I think this is part of God's judgment, justice, and protection being accomplished on earth until the ultimate or final fulfillment of the prophecies concerning the Day of the Lord. That Day will come at the end of history in the fulfillment of time as determined by God, when He with wondrous power, utterly punishes evil, thus fulfilling all His promises.

In God's Hands, Pain Is a Process with a Purpose

When we are enduring any kind of suffering, finding *anything God about it* is difficult. Joseph M. Stowell, president of Cornerstone University and the author of over twenty Christian books, refers to this as *The Trouble with Trouble*.

> The trouble with trouble is that it threatens not just our comfort and peace but our faith in God. Pain so conflicts with our concept of what we expect God to be like that trying to merge our pain with His claims [for our victory] is almost too risky to attempt head-on. It is easier to retreat into pious-sounding statements and hide under hollow phrases that have little meaning and no healing value or, more damaging, embitter our hearts and cause us to withdraw our spirits from Him.
>
> There is no hope until we understand the way God interfaces with problems, what he supplies in the process and what He seeks to accomplish. Viewing our trouble from the vantage point of truth about God equips us to make it through a crisis with hands held high in victory. Unfortunately, it is sometimes difficult to see God's place in our problems because a clear view of His role is often obscured by myths.[8]

I especially like a quote from Dr. Alan Redpath, Pastor of the Moody Church in Chicago, concerning God overseeing all that we suffer:

> There is nothing—no circumstance, no trouble, no

testing—that can ever touch me until, first of all, it has gone past God and Christ, right through to me. If it has come that far, it has come with great purpose, which I may not understand at the moment. But as I refuse to panic, as I lift up my eyes to Him, and accept it as coming from the throne of God, for some great purpose of blessing to my heart, no sorrow will ever disarm, no circumstance will cause me to fret. For I shall rest in the joy of what my Lord is.[9]

Five Myths about God's Role in Our Pain

Many times we are helped to understand what something is by learning what it is not:

Pain is not punishment. Punishment is a response to breaking a law or committing a crime. When you placed your faith in Jesus Christ, you were instantly saved by grace, no longer bound to the law. By faith, you have escaped punishment. That's not to say that you or I won't error and conduct ourselves in a less-than-godly manner. As long as we live in this fallen world, we will from time to time fall into sin. As a child of God, however, although there may be consequences for our behavior, there is no eternal punishment. This is not to say that Believers escape discipline. God disciplines His children in this life just as any loving earthly father implements discipline to correct his child.

Pain is not unproductive. Most of us would claim that a pleasurable life is one that is free of problems. In reality, that kind of life would be monotonous and unproductive. Just as we can't discern what is good without the contrast of evil, we can't enjoy what is pleasurable without the contrast of problems. Pain provides us with an immediate reality check to re-evaluate what is truly important. When tragedy strikes, we are instantly aware of the frivolous and meaningless things we've allowed to become overly important in life. Pain can actually restore many things to a proper value.

Pain is not indicative of spiritual failure. Since the dawn of time people have equated *the good life* as a sign that God is blessing. Yet, the Bible is replete with stories of righteous men and women suffering all sorts of difficulties, even some suffering unto a death as a martyr. After I suffered my sudden arrest, I had thoughts that God must not have been pleased with me—that He wanted to remove me from any earthy influence. I called my Pastor who interrupted me saying, "Pam, Pam, stop right there. Let me ask you, was there ever a time you prayed to God to do whatever it takes to get through to your husband?" I was immediately taken back in my memory to the situation, circumstance, and place when I prayed that very thing. Clearly the thoughts I'd entertained were of the devil. And in answer to my own prayer, God was with me every moment of my cardiac-arrest experience. As I am now convinced, He permitted the experience knowing the cardiac-arrest would ultimately be useful in reaching my husband. Sometimes the pain we suffer is not about us, but for others.

Pain in the end is not bad. When we understand this, we can far more easily join God in His miraculous way of using all things, even pain and suffering, for ultimate good. Romans 8:28 assures us, "And we know that for those who love God all things work together for good, for those who are called according to his purpose." Once we grasp that pain will ultimately be turned to good because God is sovereign, we have an easier time enduring the suffering and trusting God, while we seek to appropriate the authority we have over the situation. When we respond to pain in any other way, we can actually cause matters to become worse. Our response to pain takes confidence in God and a future focus.

Pain is not incompatible with a good and all-powerful God. The existence of pain and suffering is not an indictment against God. From the moment sin entered Creation, God immediately provided a way of escape—a way of redemption. His goodness and omnipotence were demonstrated in the birth, life, death, and resurrection of Jesus. God's goodness was demonstrated by Him personally taking the sin of the entire world unto Himself. His unfathomable love was demonstrated then and is demonstrated every day as He restrains evil. Yes, consider that God is busy restraining evil every moment of every day. The fact that all sin has not been completely eradicated is no indication of any lack in goodness or power. God, in His wisdom, is following a plan that encompasses all of time created, allowing the offer of redemption to be given to every person He has willed to walk this earth until the fullness of the earth's time.

Again from the writing of Joseph M. Stowell:

> The struggle about God's place in pain is not completely resolved by simply affirming that he is not the source of our trouble. No doubt some of us are willing to accept this truth—and yet our hearts cry, "If He is all-powerful, why doesn't He stop my pain?" In fact, God does stop much if not most pain and suffering from ever getting to us in the first place. If it weren't for His guardianship at the gates of our existence, we would be consumed. What God does permit Satan to inflict is subject to God's capacity to bring about glory and gain through it all. The wonder of it all is that God takes Satan's finest efforts to deface God's reputation and turns them completely to His glory![10]

Our response to God as we suffer is crucial to the process of our suffering being used for good, sooner than later. In my darkest times of trials and troubles, I pored over Scriptures. Not wanting to suffer any longer than necessary, I learned everything I could and I made all necessary adjustments to get my heart and mind lined-up with the truth of God's Word. In addition to sinful ways expressed outwardly, we can harbor sinful ways inwardly—things like unforgiveness, bitterness, envy, etc. When we know that God uses suffering to transform us for the better, cooperating with Him to shorten the process is prudent! The Israelites wandered the desert for *forty years* because of their murmuring and complaining, instead of submitting to and obeying God. According to scholars, the actual trek from the Red Sea to the Promised Land was approximately 750 km/466+ miles that otherwise could have been completed in approximately 44 days![11]

Satan's Purpose in Our Pain

Ever since Satan chose to rebel against God, his every thought and deed has been to defame God and rob Him of His glory. Satan actually sought to take God's glory unto himself, but he was denied as we read in Isaiah 14:12-17. As a result, any and all things that are important to God are targets of the enemy's intended destruction. He was unsuccessful in acquiring God's glory so now he works continually to try to prevent God from having any glory.

When God finished all His creation and declared it was good, the enemy schemed every way possible to corrupt and destroy. Satan does not care about us or our environment. He only seeks to use us and abuse us as tools to carry out his revenge against God.

Because Satan was successful in tempting the first man and women to rebel against God, all of Creation has suffered. And Satan and his demons have continued in their effort to destroy mankind and prevent us from knowing God.

The Old Testament reveals how wicked the hearts of men became under the influence of Satan, time and time again. Genesis 6:1-9:17 records how the hearts of men were turned away from God, and evil prevailed to such an extent that God grieved. In response, God caused a flood to purge the earth of evil. Not terribly long after that, mankind tried to dethrone God as we read in the story of the Tower of Babel, Genesis 11:1-9. In response God dispersed the people, confounding their language, so that they couldn't as easily plot. And Satan's effort to destroy all that is God's and all that is good continues to this day.

We can't overstate that Satan works hard to prevent people from discovering the truth of God's plan of Redemption in a variety of ways. Keeping people from learning about God's offer of redemption that allows Believers to have authority over all Creation (which includes Satan and his demons) is a major battle plan for Satan. Confounding truth and deceiving people into believing lies is Satan's doing. When people do discover truth and choose to be restored by faith in Jesus, Satan doubles his efforts to bring destruction, ever and always seeking to prevent God from receiving His glory due.

People often speak in terms of humanity being pawns in God's human experiment. This is a lie from the pit of Hell. Satan is the one who seeks to use us as pawns in his plan to destroy. God is ever working to rescue us.

Take a moment to consider the success of the enemy. When was the last time you heard Satan being blamed for war, blight, starvation, mass murder, sex trade, abortion, murder, rape, greed, or gossip? People generally blame God. When people seek to curse do they swear by Satan's name? No, they use the Lord's name in vain. Did you know that even when people say, (and please excuse me but I'm making a point), *God damn it!* they are cooperating with the schemes of the devil? God does not damn anyone. Angels and people receive life or death, heaven or hell through their choice to embrace or reject Jesus. In this sense, angels and people damn themselves.

If we understand that no evil can come our way without God permitting that evil, then our first response must be to learn God's purpose for allowing us to suffer the evil. Is the pain/suffering to cause us to deal with a sinful behavior? Is the circumstance intended to direct us to matters of our heart that are hindering our success in Christ? Is our misfortune to have us exercise our authority over the enemy? Is the disaster to drive us to pray for the protection of others and thereby become part of God's power in working out His plan? Seek God and ask Him to reveal His purpose and the response He wants from you.

Cooperating with Jesus' instruction and following His example is how we thwart the enemy. To do anything less is to hand the victory in the battle over to Satan.

Pain has a Public Purpose

Generally speaking, many who profess to be Christians have not demonstrated the vital, abiding hope that is available. We are not only failing to walk in the victory Christ died to give us, we are reflecting poorly upon our Lord, misleading others about the Christian faith by the way we respond to our sufferings. In so doing we are also helping Satan win strategic battles. If we don't know how to tap into and apply Christ's victory power in our trials, we can't experience real and certain hope for ourselves, let alone offer hope to anyone else. When I realized that our suffering and victory through suffering is not *all about me*, I changed the way I accepted my response.

Of the trials I previously shared that I suffered early in my faith, most were experienced during seasons when I was in public ministry. I was working to form a class for Community Bible Study, then once CBS was established, I worked as Teaching Director for the class. For nearly seven years, the precious women who served with me and the class members observed me living through an extended season of hardships. I was blessed by their prayers and gifts of compassion. I know I could not have survived all that happened without their love and support! At the same time, the way I endured my trials and relied on my faith was in full public view. In retrospect, I'm exceedingly glad for that. As a fairly young Believer in a position of leadership, I was forced to apply my own instruction knowing my life was in plain sight for all to see. I didn't realize then that that every Believer is in public view and the enemy of God works overtime to discredit your testimony as a means to rob God of His glory. For me, back then, having the responsibilities I did for the class was something God used to help me walk my talk. While I didn't perform perfectly, I did handle myself and my situation sufficiently through the end of the trial. Gratefully, God rewards faith not performance.

You may not be in a position of much visibility with your daily routine. But, know that if you openly claim to be a Christian, you are being watched. People are hungry for hope. Even those who have given up on finding hope are still starved for hope. With the prospect that Christianity may offer what they need, people are watching us.

There are women to this very day who occasionally contact me, sharing that their observation of my suffering and my not completely giving in to the temptation to be defeated was what encouraged them to not give in or give up when they encountered difficulties. There are people who thank my husband and me for being candid about our trials—even those most people would work hard to keep private. Why? Because by our sharing the truth about our realities, we reveal what is common to the human experience and in so doing offer hope. If God helps us through, He will you, too, if you so desire.

And one truly great praise is the lessons our children learned from us as we sloshed our way through the pain and suffering, holding out all faith in God's character, will, and intentions for humanity as recorded in His written Word.

The Benefit of the Burden of Evil

What I've come to understand is that while we live on this earth we are *entrusted* with the burden of evil, which according to God's promise and abilities will be used by God to ultimately produce good. Psalms 55:22 reads, "Cast your burden on the LORD, and He shall sustain you; He will never permit the righteous to be moved." What is especially significant about this verse is the word *burden*. This particular Hebrew word is more properly rendered as *gift* or *portion* or *providence*. This reminds us of the hope and promise of Christ's words, "In the world you will have tribulation. But take heart, I have overcome the world." (John 16:33b)[12]

God hates the evil atrocities that have occurred throughout the history of mankind even more than we do! God promises to bring justice for all the evil ever committed. God *is* working sin out of this world, consistent with His complete plan and purpose. Scripture declares, "The Lord is not slow to fulfill his promises as some count slowness, but is patient toward you not wishing that any should perish, but that all should reach repentance." (2 Peter 3:9)[13] When God set time in motion, He planned for *all* of His created human beings to have the opportunity to choose to be united with Him, or not. The fullness of time will be that point in history when the last of His beloved planned human beings exist.

The final book in the New Testament, The Revelation of Jesus Christ, forewarns us about the continued increase of both good and evil until such time as all of God's people are restored unto Him. Then the end will come.

The new heaven and earth for God's people, and the eternal place of banishment for those who willfully refuse to be united with God, will become the ultimate separation between good and evil. This will be the final point of restoration where Believers will co-reign with Christ/God as He has desired from the beginning of Creation.

Revelation 12:11, revealing what will take place in the very end of time, explains that "And they, [Believers], have conquered him [Satan], by the blood of the Lamb, [Christ's sacrifice on the cross] and by the word of their testimony, for they loved not their lives even unto death." Believers who do not give up on God, regardless of evil they suffer in this world, are assured victory experienced in part in this life and eternally in the life hereafter.

God is Justice

Again, God is the ultimate Judge and justice is His promise to all Creation. Those who trust God, His character, will, intentions, and promises, will seek Him with the assurance of hope perfectly fulfilled in the end of this present age. We are living in the process. We are living in the dash between the beginning and the end. The Bible gives us all the information we need to understand what life will be like on earth, until the end. And nowhere does the Bible say that God will cease to do great and mighty things for, in, and through His people. To the contrary, Jesus said "Truly, truly, I say to you, whoever believes in me will also do the works that I do; and greater works than these will he do, because I am going to the Father. Whatever you ask in my name, this I will do, that the Father may be glorified in the Son. If you ask me anything in my name, I will do it."[14] *In My name* means according to His position and authority, which is always one-hundred percent lined up with the will of the Father (John 15:9). Elsewhere in Scripture we are assured that our prayers, made consistent with the Father's will, shall be answered (1 John 5:14). When we pray, we need to defer to God's perfect will over our limited ability to know what would be good and perfect in any given situation.

The lesson of the book of Job confirms to us that God is supremely wise, He is perfectly just, and He is overwhelmingly sovereign even in the most intense human suffering. The story of Job, who was clearly noted in Scriptures as a righteous man, is not one for us to read and think about Job and ourselves. Rather, we need to consider what we can learn about God.

We tend to believe that those who are righteous will prosper and those who are wicked will suffer. This line of thought adversely impacts us as Believers when we suffer. When we suffer, we naturally want to find a way to stop the pain. But the only way to effectively do that is to pursue God. When we suffer, we must remind ourselves of the character, will, intent, and promises of God and seek His supreme wisdom about what we're to do in our suffering.

The Apostle Paul wrote of his affliction in 2 Corinthians 12:7-10:

> So to keep me from becoming conceited because of the surpassing greatness of the revelations, a thorn was given me in the flesh, a messenger of Satan to harass me, to keep me from becoming conceited. Three times I pleaded with the Lord about this, that it should leave me. But he said to me, "My grace is sufficient for you, for my power is made perfect in weakness." Therefore I will boast all the more gladly of my weaknesses, so that the power of Christ may rest upon me. For the sake of Christ, then, I am content with weaknesses, insults, hardships, persecutions, and calamities. For when I am weak, then I am strong.[15]

Obedience in the Trial Produces God's Good

Through the years of having to draw on my faith, pouring over Scriptures to find God's promises to stand upon, refusing to give up or give in, I've learned that the trials or hardships we endure today, is intended by God to strengthen us for tomorrow. Romans 5:3-5 encourages us:

> "…we rejoice in our sufferings, knowing that our suffering produces endurance, and endurance produces character, and character produces hope, and nope does not put us to shame, because God's love has been poured it our hearts through the Holy Spirit who has been given to us.[16]

Think about that.

God intends us to be strengthened in our faith as we suffer and endure with His help and power. But again, too few Believers know how to do this and the result is that their faith is weakened in the trial, giving Satan a victory in that battle. Remember, Satan only has as much power as we give him in our lives.

One story that has had great meaning for me is entitled *Pushing Against the Rock* by John Arcovio that appeared in *Fresh Manna*, from Spirit Led Ministries Publishing in 1996:

> There was a man who was asleep one night in his cabin when suddenly his room filled with light and the Savior appeared. The Lord told the man that he had work for him to do and showed him a large rock in front of his cabin. The Lord explained that the man was to push against the rock with all his might. This the man did, day after day. For many years, he toiled from sun up to sun down, his shoulder set squarely against the cold, massive surface of

the unmoving rock, pushing with all his might. Each night the man returned to his cabin sore and worn out, feeling that his whole day had been spent in vain. Showing signs of discouragement set the stage for Satan to whisper doubt, "You've been pushing against that rock for a long time and it hasn't budged. Why kill yourself over this? You're never going to move it." Soon the man thought of himself as a failure. Discouraged and disheartened he finally took his thoughts to the Lord, "Lord," he said, "I have labored hard and long in your service putting all my strength to do that which you have asked. Yet, after all this time, I have not even budged that rock a half millimeter. What is wrong? Why am I failing?" To this the Lord responded compassionately, "My son, when long ago I asked you to serve me and you accepted I told you that your task was to push against the rock with all your strength, which you have done. Never once did I mention to you that I expected you to move it. Your task was to push. And now you come to me, your strength spent, thinking that you have failed. But is that really so? Look at yourself. Your arms are strong and muscled, your back sinewy and brown, your hands are callused from constant pressure and your legs have become massive and hard. Through opposition you have grown much and your abilities now surpass that which you previously had. Your calling was to be obedient and to push and to exercise your faith and trust in My wisdom. This you have done. I, my friend, will now move the rock. And next I will reveal to you the work for which you are now proven and prepared to do for Me.

At times, when we hear a Word from God, we tend to use our own intellect to decipher what He wants, when actually what God wants is just simple obedience and faith in Him. By all means, exercise the faith that moves mountains, but know God is still the One who moves the mountains!

Again, don't let the perplexities you feel in your suffering be used by the enemy to draw you into isolation. Instead, be as proactive as you can to study, learn, and grow your faith. You have God's promise that He will never leave nor forsake you. Deuteronomy 31:8: "It is the LORD who goes before you. He will be with you; he will not leave you or forsake you. Do not fear or be dismayed."

With a solid understanding about the purpose of pain and suffering, with the next chapter and Section we will learn what miraculous blessings we can expect for our faith. Do you have Hebrews 11:6 memorized by now? That verse is a perfect promise to keep in your heart.

PART THREE

THE FRUIT OF FAITH

The fruit of faith can only be produced by remaining in Christ. Jesus makes it clear in His words recorded in John 15:4-5, "Abide in me, and I in you. As the branch cannot bear fruit by itself, unless it abides in the vine, neither can you, unless you abide in me. I am the vine; you are the branches. Whoever abides in me and I in him, he it is that bears much fruit, for apart from me you can do nothing."[1] By simply remaining in Christ, which is to maintain Him as preeminent in our lives, we have God's assurance for abundance.

CHAPTER NINE

Faith Fortified

Celebrate Your Abundance

You have to admit that what we humans can accomplish using our natural minds and physical abilities is truly amazing. Consider the accomplishments of the ancient Mayans, Egyptians, or Romans. Consider just the Jewish people. One could argue that through the centuries they have contributed more to change the world than any other people-group. Their modern inventions include lasers, pacemakers/defibrillators, genetic engineering, stainless steel, Cholera and Bubonic plague vaccines, the polio vaccine, the atomic bomb, and Google![1] Some say that the main and most important thing the Jewish people contributed to all of civilization was the idea of monotheism, the practice of the vast majority of religions today.[2]

As tremendously significant as the accomplishments of these ancient people groups are, nothing is more significant than the contribution God personally made for all humanity for all time and history by personally coming to this world, taking on human form to redeem anyone who wants to be rightly-related to God by faith. Think about that. Jesus was the only one to suffer to the extent that He did, by taking on the sin of the *entire world* in order to pay the debt of sin, once and for all. No other human being has or will ever suffer to the same extent He did. Yes, I know of the horrific atrocities people have inflicted on other people throughout the ages. But not one of these people was required to take on the sin of the entire world. Believers in Jesus Christ have everything to celebrate when considering Jesus alone. But God is so generous and loving that beyond redeeming us, He has made a way for us to participate in His process of ridding this world of evil. As Christians we are co-workers and joint heirs with Jesus!

The Apostle Paul wrote in Romans, "The Spirit himself bears witness with our spirit that we are children of God, and if children, then heirs—heirs of God and fellow heirs with Christ, provided we suffer with him in order that we may also be glorified with him."[3] Juli Camarin, writer and teacher on JCBlog, commenting on this same passage wrote:

> Through faith we were born into God's family. He has given us a new name, a new spirit and a new future to testify to this very fact. We are heirs of God and co-heirs with Christ Jesus. God has withheld nothing from us. Ephesians says, *"For he chose us in him before the creation of the world to be holy and blameless in his sight. In love he predestined us to be adopted as his sons through Jesus Christ, in accordance with his pleasure and will"* *(Ephesians 1:4-5)*. All of this eternal blessing grew out of His love for us. Before Christ we were helpless and hopeless without God, but through the blood of Christ we have been brought near and included in the covenant of promise (Ephesians 2:12-13).[4]

The Covenant Promise

The word covenant simply means an agreement—a legally binding agreement between different parties. Synonyms for the word covenant include contract, agreement, undertaking, commitment, guarantee, warrant, pledge, or promise.

Kay Arthur, in her book, *Our Covenant God*, explains the deep, deep meaning of what being in covenant with God is. Kay's excellent book reveals how extensive the covenant is and how the Old Testament sacrificial system was a strong symbol of God's promise as well as a visual representation of the profound significance of the covenant. She explains that to enter a covenant with God as demonstrated with Abraham (Genesis chapter 15:9-10), is to walk from death into life, and that this covenant requires the shedding of blood. Hebrews 9:22 states: "Indeed, under the law almost everything is purified with blood, and without the shedding of blood there is no forgiveness of sins."[5] This particular law dealing with the required sacrifice is found in Leviticus 17:11 where God is speaking to His people and He states, "For the life of the flesh is in the blood, and I have given it for you on the altar to make atonement for your souls, for it is the blood that makes atonement by the life."[6]

The grave seriousness of sin is brought to our understanding when we grasp the way in which God's covenant must be expressed. We know that sin brought death to humanity and all the world God created. Sin never impacts just one person, creature, or thing. In God's plan of redemption, through the Old Testament covenant, *sacrifice* was the system whereby the blood of animals provided a *covering* for our sin. Under the New Testament covenant, faith in Christ is the system that provides a *cleansing* of our sin. Both require the shedding of blood—the first was that of sacrificial animals, the final and ultimate sacrifice was the blood of Jesus Christ, the Lamb of God.

The Old Testament Law of God was not given to emphasize the legality of the covenant, but rather the *disposition* of the two parties of the covenant and to identify *holiness*—to identify the type of life that God's people are to live. Holiness means a life set apart for God—a life that believes and receives by faith and responds by obedience. Disobedience brought death. Covenant brought sacrifice. The blood brings life, restoring God's people to obedience.

Covenant, in God's intention, is eternally binding on both parties. However, even when we fail to live up to our role under this loving covenant, God will never fail to live up to His. Neither can we wander outside of His Covenant—we can move outside His will, but not His Covenant.

As Joint Heirs What Can We Expect?

Jesus personally cautioned Believers to expect suffering in this world. One passage is John 15:18-19, "If the world hates you, know that it has hated me before it hated you. If you were of the world, the world would love you as its own; but because you are not of the world, but I chose you out of the world, therefore the world hates you."[7]

But, as Jesus also said, we are not to let this concern us for He has overcome the world, (John 16:33). And the Apostle Paul, who suffered greatly in his life for faith in Christ, wrote that he cannot compare his sufferings to Christ's. All His sufferings (and ours) pale in comparison to Christ's sufferings or the inheritance that awaits us:

> For this light momentary affliction is preparing for

us an eternal weight of glory beyond all comparison, as we look not to the things that are seen but to the things that are unseen. For the things that are seen are transient, but the things that are unseen are eternal.⁸

While we can't avoid pain and suffering in this life, we have Christ's assurance that we not only have a way of eternal escape, we have supernatural abilities on earth to overcome much. To overcome does not mean to avoid. Rather, overcoming means to partner with God, allowing Him to guide us through the suffering in His wisdom, to work in and through us all the transforming work He intends in the process. The result is that good actually comes from the suffering, for ourselves, for others and all for God's glory.

Miracles have their greatest impact when they resolve suffering. Think of the many different miracles Jesus and His disciples, including all up through modern times, have performed or experienced. All were for the purpose of redemption, restoration, and declaring Jesus as the *Messiah*—the Jewish word for the Promised Deliverer.

Even Jesus turning the water into wine at the wedding in Cana was a highly significant miracle. (John 2:1-11) Weddings were the biggest and most important celebrations among the Jewish people— the weeklong party signaled the social status of the new family in the community. Certainly helping the wedding host and newly married couple avoid a major embarrassment was compassionate. But more, Jesus' action reveals how God is aware of every matter that concerns us, wanting us to follow in His ways. Hospitality is important to God as a way to demonstrate brotherly love. Turning water into wine may seem like a small miracle in contrast to delivery from demons or raising people from the dead. Yet, when Jesus was asked which is the greatest commandment, He replied,

> And he said to him, "You shall love the Lord your God with all your heart and with all your soul and with all your mind. This is the great and first commandment. And a second is like it: You shall love your neighbor as yourself. On these two commandments depend all the Law and the Prophets."[9]

In 1 Corinthians, Chapter 13, the Apostle Paul makes the point very clear that unless we have love, no matter what miraculous feats we may accomplish, we gain nothing. He instructs that faith, hope, and love are essential to abide in Christ, and asserts that the greatest of these three attributes is love.

Were we to fully embrace all that God offers, we would have abilities for compassionate miracles and victory over natural circumstances as Christ demonstrated in His earthly life. Scriptures clearly tell us that Jesus is our example. If we learn from Christ, as His early disciples did, we, too, will demonstrate miracles, signs, and wonders, bringing health, wholeness, restored relations, provisions, and more, just like Jesus said we could:

> Truly, truly, I say to you, whoever believes in me will also do the works that I do; and greater works than these will he do, because I am going to the Father. Whatever you ask in my name, this I will do, that the Father may be glorified in the Son. If you ask me anything in my name, I will do it.[10]

What Kind of Miracles Can We Expect?

Of the thirty-seven miracles[11] recorded in the New Testament that Jesus performed, not including those performed by His disciples, six were provisional, three were deliverance from demons, three were restoring life to the dead, three were defying natural elements, and twenty-two were restoration of health. Some of His miracles could be listed in more than one category such as turning water into wine being both provisional and defying natural elements.

Hebrews 13:8 states, "Jesus Christ is the same yesterday and today and forever."[12] Not only based on this passage, but on all of Scripture, I see no reason why we should not expect a miracle of any kind and at any moment!

Let's consider the miracles that Jesus performed, realizing that as He performed them, He was training His disciples. Jesus is the example for all who choose to believe in and receive Him. As stated before, Jesus proclaimed that all authority had been given to Him and that He has imparted that same authority to us, making the same power of the Holy Spirit available to us. Any true disciple of Jesus needs to learn from Him and step out in faithful effort to partner with God in obedience to Christ's command found in Matthew 28:18-20, "And Jesus came and said to them, "All authority in heaven and on earth has been given to me. Go therefore and make disciples of all nations, baptizing them in the name of the Father and of the Son and of the Holy Spirit, teaching them to observe all that I have commanded you. And behold, I am with you always, to the end of the age."[13]

Provisional Miracles: True, God knows what we need before we ask, but He loves our asking because we demonstrate our willing reliance and understood dependence upon Him. We are placed in a right communion with Him, positioning our heart, mind, soul, and strength as *all in.*

Receiving what we need and even some of what we want from God is such a blessing. But what about being a blessing? What if God used you to provide a provisional miracle to someone else? Surely those blessed families who gave to my family cash, checks, and groceries in our years of lack were especially blessed by God for their charity and compassion. Remember the Law of Sowing and Reaping?

At least at one point in our lives, we will need God to miraculously help us provisionally. We should do all we can to be in position to receive when the need arises. I can't think of a better way than to make certain we give when we can.

Deliverance from Demons: Many people declared mentally-impaired actually suffer from demonic influences. Dr. Charles H. Kraft, Director of Deep Healing Ministries from Pasadena, California, previously mentioned, understands this better than anyone else I have personally met. He writes:

> Jesus' authority was most obvious in dealing with demons. Demons never questioned Jesus' authority over them; they responded immediately. He did not beg demons to leave, as we are told the Pharisees did. Nor did He pray to God the Father to release a person from them. He assumed they should not be there and He commanded them to go.[14]

As with all of Christianity, there are things we must learn and understand before we can believe and receive and be effective so that God's kingdom is done on earth as in heaven. Because the enemy has done such a good job of deceiving people about his existence and abilities, we are, generally speaking, ill-prepared to help people become freed from demonic influence.

I'll add that hypnotism and other altered states of consciousness such as with drug or alcohol abuse can open the way for demonic influence. My understanding is that a Christian cannot be demon-possessed because his/her spirit was completely made new when they confessed Jesus as Savior and Lord. However in the mind and body, a Christian can be demon-influenced.

Restoring Life to the Dead: Of all possible miracles, restoring life to death is the most difficult to believe. At the same time miraculous resurrection of life from death is the most compelling regarding the existence and power of God. Therefore, beginning with the claim of Jesus' resurrection, such miracles warrant the highest scrutiny.

It is my researched opinion that not only was Jesus miraculously, bodily resurrected from the dead, resurrection from the dead is really still occurring according to God's perfect plan and purpose. The story of Andrew Womack's son shared in Chapter Six is one example. But there are other modern-day examples.

Scholars like Craig Keener, professor of New Testament at Asbury Theological Seminary has written a number of helpful and important books on a number of topics in New Testament studies. His most recent book is *Miracles: The Credibility of the New Testament Accounts* (Baker, 2011). In this book Craig argues that the miracles recorded in the Gospels and Acts are not fabricated myths, but historical events. In a video clip Craig talks about people being raised from the dead in modern times and he discusses some of the eyewitnesses he interviewed, including those from his own family.[15]

Steve Trullinger, the founder of The Father's Touch Ministries, claims to be the instrument God has used to restore people from death to life. He was called into the healing ministry in 1995 by God. At that time, he worked as an Associate Professor of Physics at the University of Southern California in Los Angeles. His twenty-five years as an educator and researcher helped prepare him to train healing teams and to understand the synergisms of spiritual gifts in the ministry of healing. Steve holds the firm belief that the Father trains his sons/daughters through *activation* of faith and the *demonstration* of promised miracles that Jesus said would accompany those who believe.

Closer to home for me is my personal experience with death and being revived. In 2002, I suffered sudden cardiac arrest. Sudden cardiac arrest is different from a heart attack. A heart attack is caused by some blockage to the flow of blood through the heart. Sudden cardiac arrest is where the heart abruptly stops. Until recently, the occurrence was called sudden cardiac death because no one survived. But now with the advent and accessibility of defibrillators, about five percent of witnessed victims survive. Gratefully, according to God's plan, I am among the five percent.

I was not overweight, I did not smoke, and in fact I was walking onto the tennis courts to play as usual when the exceedingly mild symptoms began. I thought I was simply nervous because I was playing with some women from my church for the first time. I stepped on the courts to warm up, but my game was way off. Not knowing that anything serious was happening, I sat down to *emotionally* collect myself. But the symptoms progressed and I was clearly physically suffering. The precious women on the court with me called 9-1-1 and then our church prayer chain.

The Emergency Medical Technicians (EMT's), arrived on the scene six minutes and twenty-one seconds after the call was made. From the moment they arrived, they began administering advanced life support. The EKG showed my heart beating around 300 beats per minute. A person my size, at full exertion—playing tennis on a good day—should have a maximum heart beat of about 190.

The alarming progress of the heart rhythms, according to the paramedic, originated in the upper chambers of my heart and went from a Sinus Ventricular Tachycardia into a Ventricular Tachycardia and then into Ventricular Fibrillation. If you don't know what that means—it was really bad. The upper and lower chambers of my heart were beating out of sync, and as my first cardiologist shared, this condition is very rare. In the V-Fib stage, my heart stopped. I died. This is fully documented with extensive medical records. Little did anyone know that they would be used by God to actually restore my life. I'm told that in an expert rush, the EMT's prepared to defibrillate my heart. Someone yelled CLEAR then two hundred joules of power surged through my body. While this was happening, I was in an entirely different dimension, one I can only describe as the threshold of heaven. I did not want to come back. I knew I was in the center of God's sovereign care, basking in His love in a way I'd never known before.

I was gone for about one minute when they defibrillated me and began calling my name. I felt my spirit/soul return to my body and not wanting to leave that experience with God, I was agitated that anyone disturbed me.

Do you think that a miracle can't occur if medical science is involved? I can't say that because not everyone who is defibrillated in virtually the exact same circumstances as I experienced is revived. Again, only 5% of witnessed victims survive. And for each minute a victim is gone, some degree of brain damage and other harmful conditions are generally experienced. I have no residual issues—no heart or brain damage and my heart is healthy enough that I take no medications.

A definition of the word *miraculous* is an unexplainable occurrence through divine or supernatural intervention, or manifestation of supernatural power resulting in an inordinately high improbable or impossible conclusion. I think my experience qualifies as a miracle.

I came into the spiritual presence of God and enjoyed a peace and love for which there are no earthly words, illustrations, or analogies that can even closely describe what I felt. The reality of our eternal existence, the existence of God, and Him being profoundly good as described in the Bible, the reality of Christ and our faith in Him to allow Believers access to God, all these things were confirmed for me *experientially*. Although I wanted to stay, in God's plan my time to leave this earth had not come. Instead, I get to remain to minister and work to help others discover and live in the same life-giving truth I have been blessed to find.

God is clearly still involved in each individual's situation, working according to His plan and purpose, sometimes through medical science and His divine intervention, and sometimes independent of medical science. But clearly divine or supernatural intervention is an essential part of the miraculous. Divine or supernatural because angels, both holy and fallen, have the ability to intervene.

Defying Natural Elements: Physics and biology tell us that miracles that defy natural elements can't happen. But neither are scientists who don't believe in miracles able to explain how the *unexplainable* occurs. Recognizing that there is a God means recognizing an agent not bound by physical laws. But to claim that miracles are impossible is a claim that cannot be proven. By definition, miracles are unique and therefore not scientifically repeated or tested. The best we have is the physical evidence before and after. As John Perry, Co-host of Philosophy Talk states: "You have to get out of the lab coat of the scientist and into the cardigan of the historian or the suit of the detective. Weigh the accounts, the testimony, and the probabilities, and make an assessment. That is all you can do. Even science does not have nearly as many real *absolutes* as the popular imagination likes to think it has."[16]

In reality, science is not at odds with God's creation—only some scientists are. Open-minded scientists, archeologists, and others actually continually discover the truths of God's universe and are amazed at the unexplainable miraculous reality of His work

Jesus bid Peter to join Him on the water. He calmed the storms and fed the multitudes with two fish and five loaves to the point of their being sated, with ample leftovers. These are Biblical miracles that defied the natural laws. But are there any modern day testimonies? Yes, as testified by Heidi Baker.

Heidi Baker, a petite blonde woman with a doctoral degree from King's College, University of London, lives with and ministers to the people of Mozambique. She and her husband Rolland are the founders of Iris Global, a missionary organization caring for thousands of children at risk, in more than thirty nations.[17] Heidi also speaks at conferences around the world, sharing God's love and telling about the amazing things He is doing. I personally heard her speak at the Revival Alliance Conference in Pasadena, California, in April 2014. What follows is a written version of a testimony she shared there.

"Marc Dupont, (a prophetic minister representing the will of the Father to the body of Christ)[18] has only called me two times in twenty years. The last time he called, we were in Maputo (Mozambique), and he said, "I don't know what's going on right now but there's a cyclone coming." I told him, "I hope not! That would be the sixth cyclone this year!" This was in 2000, and we'd definitely had about as much bad weather as we could take. Marc said, "Well you're supposed to go out and tell this one to turn around."

"I thought, *oh, please. Sweet Jesus, have mercy. I just found out I'm 5'3"—I always thought I was 5'4" and I'm supposed to go outside and tell a cyclone to turn around?*

"You know I don't call you very often," Marc reminded me. *That's true*, I thought. I was still a little unsure. He said, "God spoke to me. And you're supposed to tell the cyclone to leave."

"I had nothing to lose anyway. I decided I would try to listen to this prophet, but even so I was so embarrassed I didn't want anyone to see me praying. I snuck out to my truck and drove to the beach. The sky was dark and the rain was driving down hard in big heavy drops. There had been disastrous floods this season, and tens of thousands of people were homeless. Many of them were sick with cholera. Others were starving.

"I started to whisper, "Cyclone, go!" while desperately hoping no one would find me there. "Cyclone — go away now in Jesus' name!"

"The rain went on. I got back in my truck and drove home. But over the next few days I saw on the news that a fresh cyclone *had* been drifting closer and closer to the coast of Mozambique. Eventually it had slowed down. Then it stopped completely. It lasted a very long time, spinning around and around off the coast, but it never did touch us. (This was the tropical cyclone Leon-Eline, the longest-lived tropical cyclone on record in the Indian Ocean.)[19]

"We are worshippers of God. We love him. Out among the Makua and Makonde people we've planted 2700 churches now. We've joined one great tribe for God. When massive storms began to hammer us again in 2014, we didn't have any warning. Even if there had been all kinds of warnings on the television or radio, most of the people don't have these things. Immediately we were in great distress as the roads began to wash away. One of our bases was completely flooded out. Four hundred people in our home church lost their homes. Just like that, their few possessions were gone. The electricity went down. Clean water stopped running through the pipes. In our own house we sat sopping wet under the leaking roof and prayed desperately: "God, what's going on?" But we also prayed: "We love you! We love you in the midst of the storm! We worship you in the midst of the storm!"

"When we heard that an extremely intense cyclone had formed and that the worst of it was still moving toward us (this was Cyclone Hellen), I decided to approach it a little differently than I had approached the one in 2000. This time I didn't want to tiptoe around and whisper sheepishly. Instead I called out hundreds of our local pastors, along with all the children living on our base. We would do things totally differently. We would pray as a tribe. Even as we were gathering, dozens of houses around us looked ready to topple into the muddy floodwaters streaming through our city toward the ocean. But we stood together in the rain and began calling out at the top of our lungs: "Cyclone turn around! Turn around in Jesus' name!"

"Within days the newspapers were reporting good news: Cyclone Hellen had weakened and then dissipated at the edge of Madagascar.[20] We lost no more houses. The skies cleared. Our rainy season was over."

I believe, beyond any doubt, this was God demonstrating what He can and will do through a willing vessel with faith.

God Rewards Those Who Diligently Seek Him

I have experienced several miracles of God in my life, not the least of which is my salvation. Our son's miraculous recovery from all the complications of his seriously-premature birth, and my miraculous survival of sudden cardiac arrest are two of the more dramatic. But God provides miraculous blessings in many ways.

After the many years of suffering unemployment, underemployment, and much loss, the day came in 1996, when my husband was once again gainfully employed. His job meant that he had to drive up to two hours each way from our home in Temecula to Los Angeles, depending upon traffic, but we didn't complain! We simply made plans to move closer once the children finished the school year.

I'd grown up in Orange County and was quite familiar with the sleepy semi-rural town of Yorba Linda. On the map Yorba Linda appeared to be a good location for any future work that David might have in Los Angeles, Orange, or San Diego counties. What I didn't know was how much this once-unincorporated city had changed! The community wasn't the affordable community I remembered from when I was a young girl.

David's new job was a temporary contract, which meant that they paid him handsomely in lieu of a permanent position. By this point, our monthly overhead was exceptionally low, so we were putting good chunks of money in the bank.

I contacted a recommended realtor, Mary, and told her, "I know I'm shooting for the moon here, but we've been in a long desert experience so I'm going for it." Then I shared my *wish-list* of all the features I hoped to find in a rental home. As I shared, I was also praying and asking the Lord for His input. Like a young child making a Christmas wish-list, completely oblivious to any limitations, I found myself rattling off all sorts of features I'd never actually thought about before.

I told Mary the house needed to be a minimum of three bedrooms because I have a girl and a boy who need separate rooms. And if the house was only a three-bedroom, I needed to have a separate family and living room so I could use one of those rooms for my home office. Then I remembered David needed a home office, too, so I told her we needed a three-car garage. David could convert one of the bays into his office as he'd done before. That arrangement works best considering all the equipment he has.

As I spoke, I felt like the Lord was clearly guiding me with my *wish-li*st. Then I thought, I'd really like a wood-burning fireplace, and not one of those puny pre-fab fireplaces. Next I heard myself say, "I'd really like a pool and spa. Oh, and an RV pad." I explained that we didn't own an RV yet, but we hoped to someday. And finally I told her, "I'd really like a little bit of land, nothing enormous, but I just don't want to open my kitchen window and see my neighbors as so many homes do in Orange County." Once I realized all I'd told her that I wanted *in a rental*, I was shocked that she still wanted to work with me!

We set out in May on our first efforts to find a home to rent. This was in 1996 when the economy was still suffering and many people, just like us, had lost their homes to foreclosure and were looking for homes to rent. By the time I found something worthwhile and could get David out to see the home, someone else snatched up the house. This happened repeatedly.

In June, we finally got the paperwork back that confirmed David's eligibility for a VA loan. So we spent that month looking to *purchase* a home in our price range. Well, in Orange County, getting anything suitable in that particular price range was next to impossible, even in the down market. So now we'd spent another month looking for a home without success.

My kids hate the memory of that summer, of having to get in the car with me to drive over an hour, and spending the entire day looking at homes, as many as five days a week. I appeased them with fast-food lunches that came with a toy. Considering that we very rarely spent money on any restaurant food for the four years we were unemployed, they were very happy to have such a treat, (not knowing I was actually bribing them!).

By this time we'd managed to put quite a bit of money in savings, so I told Mary, "If we can qualify for a conventional loan with a foreclosure on our record, we could look into buying that way."

About a week or so later, Mary called to say what she'd said many times before, "I found your home." I was reluctant to place the kids in the car yet again and this time on a Friday. But needing to find a home and get through the escrow process in time for the kids to start a new school early September served as pressure to go. Back in the car we went to make the trek. We called David to have him meet us. Once we were all gathered at the address, we approached the property.

I can't adequately describe this house, which was in absolutely horrible disrepair. Tenants had occupied and tremendously abused the property. There was evidence all over demonstrating that this house had been used for drug parties. We later learned that the tenant owned a moving van rental lot and would load a van up with prostitutes and bring them to the house. The police had been called to the property more than once, and neighbors were glad to learn the tenants had been evicted.

At the entry there was a potted plant that had been allowed to overtake the porch so that we had to literally bend down as though entering a hobbit's house. Spider webs were everywhere. The wooden entry door had deep gouges no doubt caused by the tenants' German shepherd seeking to alert the residents he wanted back in. Upon opening the door, we were greeted with a stench that I hope never to encounter again!

Looking straight ahead, I saw the family room and a large brick fireplace. We turned to our left to walk through the living room, *slish, slish, slish, slish*—the carpet was wet with a very dark substance we figured out was motor oil. The tenants apparently parked a motorcycle indoors. All around the room was candle wax, left from people sitting on the floor, leaning against the wall, and free-basing drugs. There were kick and punch holes throughout the interior. As we turned into the kitchen, there was evidence of a fire—no doubt from making drugs. Looking beyond that to the outside, I saw a huge green swimming pool and spa. And I'm not talking about the tile when I say green. And beyond that was an RV pad.

We were all feeling very queasy from the experience, and I didn't want us to spend any more time in the house than necessary, so I asked, "How many car garage?" Mary said, "Three." I inquired how many bedrooms and baths?" Mary said, "Two bathrooms and three bedrooms." Then I asked about the lot size and Mary replied, "The lot is a third of an acre." Walking outside for some fresh air, I thought, *perhaps Mary has found our house after all.*

Everything about this home was original and also in great need of repair. Landscaping was horrible and over-grown, which also meant a bad pest problem. The fences were literally falling down, and the roof leaked like a sieve. There was so very much work to do everywhere we looked. But we were elated! We could not believe that everything I *prayerfully wished* for was in this one home!

We were the first and only ones to see the home since it had been listed for sale. We made an offer. The seller couldn't believe anyone wanted the house. She just wanted to unload the property and be done, which meant she worked with us on price. We amazingly qualified for a loan even with a foreclosure on our record. The back story to this miracle was inspired by God.

One day, likely in 1992, when David opened the mail, he found a rejection letter from an employer where he'd applied for work. He tossed the letter into the trash and walked away. I had a feeling of compassion come over me and I pulled the letter from the trash and tucked the missive away. How morbid is that? Who would want to save a rejection letter? Well, I not only saved that one but nearly every other one he received from 1992-1996. Presenting these to the lender proved that David and I were simply caught in the horrible economy and had been doing everything possible to become gainfully-employed. Those letters along with our responsible ownership of two prior properties, along with no bankruptcy, allowed the lender to conclude we were not a loan risk.

Without a doubt, I believe God had been orchestrating details all along that would ultimately allow us to buy the home that had every single feature that I *wished* for, in a down market, with a motivated seller, giving us almost instant equity. The equity enabled us to clean and cosmetically fix the home and repair fences before we moved in. Soon after we replaced the roof. Some months following, Frank and his family moved in next door. He repairs pools for a living. David is a licensed architect. Frank wanted to do an addition on his home. Our pool needed repair. You can't tell me that wasn't God, too!

As I shared earlier, both my husband and I know that by our going through the four painful years of part-time work and unemployment, and suffering everything that came included, we gained far more than we ever lost. We now have a faith and belief in God that is stronger than our faith would ever otherwise be.

When we see God's work in our trials we are encouraged and enabled to stand firm on other promises God has made us that are yet to be fulfilled. When we consider all that God has already done to secure our eternal future, should we have any sense of fear that He will let us down in the present?

Expect the Miraculous

I firmly believe that miracles pass by us every day. They go unnoticed because of our focus. We will always move in the direction of our vision and focus. What are you focused on? Are you focused on the problems and sufferings and trials, or are you focused on the promises of God to help you through them? Are you focused on the present realities or the promised resolutions?

For us as Believers, the moment we became Christians we were called to live in the realm of *all things are possible*. But to walk in that realm requires that we stop living according to our human understanding. As Believers, we are new creatures in Christ who never existed before. We are now completely spiritually-regenerated and we have the distinct ability to live from that new and perfect spirit and to enjoy all that Christ died to provide us.

God is pleased when we expect Him to do what He says He will do. He loves our praying back the promises He made to us, reminding Him of what He said. Of course, He doesn't need to be reminded! Rather, He knows that when we pray back His promises, we are convinced and expecting Him to act. From that mind-set we are in the best position to receive from Him—with the confidence that we are praying according to His will (1 John 5:14-15).

If we are not experiencing the fullness of what God has promised—the abundant life that Christ died to provide, including a perfect peace and joy even in the midst of trials—the cause is our limited thinking, understanding, and a wrong focus.

Garris Elkins is Senior Leader at Living Waters Church in Medford, Oregon. He shared what follows that prophetically reveals the heart of God:

You are seeing painful things that have produced scars and wounds in your life and in the lives of the people you love. You think these things will always remain. You might even feel helpless to bring about change. Don't forget that I am involved in the events of your world. I can take the deepest pain and transform it in to great joy and celebration.

As I raised My Son to life, I will do the same for those who put their trust in Me. My greatest purpose is discovered on the other side of what you call impossible. I am the God who can transform a marred and disfigured circumstance into a thing of beauty.[21]

Another story from Scriptures of amazing faith is that of an unnamed outcast woman who lived in area of Galilee at the time of Jesus' life on earth. The story is found in Matthew 9, Mark 5, and Luke 8. Her faith was such that Jesus commended her, and though she's unnamed, she has earned a place of esteem and honorable mention in God's Word. She is referred to as the woman with the issue of blood.

From the Scriptures we learn that this frail woman had suffered a type of hemorrhaging for twelve years. In Jewish religious culture of the day, such a condition meant that she was ceremonially unclean and everyone and thing she touched was then defiled. She no doubt lived a lonely, obscure life for the entire twelve years of her ailment. She had heard of Jesus. All she had heard about Him revived her hope—a hope that no doubt had been entirely drained just as her finances had been. During the twelve years, she'd visited every physician possible to find a cure and she'd spent all her financial resources in the process. Instead of the doctors being able to help her, her condition worsened. All that resulted from her issue of blood likely included feelings of utter dejection and depression. She didn't have any influential advocates such as the Roman Centurion had. (Matthew 8:5-13) Even the Jewish leaders could offer her nothing as she was considered untouchable. Legally she couldn't even pursue Jesus for help as the Syro-Phoenician woman did. (Mark 7:24-30)

As an outcast, and in her weak and anemic state, when she heard about Jesus and that He would be passing through her village, she said to herself, *If I touch even his garments, I will be made well.*[22] The Amplified Bible states, "For she *kept saying*, If I only touch His garments, I shall be restored to health." She proclaimed what Jesus had available to her by *saying*. Jesus taught as recorded in Matthew 17:20, if we have faith as a mustard seed, we can *say* to the mountain, *Move from here to there* and the mountain will be moved; and nothing will be impossible for us.

Did she have a specific Scripture to base her specific belief of healing upon? No. Did she have a *rhema*/spoken word from God to give her the confidence to believe for her miracle? I don't think so. Instead, I conclude that she had heard of the character, will, and intent of Jesus as He'd blessed many others. She'd heard of the claims Jesus made of Himself. She counted herself worthy by her faith in Jesus to receive from Him.

Wholly inconsistent with the cultural claims of her day, what this woman heard, understood, and accepted about Jesus, convinced her that she was not outside the realm of His compassion and ability to help. Jesus had demonstrated repeatedly that He was [and is] willing and able to heal everyone without exception, if they so desired. While this woman's physical body was frail, her faith certainly was not. By faith, she sought to appropriate what Jesus was willing to give. Acting in faith is believing that we will receive according to what God has already offered. He initiates and we respond by faith, believing the promise is ours.

This unnamed woman's statement of faith was, "If only I may touch His clothes, I shall be made well." Recall that Jesus taught "Truly, I say to you, whoever says to this mountain, 'Be taken up and thrown into the sea,' and does not doubt in his heart, but believes that what he says will come to pass, it will be done for him. Therefore I tell you, whatever you ask in prayer, believe that you have received it, and it will be yours.'"[23]

Reread the last two sentences in the previous paragraph and notice the two easily-overlooked words that I italicize here: "but believes that those things *he says* will be done..." If the text were written *He says*, the meaning would be that we receive what God says. But *he* is written in the lower case, giving us insight to the importance of stating and proclaiming our needs, expecting that we will receive, according to God's will. Scriptures explain that we can ask anything according to the Father's will and our request shall be done (1 John 5:14-15).

As an unclean outcast, this emaciated woman braved the religious scrutiny and crush of the crowds and somehow managed to get close enough to Jesus to touch the hem of His garment. Immediately He knew His healing power had been released. He stopped and turned to the mass of people and asked:

> "Who touched my garments?" And his disciples
> said to him, "You see the crowd pressing around

> you, and yet you say 'Who touched me?' And he looked around to see who had done it. But the woman, knowing what had happened to her, came in fear and trembling and fell down before him and told him the whole truth. And he said to her, "Daughter, your faith has made you well; go in peace, and be healed of your disease."[24]

We must thoroughly understand what took place. This woman's faith empowered her to overcome her weakened physical condition and make touching Jesus' garment her unwavering goal. Her faith allowed her to disregard the centuries of religious tradition that defined her an outcast, confident by faith that she was worthy. Had she acted according to Jewish instruction, she would not have dared to be in crowds of people believing that she would defile them and even defile Jesus upon touching His garment. Her faith alone allowed her to overcome:

1. her weakened physical condition—she managed to fight through the crowds;
2. her culture's religious mind-set—Jewish leaders did not believe Jesus was the Messiah;
3. her physical ailment of over twelve years—she indeed was healed;
4. her restricted place in society—she had confidence that her faith in Jesus qualified her to receive;
5. all limitations moving forward in her new life with faith in Christ—she gain experiential knowledge that nothing is impossible with faith in God.

Look how extensively faith can benefit not only on a personal basis but also those who learn of the testimony. This unnamed woman with the issue of blood is included in the pages of Scripture and is able to encourage and empower others until the end of time. Let's indeed celebrate our abundance which includes sharing in the joys of others!

What Will Your Abundance Look Like?

What do you need from God? Have you satisfied the conditions of receiving His promises? Is what you need within the character, will, and intent of the Father to grant? Is there any reason you can't have what God has offered you? Do you believe you have every reason to celebrate God's fulfilled promises in your life before you actually secure them? Scriptures promise, if we believe, we shall receive. Do you believe?

With the next and last chapter, I want to help you become utterly convinced that as a Believer in Christ, you are in perfect position to receive from Him, abundantly more than you could ever hope or imagine.

CHAPTER TEN

Faith Magnified
Hope Renewed

Overcoming traditions and things we've been taught to believe can be the most difficult hurdles to move past. I marvel at the woman with the issue of blood and her example for us all, explored in the previous chapter.

To realize that what we choose to believe can either bring us victories, including the miraculous, or not, is astounding. What we willfully perceive from our limited viewpoints either hinders us or propels us. That we nurture our faith, consistently bathing our minds with truth, is so important. Wisdom and discernment are attributes we need to continually seek from God, lest we be deceived.

Discerning Miracles

Satan has the power to perform supernatural feats. In fact, this was the caution of the religious leaders of Jesus' day. The Sadducees and the Pharisees claimed that the miracles Jesus performed were of the devil. (Matthew 12:24) In the Old Testament, Exodus 7:8-13, we read how Pharaoh's magicians performed various perceived miracles, by drawing on the powers of darkness. While Satan's power is limited, he can and does perform what appear to be miracles in order to deceive. John 8:44 says that Satan is a liar and the father of lies. Satan can make himself appear as an angel of light. (2 Corinthians 11:14) He does everything possible to draw people away from God, including counterfeit signs and wonders.

During the tribulation, the Antichrist will use all sorts of displays of power through signs and wonders that serve the lie. (2 Thessalonians 2:9) These amazing displays are explicitly stated to be empowered by Satan. Jesus warned that the end times will be characterized by the treachery of counterfeit prophets who "will appear and perform great signs and wonders to deceive." (Matthew 24:24)[1]

Clearly there is no reason to believe that *miracles*, both Satanic and of God, are not available through to the end of the New Testament era. However, discernment and wisdom are essential in the evaluation of miraculous events. We must test all spirits according to 1 John 4:1, "Beloved, do not believe every spirit, but test the spirits to see whether they are from God, for many false prophets have gone out into the world."[2] Any time we are in doubt, we are to make sure that what is being taught lines up with what Scripture says. If the miracle worker is teaching something contrary to God's Word, then his alleged miracles, no matter how convincing they seem, are a demonic delusion.

Rather than allow fear and confusion, which are of the enemy to prevent us from believing in miracles from God, let us draw nearer to God with the expectation that when we do He will draw nearer to us.[3] Rather than grieve the heart of God by dismissing His good and perfect gifts, which assures our missing out on receiving them, let us seek after Him for all He wants to do in and through us for His glory and our benefit. Let us pray to Him with thanksgiving and submission, and trust Him to respond perfectly with respect to all He has planned for the redemption of Creation, and each of us individually.

Believe and Receive

Teaching about the indwelling of the Holy Spirit, the Apostle John explains that in our newly regenerated state we are like He *is* while we are *in this world*. 1 John 4:17 reads: "By this is love perfected with us, so that we may have confidence for the day of judgment, because *as he is so also are we in this world*. [Emphasis added]

In Christ's current state He has overcome the world. In Christ's current state He is not subject to *anything* of this world. Those of us who abide in Christ experience God's love, and Christ's imputed righteousness that enables us to escape judgment, and we can experience His victory power as He demonstrated *in this world*.

We will receive according to what we believe, providing what we believe is consistent with God's will. Do you believe Scriptures? According to Scripture, the Lord has promised to bless the obedient Believer with all heavenly and earthly blessings. 2 Peter 1:3 and 3 John 1:2:

> His divine power has granted to us all things that pertain to life and godliness, through the knowledge of him who called us to his own glory and excellence, by which he has grated to us his precious and very great promises, so that through *them* you may become partakers of the divine nature…that you may be in good health, as it goes well with your soul.[4] [Emphasis added]

The Lord has also promised prosperity to those who obey and worship the Lord. Deuteronomy 30:9-10:

> The LORD your God will make you abundantly prosperous in all the work of your hand, in the fruit of your womb and in the fruit of your cattle and in the fruit of your ground. For the LORD will again take delight in prospering you, as he took delight in your fathers, when you obey the voice of the LORD your God, to keep his commandments and his

statutes that are written in this Book of the Law, when you turn to the LORD your God with all your heart and with all your soul.[5]

Isaiah and Jeremiah are an Old Testament Prophets. From Isaiah 55:10-11 we read:

> For as the rain and the snow come down from heaven and do not return there but water the earth, making it bring forth and sprout, giving seed to the sower and bread to the eater, so shall my word be that goes out from my mouth; it shall not return to me empty, but it shall accomplish that which I purpose, and shall succeed in the thing for which I sent it.[6]

Given misleading modern-day teachings concerning prosperity, understand that God wants to bless each of us in particular ways specific to our unique life and our particular potential impact within God's plan and purpose. While all manner of blessings are available according to God's Word, they are granted according to God's will and purpose.

From Jeremiah 1:12, we read:
> Then the LORD said to me, 'You have seen well, for I am watching over my word to perform it.'

To those who might tend to discount promises from the Old Testament, please consider that Jesus is the fulfillment of the Old Testament Law opens the way for our experience of God's promises. Matthew 5:17-18 and 2 Corinthians 1:20 state:

> Do not think that I have come to abolish the Law or the Prophets; I have not come to abolish them but to fulfill them. For truly, I say to you, until heaven and earth pass away, not an iota, not a dot, will pass from the Law until all is accomplished. ... For all the promises of God find their Yes in Him. That is why it is through him that we utter our Amen to God for his glory.[7]

According to Acts 16:30-31, all we have to do be in right standing with God, redeemed and restored, is to believe in Jesus as Savior and Lord. This belief is essential faith unto Salvation.

According to Matthew 21:21-22, even beyond salvation, if we believe—if we have faith and do not doubt—we will receive whatever we ask that is consistent with the will of God the Father, by the power of His Holy Spirit. This is effective faith that produces amazing results.

Unbelief displeases God and often causes Him to not grant supernatural miracles. Why would He give a gift that a person does not believe in and therefore does not want? Conversely when we truly believe, He is greatly pleased to lavish good gifts upon us. I share my next story with you to help demonstrate what can happen when we dare to believe God for the impossible.

Our Maui Miracles

David and I had made plans to visit Maui for the first time with our kids in 2002. Well, he lost his job just before our trip. Our reservations had been made for months. To not go would mean losing a lot of money on the airfare for the four of us as well as the deposit for our accommodations. We couldn't afford not to go, so we did.

Needing to keep the trip as thrifty as possible, we agreed to sit through a time-share presentation in order to get some credit for our hotel costs and we planned to eat all our meals in our room. As we sat through the presentation, unemployed yet again, we had no intentions of buying. Every time we said, "No," the agent offered something else to entice us. This happened repeatedly to the point of ridiculousness. Either the agent was new or seeking a quota for an award or something.

I asked the salesman to allow my husband and me to speak in private. I said to David, "They have made this so attractive we *can't* say no! What if we go ahead and fill out the paperwork and if the paper goes through even though we're *between jobs*, we'll have a timeshare." He agreed. The approval went through and we do have a timeshare! That's our first Maui Miracle. (Some may not see buying a timeshare as miraculous but given our years of lack, we definitely do!)

Ever since then we've used our credit card for nearly everything to get travel points while we pay the card off monthly. With the travel points and the timeshare, we are able to travel for next to nothing. We returned for family vacation often in the years afterward. But in 2009, our kids were grown, so David and I made plans for just the two of us to go.

On our way there, by the end of the five-hour flight, I wasn't feeling very well. By the time we got to our hotel, I was definitely not feeling well. During the night and all the next day I was clearly sick. While David was out lounging around the pool enjoying all that the south Pacific tropical paradise offers, I was sick in bed writhing in pain with flu-like symptoms.

I prayed and prayed to God about our continued trial of part-time work and unemployment and my being sick when we are in Maui on top of all that, too. I also prayed to God asking why my ministry work had been so stunted instead of progressing nicely. I asked God, "Why have I had so many false starts?" I discerned His response in my spirit, *You haven't had false starts, you've had false stops*. That took me by surprise and few moments later I asked, "Why?" Next I "heard" *Beelzebub*. I thought *Beelzebub? That's a name given to Satan that means Lord of the flies.*[8] *He's been the one pestering me and possibly David with his job situation for all these years?* And I got really angry! I went to warfare prayer at that very moment and continued all day and night until the next morning when I physically felt better. But I was still angry with the enemy.

David and I decided to go poolside together. I soaked up the sun while he took his fins and snorkel into the ocean. He was gone a very long time. When he finally returned, he was clearly shaken and all cut up and bloody from swimming against the coral. He's an experienced swimmer and this was not normal. I asked him what happened and he explained that he lost his wedding ring while swimming in the ocean.

That was all I needed to hear and I set off in warfare prayer all over again. To think that Beelzebub would try to take one more thing from us! You've never known a person to pray as fervently as I did. I also called my spiritual mom, Penny Olivierie, a strong prayer warrior and told her what happened. I knew I could count on her prayers. I didn't know how, but I fully expected God to make Satan restore the ring. I know I sound like I'm insane in this matter and that Penny is out of her mind, too, for agreeing to pray for the recovery of the ring. But we prayed.

The value of the ring wasn't as important to me as was the significance. Our marriage had suffered so very much already. To lose the ring and what the ring symbolized was unacceptable. I prayed in the Spirit like I never had before.

I remember walking to the shore line praying, "God, if You want a fish to bring David's ring up in its mouth, You can do that. If You want it to miraculously show up in David's pocket. You can do that. If You want us to return to the hotel room and find it there You can do that." I was praying confidently expecting that nothing is impossible with God. And I'll be honest, I was really mad! *Beelzebub* was not about to get one more thing from us!

David went back out later in the day to see if he could find his ring. I know how absurd that sounds. But I was reminded of the day my car was stolen—I couldn't believe the car was gone so I just kept looking for it—even looking in the closet inside the house. I couldn't believe my car was gone. But regarding the ring, I refused to believe the loss, confident that God can do the impossible. While David was searching, I was praying.

A storm came in that night. But not just any storm. A hurricane. Hurricane Felicia to be precise. The wailing of the wind roared hard outside, there were tremendously strong gusts that blew with torrential rains all night long. There was one point when the loudspeaker announced we were to evacuate. Completely startled by this, we got out of bed and started figuring out how to comply when the voice over the speaker told us to stay put and listen for any further instructions. I had been intently praying since the day I was sick, so I was in full gear to continue. Not only for safety in the storm, but to find the ring!

The next morning after a few hours' sleep, we woke to light tropical showers and evidence that the sun would show up soon. We ate breakfast and went back down to the pool area. I took my post on the lounge chair and kept praying. After about an hour, David decided to see if he could find the ring. About an hour later while my eyes were closed, praying, I felt something very heavy and solid drop on my chest. I reached with my right hand to grab the object and sat up bolt straight. I saw David standing next to me. My mouth and eyes were wide open and I finally found the courage to take my clutched hand away from my chest, open it to look, and there was—David's ring!

David said he swam and prayed and just felt the Lord leading him to look back at the hotel. He lined himself up to the place he thought he lost his ring the day before and kept swimming and looking. After a while something glistened and caught his eye. Swimming over to the gleam, he said the ring was sitting in a small circular coral outcropping with sand in the center, perfectly displayed as if in an oceanic jewelry store.

Are you getting this? David finds his ring, in the *ocean* after nearly twenty-four hours, *after* Hurricane Felicia had ravaged the shoreline. Even if you don't agree that getting our time-share was a miracle, you must agree that finding David's ring is definitely a Maui Miracle.

Only Faith that's Been Developed Produces Miracles

I had never prayed that way, and actually haven't since prayed quite the same—though I know I can now, when the need arises. I prayed believing God can do anything. I prayed believing in the character, will, intent, and promises of God. I prayed knowing that the enemy has no authority over me or my husband, demanding with the authority I have in Christ that Satan return what is rightfully mine (and my husband's). I prayed according to the promises and revelation of truth in Scriptures. I prayed aloud, to declare my faith to all listening spirits. I prayed without ceasing. I prayed believing. And God answered.

The belief I had that God could cause my husband's ring to be found however and wherever He liked, and my request for Him to please produce the ring, demonstrated my faith in Him. I didn't care how God produced the ring. I knew He could and I asked and looked forward to the return with eager expectation. My belief was based on Scripture, along with all the prior life experiences that had developed my faith.

I hope this is one reality that you are able to embrace like never before: the trials we suffer today are intended by God to prepare us and develop our faith for what lies ahead.

The early disciples of Jesus were not pillars of the faith from the start. Their faith was developed over time by experience. Rather than seeing your trials and tribulations only for the hardship they bring, seek to focus on what God is doing—how He is perfecting you in the process.

Radical Faith Looks Like Denial to Unbelievers

To believe for the supernatural to manifest in the natural is not natural, but is supernatural. For this reason those whose focus is based on the natural cannot experience the supernatural.

To unbelievers, when Christians act on faith according to the promises of God, we look like lunatics. What would unbelievers say about me declaring that God could have my husband's ring brought up on the shore by a fish? Even Christians who know the Biblical story of the Christ ordering a fish to present a coin to Peter (Matthew 17:24-27), could think I was crazy! Yet, as I shared, my husband's ring that was lost in the Pacific Ocean was found because God saw our faith and rewarded us for agreeing with His declaration in Hebrews 11:6.

When your hope is firmly rooted in belief in Jesus, and you operate your life by your new spirit, obedient to the Word of God, aided by the power of the indwelling Holy Spirit, you are in position to demonstrate effective faith and expect God to fulfill His amazing promises in your life. Will you believe?

CHAPTER ENDNOTES

Introduction

1. *The ESV Study Bible®*, ESV® Bible, Copyright 2008 by Crossway. The Holy Bible, English Standard Version® (ESV®) Copyright © 2001 by Crossway, a publishing ministry of Good News Publishers, ESV Text Edition: 2011, Hebrews 11:6, 2380.
2. Ed Stetzer, *The State of the Church in America: Hint: It's Not Dying* (May 9, 2014), The Exchange, http://www.christianitytoday.com/edstetzer/channel/utilities/print.html?type=article&id=112392.
3. *The ESV Study Bible®, op. cit.*, John 5:6b, 1379.
4. *Ibid.*, John 5:1-9, 1380.
5. *Ibid.*, John 21:25, 1409.
6. *Ibid.*, John 14:12-14, 2052-2053.

Chapter One

1. *The ESV Study Bible®*, ESV® Bible, Copyright 2008 by Crossway. The Holy Bible, English Standard Version® (ESV®) Copyright © 2001 by Crossway, a publishing ministry of Good News Publishers, ESV Text Edition: 2011, Hebrews 11:6, 2380.
2. *Ibid.*, Genesis chapters 1-3, 49-47.
3. *Ibid.*, John 16:33, 2058.
4. *Ibid.*, John 10:10b, 2043.
5. Richard T. Ritenbaugh, "Are You Living the Abundant Life?," *Forerunner*, "Ready Answer," July 3, 2014, http://www.cgg.org/index.cfm/fuseaction/Library.sr/CT/RA/k/1062/Living-Abundant-Life.htm
6. *The ESV Study Bible®, op. cit.*, 1 Corinthians 2:9, 2194.
7. *Ibid.*, Ephesians 3:20, 2267.
8. *Ibid.*, John 17:3, 2058.
9. *Ibid.,* Luke 10:19-20, 1976
10. *Ibid.*, 1 Corinthians 6:19-20, 2199.
11. *Ibid.*, Romans 8:32, 2172
12. Brainy Quote, http://www.brainyquote.com/quotes/quotes/b/blaisepasc395508.html, November 3, 2014.
13. *The ESV Study Bible®, op. cit.*, Jeremiah 17:9-10, 1405.
14. *Ibid.*, Colossians 3:23, 2299.

15. *Ibid.*, Matthew 6:19-20, 1832.
16. *Ibid.*, Matthew 6:25 and 6:31-32, 1833.
17. *Ibid.*, Jeremiah 9:23-24, 1393.
18. J.I. Packer, *Knowing God*, (Downers Grove, IL: Inter Varsity Press, 1973), 34.
19. *Vines Expository Dictionary of Biblical Words*, ed. W.E. Vine, Merrill F. Unger, and William White, Jr. (Thomas Nelson, Inc.1985), 131.
20. *The ESV Study Bible®*, *op. cit.*, Mark 8:29, 1910.
21. *Ibid.*, John 3:3-8, 2024-2025.
22. *Ibid.*, John 3:10-21, 2025-2026.
23. Charles H. Kraft, *I Give You Authority: Practicing the Authority Jesus Gave Us*, (Bloomington, MN 2012), 185.
24. *The ESV Study Bible®*, *op. cit.*, Isaiah 14:13-14, 1267-1268.
25. Kraft, *op. cit.*, 22.
26. *Ibid.*
27. *The ESV Study Bible®*, *op. cit.*, 2 Timothy 3:5-7, 2341.
28. *Ibid.*, Luke 1:30-33, 1944-1945.
29. *Ibid.*, Luke 1:35, 1945.
30. *Ibid.*, Hosea 6:2, 1630; Matthew 12:38-40, 1846 and; John 2:19, 2024.
31. *Ibid.*, 2 Corinthians 5:1-4, 2229.
32. *Ibid.*, Romans 10:8-13, 2125.
33. *Ibid.*, , Romans 12: 1-2, 2178.
34. *Ibid.*, 2 Corinthians 10:4-5, 2235.
35. *Ibid.*, 1 John 2:15-17, 2432.
36. *Ibid.*, Revelation 12:11, 2480.

Chapter Two

1. *The ESV Study Bible®*, ESV® Bible, Copyright 2008 by Crossway. The Holy Bible, English Standard Version® (ESV®) Copyright © 2001 by Crossway, a publishing ministry of Good News Publishers, ESV Text Edition: 2011), Colossians 1:27, 2295.
2. Logical, Vocabulary.com, http://www.vocabulary.com/dictionary/logical, November 5, 2014.
3. BELIEVE Religious Information, http://mb-soft.com/believe/text/logos.htm, November 5, 2014.
4. *What is the Rhema Word?*, Got Questions?, http://www.gotquestions.org/rhema-word.html, October 28, 2014.
5. *What is a Rehma?* Scripture for Personal Application http://ati.iblp.org/ati/family/articles/concepts/rhema/, November 12, 2014.

6. *The ESV Study Bible®, op. cit.*, Hebrews 11:6, 1566.
7. *Ibid.*, Matthew 8:10, 1250-1251.
8. *Ibid.*, Matthew 17:20, 1267.
9. *Ibid.*, 1565.
10. E. W. Kenyon and Don Gossett, *Words that Move Mountains*, (New Kensington, PA: Whitaker House, 2009), 34, 35.
11. *The ESV Study Bible®, op. cit.*, Philipians 2:3, 1524.
12. *Ibid.*, James 4:3, 1574.
13. *Ibid.*, John 16:33b, 1401.

Chapter Three

1. E. W. Kenyon and Don Gossett, *Words that Move Mountains*, (New Kensington, PA: Whitaker House, 2009), 21, 22.
2. *The ESV Study Bible®*, ESV® Bible, Copyright 2008 by Crossway. The Holy Bible, English Standard Version® (ESV®) Copyright © 2001 by Crossway, a publishing ministry of Good News Publishers, ESV Text Edition: 2011, 2 Corinthians 1:22, 2224; 2 Corinthians 5:5, 2229 and; Ephesians 1:14, 2263.
3. *Ibid.*, John 14:16, 2053; Romans 8:34, 2172; Hebrews 7:25, 2372.
4. *Ibid.*, John 14:12-14, 2052-2053.
5. *Ibid.*, Matthew 16:13-19, 1854-1855.
6. *Ibid.*, 1 John 4:17, 2435.
7. *Ibid.*, 2 Peter 1:1-4, 2418.
8. *Ibid.*, 1 John 4:4, 2435.
9. Kraft, *op. cit.*, 37, 38, 39 and 43.
10. *The ESV Study Bible®, op. cit.*, Philippians 1:6, 2280.
11. *Ibid.*, Romans 2:11, 2160.
12. *Ibid*, Ephesians 2:10, 2265.
13. *Ibid.*, Jeremiah 17:9-10, 1405-1406.
14. Terri Fivash, *Spiritual Toolbox*, (Berrien Springs, MI, 2014), 22-24.
15. *Ibid.*, 24.
16. *Ibid.*, 26 and 28.
17. *Ibid.*, 28 and 30.
18. *Ibid.*, 30.
19. *Ibid.*, 32.
20. *Ibid.*, 36.
21. *Ibid.*, 34.
22. Kenyon and Gossett, *op. cit.*, 36 and 68-70.

Chapter Four

1. *The ESV Study Bible®*, ESV® Bible, Copyright 2008 by Crossway. The Holy Bible, English Standard Version® (ESV®) Copyright © 2001 by Crossway, a publishing ministry of Good News Publishers, ESV Text Edition: 2011, Matthew 4:6-7, 1825.
2. *Ibid.*, 2 Peter 3:9, 2422.
3. *Ibid.*, Romans 8:2, 1465.
4. *Ibid.*, John 12:23-26, 2048.
5. *Ibid.*, Matthew 5:17, 1828.
6. *Ibid.*, Romans 3:27, 1460-1461.
7. *Ibid.*, John 1:17, 2020.
8. *Ibid.*, Genesis 1:26, 51.
9. Terri Fivash, "Spiritual Laws," (May 2014), http:www.terrifavish.com/spiritual-laws/ July 5, 2014.
10. *The ESV Study Bible®*, *op.cit.*, Galatians 6:7-8, 2255.
11. *Ibid.*, Matthew 13:23, 1848.
12. *Ibid.*, Matthew 13:24-28, 1848.
13. *Ibid.*, 2 Corinthians 9:6, 2234.
14. *Ibid.*, Romans 10:17, 2175.
15. *Ibid.*, Mark 1:10-12, 1893.
16. Fivash, *op. cit*, July 5 2014.
17. Compilation from: http://www.preceptaustin.org/notes_on_attributes_of_god_(2b).htm; http://joshmcdowellmedia.org/PromiseKeepers/DiscoverGodAttribute.pdf and; http://www.blueletterbible.org/faq/attributes.cfm, (May 2014), July 5, 2014.
18. Dr. Charles Stanley, "How Do I Talk With God?" http://www.intouch.org/you/article-archive/content/topic/how_do_i_talk_with_god_article#.VCRT22ddWSo, September 25, 2014.
19. *The ESV Study Bible®*, *op. cit.*, Proverbs 29:18, 1166.
20. *Ibid.*, Hosea 4:6, 1627.
21. *Ibid.*, Hebrews 11:1, 2379.
22. *Visualization*, Let Us Reason Ministries, http://www.letusreason.org/NAM22.htm, September 27, 2014.
23. *The ESV Study Bible®*, *op. cit.*, Jeremiah 23:16, 1416.
24. *Ibid.*, 1 John 5:14-15, 2437.

Chapter Five

1. Oswald Chambers, *My Utmost for His Highest*, (Westwood, NJ, Barbour and Company, Inc., 1963), 37-38.
2. *The ESV Study Bible®*, ESV® Bible, Copyright 2008 by Crossway. The Holy Bible, English Standard Version® (ESV®) Copyright © 2001 by Crossway, a publishing ministry of Good News Publishers, ESV Text Edition: 2011, James 1:2-8, 2391.
3. *Ibid.*, Jeremiah 29:11, 1424.
4. *Ibid.*, Romans 8:28, 2171.
5. *Ibid.*, Hebrews 11:6, 2380.
6. Jon Ruthven, "What's Right About the Faith Movement" (May 8, 2014) http://hopefaithprayer.com/word-of-faith/whats-right-about-the-faith-movement/ July 3, 2014.
7. *Ibid.*
8. *The ESV Study Bible®, op. cit.*, John 5:19-21; John 5:30, 2030-2032 and; John 12:49, 2050.
9. Charles H. Spurgeon, "The Secret of Failure," sermon delivered in 1896, http://www.spurgeon.org/sermons/2454.htm, July 9, 2014.
10. *The ESV Study Bible®, op. cit.*, Matthew 17:20-21, 1267.
11. *Ibid.*, Matthew 13:54-58, 1850.
12. Spurgeon, op. cit., July 9, 2014.
13. *Thompson Chain-Reference Study Bible*, ed. Frank Charles Thompson, New King James version, (Thomas Nelson, Inc., 1982), Psalm 27:13, 716.
14. *The ESV Study Bible®, op. cit.*, Matthew 6: 25-26, 1833.
15. *Ibid.*, Matthew 6:30-33, 1833.
16. *Ibid.*, James 5:13-16, 2399.
17. *Ibid.*, 1 John 3:16-18, 2434

Chapter Six

1. Reference to Luke 1:37.
2. *The ESV Study Bible®*, ESV® Bible, Copyright 2008 by Crossway. The Holy Bible, English Standard Version® (ESV®) Copyright © 2001 by Crossway, a publishing ministry of Good News Publishers, ESV Text Edition: 2011, Revelation 12:11, 2480.
3. *Ibid.*, Matthew 16:18, 1266.
4. *Ibid.*, Romans 4:20-25, 2165.
5. Transcript of testimony of Andrew Womack as told when interviewed on *Christian Philosophy* television show, October 20, 2005, used with permission.

6. *The ESV Study Bible®*, *op. cit.*, Romans: 10:17, 2175.
7. *Ibid.*, 2 Corinthians 5:7, 1499.
8. *Ibid.*, Isaiah 55:11, 953.

Chapter Seven

1. *The ESV Study Bible®*, ESV® Bible, Copyright 2008 by Crossway. The Holy Bible, English Standard Version® (ESV®) Copyright © 2001 by Crossway, a publishing ministry of Good News Publishers, ESV Text Edition: 2011, Hebrews 11:6, 2380.
2. *Ibid.*, Ephesians 2:8, 2265.
3. *Ibid.*, James 1:5-8, 2391.
4. *Ibid.*, Psalms 84:11, 1044.
5. *Ibid.*, Ephesians 6:10-18, 2273-2274.
6. Charles H. Kraft, *I Give You Authority: Practicing the Authority Jesus Gave Us*, (Bloomington, MN 2012), 185.
7. *The ESV Study Bible®*, ESV®, *op. cit.*, Genesis 1:27-28, 51-52.
8. *Coffman's Commentaries on the Bible*, (May 2014) http://www.studylight.org/commentaries/bcc/view.cgi?bk=18&ch=8&vs=5-6 , July 7, 2014.
9. *The ESV Study Bible®*, *op. cit.*, John 19:30, 2068.
10. *How is Satan god of this world? (2 Corinthians 4:4)*" (May 2014) http://www.gotquestions.org/Satan-god-world.html, July 7, 2014.
11. Kraft, *op. cit.*, 34 and 35.
12. *Spiritual Gifts* (May 2014), http://www.cmalliance.org/about/beliefs/perspectives/spiritual-gifts, July 7, 2014.
13. *Have the Charismatic Gifts Ceased?* (May 2014), http://carm.org/questions/about-doctrine/have-charismatic-gifts-ceased , July 5, 2014.
14. *The ESV Study Bible®*, *op. cit.*, John 16:13-15, 2057.
15. *Ibid.*, 1 Corinthians 12:1-7, 2209.
16. Tom Pennington, *Strange Fire-A Case for Cessationism*, The Cripple Gate, (October 17, 2013), http://thecripplegate.com/strange-fire-a-case-for-cessationism-tom-pennington/, September 30, 2014.
17. *Ibid.*
18. *Seventy Disciples*, http://en.wikipedia.org/wiki/Seventy_disciples, July 10, 2014.
19. Micael Grenholm, *A Response to Tom Pennington's Seven Cessationist's Arguments*, (October 19, 2013), Holy Spirit Activism, http://holyspiritactivism.wordpress.com/2013/10/19/a-response-to-tom-

penningtons-seven-cessationist-arguments/, September 30, 2014.
20. Ibid.
21. Pennington, op. cit., September 30, 2014.
22. *Thompson Chain-Reference Study Bible*, ed. Frank Charles Thompson, New King James version, (Thomas Nelson, Inc., 1982), 1 Thessalonians 5:19-22, 1536.
23. Ibid., 1 Corinthians 13:13, 1490.

Chapter Eight

1. *The ESV Study Bible®*, ESV® Bible, Copyright 2008 by Crossway. The Holy Bible, English Standard Version® (ESV®) Copyright © 2001 by Crossway, a publishing ministry of Good News Publishers, ESV Text Edition: 2011, Hosea 4:6, 1627-1628.
2. Ibid., Romans 12:2, 2 Cor 10:4-5 and James 4:7, 2178, 2235 and 2397.
3. Bruce Yocum, *Forming the Christian Mind* (May 29, 2013), July 7, 2014http://www.swordofthespirit.net/bulwark/july07p1.htm.
4. Ibid.
5. John MacArthur, *Is God Responsible for Evil?* http://www.gty.org/resources/articles/A189/Is-God-Responsible-for-Evil, July 5 2014,
6. *Matthew Henry's Concise Commentary*, http://biblehub.com/commentaries/mhc/isaiah/45.htm, July 7, 2014
7. Ibid., 142
8. Joseph M. Stowell, *The Upside of Down*, (Chicago, IL, Moody Press, 1991), 30-31.
9. Alan Redpath, *Victorious Christian Living, Studies in the Book of Joshua*, (Grand Rapids, MI, Flemming H. Revell Company, a division of Baker Book House Company, 1955), 166.
10. Stowell., op. cit., 37-38
11. *The Exodus Route: Travel times, distances, rates of travel, days of the week*, http://www.bible.ca/archeology/bible-archeology-exodus-route-travel-times-distances-days.htm, July 7, 2014.
12. *The ESV Study Bible®*, ESV® op. cit., John 16:33, 2058.
13. Ibid., 2 Peter 3:9, 2422.
14. *The ESV Study Bible®*, op. cit., John 14:12-14, 2052-2053.
15. Ibid., 2 Corinthians 12:7-10, 2238-2239.
16. *The ESV Study Bible®*, ESV® Bible, Copyright 2008 by Crossway. The Holy Bible, English Standard Version® (ESV®) Copyright © 2001 by Crossway, a publishing ministry of Good News Publishers, ESV Text Edition: 2011, Romans 5:3-5. 2165.

Part Three Divider

1. *The ESV Study Bible®*, ESV® Bible, Copyright 2008 by Crossway. The Holy Bible, English Standard Version® (ESV®) Copyright © 2001 by Crossway, a publishing ministry of Good News Publishers, ESV Text Edition: 2011, John 15:4-5, 2054.

Chapter Nine

1. Jspace Staff, *Ten Jewish Inventions that Changed the World*, (February 25, 2014), http://www.jspacenews.com/10-jewish-inventions-changed-world/, September 25, 2014.
2. *The Contributions and Achievements of the Ancient Hebrew, Greeks and Romans*, http://www.123helpme.com/view.asp?id=133551, September 25, 2014.
3. *The ESV Study Bible®*, ESV® Bible, Copyright 2008 by Crossway. The Holy Bible, English Standard Version® (ESV®) Copyright © 2001 by Crossway, a publishing ministry of Good News Publishers, ESV Text Edition: 2011, Romans 8:16-17, 2171.
4. Juli Camarin, *Sharing in His Sufferings Means Sharing in His Glory, Romans 8:17*, (December 7, 2009), http://www.jcblog.net/romans/8/314-romans-817-sharing-in-his-suffering-means-sharing-in-his-glory, September 25, 2014.
5. *The ESV Study Bible®*, op. cit., Hebrews 9:22, 2376.
6. *Ibid.*, Leviticus 17:11, 239-240.
7. *Ibid.*, John 15:18-19, 1399.
8. *Ibid.*, 2 Corinthians 4:17-18, 2229.
9. *Ibid.*, Matthew 22:37-40, 1870.
10. *Ibid.*, John 14:12-14, 2052-2053.
11. Mary Fairchild, *The Miracles of Jesus*, http://christianity.about.com/od/biblefactsandlists/a/Miracles-Of-Jesus.htm, July 20, 2014.
12. *Thompson Chain-Reference Study Bible*, ed. Frank Charles Thompson, New King James version, (Thomas Nelson, Inc., 1982), Hebrews 13:8, 2385.
13. *Ibid.*, Matthew 28:18-20, 1888.
14. Charles H. Kraft, *I Give You Authority: Practicing the Authority Jesus Gave Us*, (Bloomington, MN: Chosen Books, 2012), 257.
15. John Byron, The Biblical World, (August 8. 2012) http://thebiblicalworld.blogspot.com/2012/08/craig-keener-reports-of-raising-from.html, November 11, 2014.
16. John Perry, *Miracles*, Philosophy Talk–Community of Thinkers, entry by Nathan Heopner [not verified], (November 2, 2011),

http://www.philosophytalk.org/community/blog/john-perry/2013/12/miracles, October 1, 2014.
17. *About Us*, https://www.irisglobal.org/about, October 21, 2014.
18. *About Marc Dupont Ministries*, http://marcdupontministries.com/about/, October 21, 2014.
19. *Cyclone Leon-Eline*, http://en.wikipedia.org/wiki/Cyclone_Leon%E2%80%93Eline, October 21, 2014.
20. *Cyclone Hellen*, http://en.widipedia.org/wiki/Cyclone_Hellen, October 21, 2014.
21. Garris Elkins, *Something Beautiful is Coming*, (September 19, 2014), http://www.elijahlist.com/words/display_word.html?ID=13887, September 25, 2014.
22. *The ESV Study Bible®*, op. cit., Mark 5:28, 1902.
23. *Ibid.*, Mark 11:23-24, 1919.
24. *Ibid.*, Mark 6:30b-34, 1902-1903.

Chapter Ten

1. *What Does the Bible Say About Demonic Miracles?* GotQuestions.org, http://www.gotquestions.org/demonic-satanic-miracles.html, July 29, 2014.
2. *The ESV Study Bible®*, ESV® Bible, Copyright 2008 by Crossway. The Holy Bible, English Standard Version® (ESV®) Copyright © 2001 by Crossway, a publishing ministry of Good News Publishers, ESV Text Edition: 2011, 1 John 4:1, 2434.
3. Reference to James 4:8.
4. *The ESV Study Bible®*, *op. cit.*, 2 Peter 1:3 and 3 John 1:2, 2418 and 2445.
5. *Ibid.*, Deuteronomy 30:9-10, 374.
6. *Ibid.*, Isaiah 55:10-11, 1342.
7. *Ibid.*, Matthew 5:17-18 and 2 Corinthians 1:20, 1828 and 2224.
8. *Bible Study Tools Online*, http://www.biblestudytools.com/dictionary/beelzebub/, September 3, 2014.

About the Author

Pamela Christian's ministry began in the early 1990s as a Teaching Director for Community Bible Study, an independent, interdenominational, international organization. This was followed by invitations to speak across the country for various organizations, which she continues to enjoy with great enthusiasm to this day. Her initial writing work included the development of workbooks for her retreats and conferences. This soon expanded to publication in book compilations, magazines and several e-books.

Her speaking and writing career translated perfectly into other media, including hosting talk shows on Christian radio, television, and voice-over work. With a certificate in apologetics from Biola University, her first passion is to help others in matters of faith. Her favorite pastimes are food, family, and friends. Weekends when she's not speaking or writing, you'll find her cooking and entertaining—expressing her second passion for food, wine, and travel. Pam is a member of International Society of Women in Apologetics, and other professional organizations.

Pam and her husband live in Orange County, CA, with their two grown children living nearby. To book Pam to speak or learn more visit www.pamelachristianministries.com

Get all the books in the

FAITH TO LIVE BY
Book Series.

"So now faith, hope and love abide,
these three; but the greatest of these is love." (1 Corinthians 13:13)

Examine Your Faith!
Finding Truth in a World of Lies

Essential faith, which is saving faith.
(2013)

Renew Your Hope!
Remedy for Personal Breakthroughs

Effective faith, which is hope.
(2014)

Revive Your Life!
Rest for Your Anxious Heart

Excellent faith, which is love.
(Future publication)

To be sure you don't miss the release of all Pam's books, events and more, sign up for her bi-monthly EZine!

www.pamelachristianministries.com

Pamela Christian Ministries

18032 Lemon Dr. #C206, Yorba Linda, CA 92886

info@pamelachristianministries.com

OTHER TITLES BY PAMELA CHRISTIAN:

The companion **Study Guide** for Examine Your Faith! Finding Truth in a World of Lies, is excellent for individual and small group study. Available in print or Kindle versions.
- **Series:** Faith to Live By
- **Paperback:** 84 pages
- **Language:** English
- **ISBN-13:** 978-1497359901

Those Interested in the history and origin of the Bible and learning an inductive method for independent Bible Study will enjoy this workbook. The A-F-R-E-S-H method allows for in-depth and applied study of God's Word. Available in print or Kindle versions.
- **Paperback:** 86 pages
- **Language:** English
- **ISBN-13:** 978-1456541156

WATCH FOR THE RELEASE OF BOOK THREE IN THIS SERIES:

REVIVE YOUR LIFE!
REST FOR YOUR ANXIOUS HEART

It is vital that we understand God's absolute, unconditional love for us. When we learn to abide in His love, we have a confidence for our life's significance and purpose that otherwise does not exist.

Expected publication 2015

BENEFITS OF SUPPORTING PAMELA CHRISTIAN MINISTRIES

When you purchase direct from Pamela Christian Ministries, you help support not only her ministry work but other ministries that share the Gospel Message of Jesus Christ. For ever ten books sold from the *Faith to Live By* book series, through our web site, one book is donated to evangelistic/missionary efforts for their use in spreading the Gospel. You may purchase direct from our secure web store on our site with your credit card or Pay Pal® account.

http://pamelachristianministries.com/store

If you have a ministry you'd like to support by way of promoting the sale of Pam's books yourself, please inquire about our Affiliates Program.

http://pamelachristianministries.com/affiliates/index

Please direct all inquiries and questions to:

info@pamelachristian ministries.com

If access to the Internet is not viable for you, please use the order form provided on the next page.

Renew Your Hope!

TO ORDER COPIES OF THIS OR ANY OF PAM'S BOOKS:

If you liked this book of Pam's, you'll like others for yourself or to give as gifts. Use this form to order by mail.

Name:_____
     First and Last

Shipping Address:_____
     Street and Suite/Apartment number if applicable

     _____
     City, State and Zip

Phone Number:_____
     Area code and number

Email Address:_____

Please be sure to provide a phone or email address in case we have any question about the proper fulfillment of your order.

TITLE	RETAIL	QUANTITY	TOTAL
Examine Your Faith! Finding Truth in a World of Lies	$16.99	_____	_____
Examine Your Faith! Study Guide	$7.99	_____	_____
Renew Your Hope! Remedies for Personal Breakthroughs	$16.99	_____	_____
Renew Your Hope! Study Guide	$7.99	_____	_____
His Word Afresh, My Life Anew!	$11.99	_____	_____

TOTAL: $_____

California residents add 8% tax $_____

Add $3.00 postage for each book* $_____

GRAND TOTAL: $_____

*Shipping limited to the United States

Please send this form with your check or money-order payable to:
Pamela Christian Ministries
18032 Lemon Drive #C206
Yorba Linda, CA 9